THE CONSULTANT'S GUIDE TO HIDDEN PROFITS

The 101 Most Overlooked Strategies for Increased Earnings and Growth

Herman Holtz

JOHN WILEY & SONS, INC.
New York • Chichester • Brisbane • Toronto • Singapore

Copyright © 1992 by Herman Holtz.
Published by John Wiley & Sons, Inc.

This publication is designed to provide accurate and authoritative information in regard to the subject matter covered. It is sold with the understanding that the publisher is not engaged in rendering any legal, accounting, or other professional service. If legal advice or other expert assistance is required, the services of a competent professional person should be sought. From a *Declaration of Principles jointly adopted by a Committee of the American Bar Association and a Committee of Publishers.*

Library of Congress Cataloging-in-Publication Data:
Holtz, Herman.
    The consultant's guide to hidden profits: the 101 most overlooked strategies for increased earnings and growth / by Herman Holtz.
       p.   cm.
    Includes index.
    ISBN 0-471-55496-0
    1. Business consultants. 2. Consultants. I. Title.
HD69.C6H622 1992
001'.068–dc20   92-11307

Printed in the United States of America
10 9 8 7 6 5 4 3 2 1

⹀ PREFACE ⹀

Since I first began writing about consulting, I have again and again received confirmation of my premise that most independent consultants and aspirants to consulting need guidance in marketing more than they need anything else. Readers were quick to agree with this premise, confirming it over and over again for me in many ways. For example, the computer consultants' forum of CompuServe established a study group that has been conducting studies and reviews of books on consulting by various authors, one of them my own book. I followed these reviews closely, and I found that interest in marketing reaffirmed here, as it was elsewhere.

Despite this experience, an impression that emerges after eight years of writing for and communicating with much of the population of independent consultants in our society is that, while they welcome all material intended to aid them in marketing their services, they often fall short in translating and implementing the ideas offered them. The purpose of this book is to close this gap.

But let us digress a moment to look at some basic characteristics of consulting and independent consultants and see whether we can gain some useful insights thereby. Are independent consultants "different" in some way? Do we have special needs that other entrepreneurs and independent professionals do not have? Do we have special problems that other independent practitioners do not have?

One thing is clear: Certain kinds of ventures have higher attrition rates than do most others. Consulting is one of those. There are probably a number of reasons for the noticeably high rate of consulting dropouts, especially during the first year.

First, a large percentage of those who undertake to become consultants are not truly committed to consulting as a career. They enter into consulting casually and as a temporary measure because they are without jobs at the moment, believe consulting to be an easy way to earn a living, or simply want to sample it for a time to see how it compares with working for a salary. A rather large percentage of these individuals forsake independent consulting quickly enough when an attractive salaried job becomes available. Or they find consulting less attractive than it seemed at first, and since they are not really committed to the field, they have little hesitancy about leaving it almost as casually as they entered it. Or they simply are having too difficult a struggle to survive in it and are unwilling – or perhaps even unable – to continue the struggle.

Then, a significant number of independent consultants, possibly even most, are dedicated professionals and technicians in their basic specialty. They love the work they do, solving problems and rescuing projects in distress. Soon enough, however, they discover that such romantic achievements are not everyday or routine occurrences. Much of consulting is like other work: repetitive, dull routine, with necessary attention to mundane administrative details.

For many, the bad news is the discovery that they must be able business men and women, attending to all the business-related details of consulting – for it is a business. They must master the art of consultant-client relations. They must learn tact and diplomacy. They must master the financial and legal elements of conducting a business, even with the help of a CPA to handle their books and taxes and a lawyer to deal with legal problems. Unwilling or unable to compromise and to cope with mundane business affairs, and disillusioned to find that they cannot spend 100 percent of their time at their beloved technical work (running any one-person business enterprise is likely to require about one-third of your time in overhead work), they return to salaried employment, where they can spend 100 percent of their time working at their technical and professional specialties and be unconcerned with business problems. And the most distasteful problem, for many, is that of marketing – winning clients.

Most of those others who do not linger long in the ranks of independent consultants are probably much better technicians and consultants than they are marketers, and they find themselves struggling to win enough clients to survive. These are the consultants most in need of help. They earnestly wish to make a success of their independent practices, but need a bit of help in marketing. That individual is the reader and the practicing independent consultant for whom this book is intended.

Marketing is often confused with selling. It's easy to understand why, for selling is part of marketing, a most important part. It's the process of finding the client and getting the order. Marketing is a bit broader in its approach: It's the process of deciding what clients and what orders to pursue – what to sell and how to sell it.

This may seem to be defining the obvious. We are talking about selling consulting services, are we not? And we know what those are, do we not?

The fact is, however, that we do not all know what consulting services are. There are some who define consulting quite narrowly, insisting that it is problem solving and advice giving and that anything else is not consulting or any part of consulting. (Some like to call those other activities "free-lancing," as though the euphemism makes a difference of some sort.)

There are others who define consulting on a quite broad basis, to include being employed as a technical or professional temporary, lecturing, writing books, publishing newsletters, and performing sundry other initiatives. The spectrum of activities is broad because the number and variety of consulting specialties is broad and growing. There are few fields for which special skills and knowledge are required that do not support independent consultants. Many of today's special career fields have developed several levels of specialization. In the computer field alone, the first level is hardware versus software specialization, but then each of these almost immediately displays various sublevels and fields.

But it isn't all high-tech specialization. Modern society and modern problems of society have produced consultants. There are consultants in security. Some specialize in the physical security of fixed installations – locks and alarms. Some specialize in industrial security, safeguarding proprietary information from the prying eyes of competitors and from industrial sneak thieves. Some specialize in physical security of the individual, functioning as antiterrorist consultants. But as locksmiths have become security consultants and former police officials have become antiterrorist consultants, writers and editors have become editorial and publication consultants, and office managers have become consultants in office layouts and work procedures. Thus, the number of opportunities to become independent consultants grows continuously, with the growth of career specialties.

Given this enormous diversity, it would be surprising if we could reach any kind of closely defined agreement on just what consulting is and how to practice it. In fact, practices vary widely, as they should and as they must, if the typical independent practitioner is even to survive, much less prosper. That is what this book is really about: the many ways in which you can market your consulting service. Perhaps it is even about the many ways in which you can define your consulting service. But the distinction is academic, for they are really the same thing. The premise is that consulting is not a simple proposition for most of us. Quite the contrary, the practice of consulting varies considerably with necessity, as dictated by the nature of the specialization, the problems that need to be solved, the expectations of the typical client, and the talents and instincts of the practitioner – you.

Accordingly, what you are about to find in the pages that follow is a potpourri of ideas, information, suggestions, and methods that I and others have chosen to use as part of, or even as the heart of, our individual independent consulting practices. It is unlikely that you will find all of these appropriate to your own needs and desires or even suitable for your own purposes. That is as it should be. Consulting provides custom services, and it is a highly individualized career: Only you can make the final decisions as to what it shall be for you. Thus, I have tried to offer a smorgasbord here. The array is spread before you for your inspection and your introspection. Study the buffet, and choose what appeals to you and what seems most useful or most suitable for your needs, as you perceive them. For example, feel free to adapt, modify, and experiment with any of the ideas presented. Use them to start you thinking, and spin off new variants.

Above all, don't be influenced by anyone else's definition of consulting as you ought to practice it. You must define it for yourself, as we all must.

Be prepared for a few surprises. You are likely to find consulting a much more diverse career than you had imagined, at least as I define it. In fact, you are likely to arrive, finally, at a career specialty considerably different from the one you envisioned when you undertook to become an independent consultant. A great many of us do.

HERMAN HOLTZ

Wheaton, Maryland
September 1992

= CONTENTS

The major points of networking. Writing proposals: Is it
a high-risk game? The RFP package. The pros of
marketing via proposals. The cons of marketing via
proposals. Typical problems with the RFP. The major
hazard. Gathering market intelligence. A special problem
or two. Proposal formats. Capability brochures.

CONSULTING IS A BUSINESS

You can afford to be "only" a professional while you are on someone else's payroll, working for wages. When you become an independent consultant, you had also better become a businessperson if you want your consultancy to survive.

MANY ARE CALLED . . .

Many thousands of individuals set out to become independent consultants every year, and their numbers increase steadily as encroaching technology overshadows and dictates more and more the conduct of our industries and businesses, and even that of our daily lives. If all those individuals succeeded in their new ventures, we would soon be awash in independent consultants, and there would be no one left to slop the hogs and milk the cows, much less carry out the garbage. Fortunately, from that viewpoint, but unfortunately, from the viewpoint of the fledgling independent consultant, few of these eager aspirants survive the first year. The vast majority succumb to a wide variety of business ills, of which probably the most common is forgetting or failing to realize that consulting is a business. You may regard it as a profession or even as an art – and it may be both of those things – but it is also a business. It stands or falls on the same principles that other businesses stand or fall on.

SMITTY'S LAW

Any mind—even the mediocre one—can find complex solutions to problems and complex explanations for anything that needs explanation. By contrast, great minds tend to simplify. That is because they perceive the essence of things: They cut through all the window dressing and distractions that surround so many propositions. The possessors of such minds have an instinct for getting to the heart of the matter quickly. Smitty, a business associate of many years ago (I called him "Smitty" for so many years, that I have forgotten his given name), had that ability. He said to me, over one memorable lunch, "I don't really find business that difficult or complicated. If something you are doing is making money for you, keep doing it. If it is not making money for you, stop doing it."

Oversimplified? Perhaps. On the other hand, I have never been sure that the term is not itself an oxymoron. Is the introductory sentence of a news story oversimplified? Or is it the lead, the framework, or the background upon which the detailed story can be mounted? Yes, there is a great deal more to be said about the successful conduct of a business, but "Smitty's law" does sum up not only the goal of a business, but the necessary condition for its survival: making sure that income is at least slightly greater than outgo. Without a clear understanding of that simple principle, no clear understanding of business is possible. What is truly amazing is how frequently otherwise clear-headed, bright individuals either fail to understand the principle or choose to ignore it. Perhaps they think, as did the alchemists of old, that they can make gold from base metals—take a living out of a venture that fails to take in more money than it pays out.

THE CONVENTIONAL WISDOM ABOUT FAILURE

A great many experts—those economists who write newspaper columns and who are executives with such organizations as the U.S. Small Business Administration, Dun & Bradstreet, and Price Waterhouse, to name a few—offer a great many theories about why small businesses fail so often, and increasingly so in the past few years. Here are a few of the causes they cite:

- Poor general management
- Poor accounting systems

- Undercapitalization
- General inexperience
- Inventory problems
- Underpricing

It is surprising how rarely these experts list shortcomings in sales and marketing as a cause of business failure. Wouldn't you suppose that insufficient sales would contribute significantly to the failure of a business? (Perhaps economic theorists don't concern themselves with the mundane matter of sales volume.) In any case, let's look at some of the areas they mention.

The fact is that there are many examples of businesses that suffer from any number of the things they cite, but that survive nevertheless and may even be considered successful. Their survival is due to the simple fact that one thing they don't suffer from is a lack of sales success. The shortcomings that handicap the business and limit its success don't bring about its downfall, as long as it markets its product successfully. The plain truth is that the business with a healthy sales volume can tolerate and survive a great many problems. Many large, highly successful businesses suffer severe problems in accounting, inventory, capitalization, and management generally. Anyone who has worked for a large corporation has observed almost innumerable examples of waste and inefficiency, although the corporation goes on, paying its employees, paying its bills, and being successful by any of the standards we normally apply to measure business success. The many shortcomings cut into profits, but they aren't what puts them away, in those cases where such organizations do fail; marketing failure does that.

1

Of all business problem areas, attack shortcomings in sales volume first. The business with strong sales can survive other systemic weaknesses.

The reverse is also true: Suppose all the areas of management and other business activity cited are handled magnificently, but there are not enough sales. In those circumstances, the business must fail: No business can survive an insufficiency of sales, the failure of its marketing functions.

Look at it this way: All those management and administrative areas are "outgo" activities: They cost money. Marketing and sales are "income" activities: They bring money in. Doesn't that alone say something about the necessary balance between them?

Still, despite the fundamental truth of Smitty's law, business is not really that simple. It isn't always easy to know which of your activities are losing money and which are making money – that is, which sales are most profitable, which are least profitable, and which are unprofitable or, at least, so marginally profitable as to be not worth doing. If you don't have some means of getting that kind of information, you can have healthy sales and still be losing money. That's one reason for the need of a good accounting system, and, to some extent, it's what the experts have in mind when they point to accounting weaknesses as a cause of failure. Only with adequate accounting do you truly *know* (not merely guess) whether some activity is profitable or not. Even more to the point, without adequate accounting you don't know *why* a given activity is or is not profitable – for example, whether your costs and pricing for that activity are what they ought to be.

2

Business without numbers isn't business. Make establishing an accounting system your second priority after marketing. That way, you can be sure you are finding hidden profits – and not losses – in your marketing efforts.

You do need to be capitalized, especially if you must carry open accounts or make large capital investments. But even without those burdens, you must assume that your new practice will not begin to produce income immediately, although it will begin to produce outgo from the first day on, as well as a minimal investment in business cards, stationery, and some other necessary business appurtenances.

I assume that you are expert in the services you render, but if you are not experienced in managing a business, you may have to find someone to guide you in getting established, at least during the early days, when you are trying to organize an office, install your systems, and meet any legal obligations, such as licensing or registering a business name. This may be the time you most need a business advisor of some sort. (Suggestions for getting this kind of help are offered later.)

BUSINESS *IS* MARKETING–BUT IT IS ALSO ACCOUNTING

Make sales and marketing a priority – probably the highest priority. Don't overlook the importance of accounting, however; it tells you how you are doing. As Smitty said, "It tells you what you should keep doing, because you are making money at it, and what you should stop doing, because you are losing money at it." It is how you know, for example, which sales are best for the health of your business and which are not.

3

Beware of accounting systems and services that do not furnish information on a *timely* basis. Perhaps the large corportion can afford to wait until December to find out whether it made or lost money in September or October, but that kind of feedback can destroy your practice quite swiftly. Even when you have a public accountant keep your books, you generally get information, not for the month just elapsed, but for a month that is from 30 to 90 days in the past.

To overcome this problem, we keep our own books (which is really quite simple for a small service business) on a daily basis, with biweekly summaries, and have a public accountant do our taxes once a year. That way, we can observe and balance costs against income continuously, detect any sharp changes in either, judge when we can afford a capital investment we wish to make, and otherwise make reasoned management decisions.

What? You think you can tell that for yourself, without an accounting system? So many have said that or something like it, that their statements ought to be among those known as "famous last words." They often are the last words – of the business, that is. There is no substitute for data – not opinions, estimates, or gut feelings, but *data.* Yes, there are some entrepreneurs who fly their businesses successfully by the seat of their pants, but the business graveyards are full of the bones of others who tried that act and couldn't pull it off. It is a high-wire act and no small risk to attempt. These are different days – days of extraordinarily high and diverse taxes and of complex tax structures, for one thing. Costs are high: Undetected losses can drain capital at a faster rate than ever before. It is also a time of easy credit: Despite the current cautiousness of banks with regard to making business loans without reassuring collateral, most of us have many thousands of dollars' worth of credit in the form of our gold credit cards, which are incredibly easy to get today. Many consultants use these cards as a resource when they can't get ordinary small-business loans from their local banks. It's quite easy to lose a great deal of money and get irretrievably deep into debt this way if you do not have an accounting system that gives you almost daily overviews of the condition of your business.

So get an accounting system that will provide you with timely and accurate information for making management decisions. It tells you what you need to know when you are considering whether you should accept a brokered assignment or whether you ought to look for another printer. Without this information, you are flying blind, without compass or vision.

THERE ARE MORE WAYS TO FAIL THAN TO SUCCEED

A great many people have published, lectured on, and offered their alleged keys to success, based on the premise that these keys are secret. No one pretends, on the other hand, that the keys to failure are secret, although they are not all that well known, either. They can't be well known, because I have seen so many business people self-destructing through such patently suicidal business practices as those described and implied here. I did not make them up, either. They are the keys to failure that I have observed others use most effectively to drive off their clients, their profits, and their business. Use them freely if you want to see your enterprise fall on its face rapidly. But first, read about a sad, sad tale from a few years ago that illustrates one of the most senseless practices there is—one that arises, I think, out of a peculiar kind of arrogance resulting from success.

There was an engineer, Sam G., who had worked for the Navy Department for some years before he set up his own independent consulting company. Not surprisingly, he pursued and won the bulk of his work from the Navy Department, which tends to be its own prime contractor and therefore awards many subcontracts. The Navy kept Sam and his little engineering firm busy with one contract after another. His company grew steadily, until he had a staff of about 35 people and had become rather well known in the area. By that time, as a result of both his employment by and his contracting with the Navy Department, Sam knew so much about the Navy's projects and plans that he hardly had to listen to what they said or wrote when they described their needs and invited bids and proposals. At least, he thought it had become a waste of time to listen to or even deal with the technical people running the Navy's programs. Sam was quite sure that he knew the work better than those fellows did, and he was also sure that he knew much more than the higher ranking officers in the Navy division for which he did most of his work. (Many of those officers were not highly knowledgeable technically, and they relied on their staffs to advise them on the technical merits of any program.) Sam therefore began to take issue with much of what the technical people said they needed and wanted, explaining that he knew what they really needed, and they could depend on him to deliver what they needed.

Soon, Sam started to become unlucky in his bids and proposals. His company began to fade from sight, and it became defunct much more rapidly than he had built it up. It was gone almost overnight. His story is the inspiration for the following summation of ways to self-destruct, although it is not a unique story; I have witnessed similar debacles resulting from analogous examples of companies becoming "fat, dumb, and happy," as observers have often described the condition.

SOME HIGHLY RECOMMENDED WAYS TO SELF-DESTRUCT

Do the following things only if you want to fail. Be scrupulous in avoiding them, however – even do the opposite – if you want to survive:

- Always remember that you are the consultant and the expert, and don't let your client forget it either. You know more than the client does about the problem; that's why you were hired. Let the client have her say – show your tolerance and fair-mindedness by waiting patiently throughout the client's wrongheaded and ignorant description – and then tell her where she is wrong. If the client wishes to argue, by all means stick to your guns. The client expects you to be completely honest and insist on whatever it is that you know is really needed.

- Be clever in your charges. Set the rate low, but estimate your working hours generously enough to make up for the low rate. Clients look at rates, not at the bottom line, no matter what they say.

- As an alternative, use sliding rates, according to how busy you are, who the client is, and how trusting the client is, among other variables. So what if a client gets offended occasionally when he thinks your rate is out of line? There is always another client eager to use your exceptional talents.

- Put up a front and don't spare the costs: Rent impressive offices in a prestigious office building, buy only the best furniture, use expensive stationery, drive a car you really can't afford, and dress the part of a highly successful specialist.

- Don't waste your time marketing when you are busy and making some money. Keep making money and maximize those hours. You can't make money when you are wasting your time marketing. You can do that when things are slow and you need new work.

- Hire the cheapest help you can find when you need help. The people you hire may not be too good, but your client won't know the difference. You can handle any problems that come up.

- Don't putter around with the little jobs. They're small potatoes, even if they are individually profitable. Think big, and go directly after the big companies and the big projects. Be sure to let clients know that you are not interested in small jobs. You want the major programs.

- Keep strict business hours, as all successful businesses do. If you close at 5:00 P.M., don't accept calls or visitors at 5:05. They can wait until tomorrow. Make clients recognize that you are a successful business; they will respect you more if you compel them to do business on your terms.

- Ingratiate yourself with new clients by telling them useful things you have learned about their competitors while working for the competition. (Don't be afraid to embellish the truth a bit when it will help. It's like advertising, which everybody knows is always a little exaggerated.)

- Tell clients what you think of your own competitors, and don't be afraid to knock the ones who deserve it. Business is tough, and you have to get "down and dirty" when you are trying to beat your competitors out for clients and contracts.

- It's nice to be goody two-shoes, but it's a hard world and you have to look after yourself. When your client wants you to advise her on some course of action, be sure to consider what course of action is in your best interest too.

The real intent in offering this list is not just to stress the fact that you should avoid doing these things and to strive to do the opposite. You're smart enough to know that. But you may have an associate or an employee or two who are not quite as smart as you are. That is why the list is helpful!

THE SHORT SURVIVAL COURSE

The flip side of the preceding list of injunctions suggests what you should do to survive that critical first year, and probably the second and other succeeding years as well. Many practices do not achieve stability and a sound business base for several years. Expect to go on building your base. The overnight success one often hears about exists far more in fiction and in the fond hopes of budding entrepreneurs than it does in reality. However, to balance the don'ts listed, following are some situations you might very well encounter and brief discussions of what to do in each case.

When the Client Is Wrong

Clients are frequently wrong, especially when they are clients of consultants who are experts. First, you need to determine whether any harm can result from their being wrong – for example, will it affect your ability to do a good job at whatever needs to be done? If not, smile pleasantly, ignore the problem, and get on with business. As a case in point, suppose the client offers me a draft that he or she says "only needs a little editing," whereas it obviously needs rewriting. I agree, I price the job for rewriting, I do it, and everyone is happy. However, when the problem stands in the way of getting the job done honestly and effectively, you need to take some action. What you don't need or want is confrontation, nor do you want to prove the client wrong. You need the classic "yes, but" response here. When the American Can Company told us that their maintenance mechanics needed training in machine maintenance, we knew that that was a pure assumption, and there was no way we could be sure of it as a premise for developing a training program. Our response, therefore, was essentially, "Yes, we can see that, but we need to do some testing to see what subjects they need most so we can weight the program properly." Our tests then revealed that the mechanics' chief problem was their inability to read the schematic drawings of the machines. We then had no trouble persuading the client to accept the training program in blueprint reading that we proposed.

4

The client *isn't* always right—but don't let confrontation stand in the way of selling your services. If you can solve the client's problem and make him or her happy, it matters little whether the client fully understood the nature of the problem in the first place.

How Much Should You Charge?

There are several "right" ways to charge for consulting services, depending on the nature of the work, the type of project, your preferences, what has become accepted as the most widespread practice in your field, and what typical clients expect and will accept. You can charge an hourly rate or a daily rate, as many do, or you can charge a fixed "for the job" price. You can even use combinations of these: If your jobs are usually best priced on a daily rate, the occasion may arise when it makes sense to charge an hourly rate or even a fixed price. Be consistent, however. If you have a daily or hourly rate, it ought to be the same for everyone. If you set different rates for different clients, the word will soon be passed around, and every client will want to bargain with you for your best rate. At the same time, no matter what you charge, every client will believe that you have not given him or her your best rate, and that alone makes it difficult to have favorable relations with your clients. If there are necessary exceptions to whatever are your standard practices, be sure that they are in fact exceptions and necessary. If you are working on an hourly or daily basis, keep scrupulously accurate records. One thing a consultant needs and must guard jealously is a reputation for integrity.

Costs Need to Be Managed

Too prosperous an appearance can hurt you more than it helps. Use judgment here, and tend always to the conservative side. When I decided that it was too expensive and completely unnecessary to maintain a suite of offices in a downtown office building, I set up an office at home. I had some trepidation as to whether this would harm my reputation or my appearance of being entirely businesslike. I began to feel better about it

when one of my clients, a Dun & Bradstreet vice-president, congratu-
lated me on my wisdom in cutting my overhead. I don't even use printed
letterheads today. Instead, I use a good grade of blank paper, and my
laser printer prints the letterhead each time it prints out a letter. It looks
as good as any preprinted letterhead and has the advantage that it is
uniquely mine: I designed it. I have extended that practice to other
printed items as well: I combat high printing prices for labels and other
forms – cut them by about one-half in most cases – by manufacturing my
own.

5

Needlessly extravagant offices and accessories are lost profits. Find out
what appearance your market really expects, and fill that need
accordingly.

The Right Time for Marketing

Most of the time, I am working on a job I contracted for six months to a
year earlier and sold several months before that. Meanwhile, I am
spending some part of my time in marketing, no matter how busy I am. If
I wait until all my projects are completed to start marketing, I will be idle
for at least six months, and possibly a year or more. I don't decide
arbitrarily when to market; I am marketing all the time. I am never too
busy to spend some of my time thinking about where and how to pursue
new business and doing something about it, such as writing and sending
out proposals.

6

Keep marketing your product or service. While you are working on one
job or project, sell another. While you are simultaneously doing three,
four, or even more jobs, market others. If you don't market while you
work, sooner or later you will find yourself without work.

Poor Help Comes Cheap

Expensive help is not always good, and cheap help is not always poor,
but the negations of these statements are the premises you must start
with when looking for assistance. I am suspicious of anything that seems

to be too cheap, including part-time help, such as moonlighters, many of whom I have paid to do jobs I had to do over in unhappy past experiences. Generally speaking, you must pay the price for top-quality work, and you must never give your clients less quality than that if you want them to remain your clients. I have sometimes redone work I knew the client would accept, but I wouldn't accept as being good enough. The philosophy of that sneering phrase, "Close enough for government work," is not good enough for me, and it should not be for you if you want to build and keep a good reputation.

Small and Large Potatoes

I have taken on government jobs for as little as $75. Small potatoes, you say? But I did more than $20,000 worth of work for that same agency subsequently. And a $2,400 job grew to almost $65,000 over time in another case. It is analogous to something they say in show business — that there are no small parts, although there are some small actors and actresses. I found that small jobs were not only a frequent entree to larger jobs, but were usually much easier to win than large ones, easier to do, virtually without risk, and quite often far more profitable for the time required to do them.

7

Don't throw away the "small" jobs. Though they may pay less, they may be just as valuable as large jobs in the long run. They often lead to larger jobs, are easy to obtain, and may even pay more than a large job on a per-hour basis.

What Are Your Office Hours and Who Sets Them?

As one millionaire businessman has said, he never works more than a half day, and he recommends it to all. He says it shouldn't make any difference to you which 12 hours you prefer to work. I find that I work some 12-hour days, and I have occasionally worked 24-hour days. But I also work some 4-hour days, some 2-hour days, and some days not at all, according to what the business demands of me at the moment. I am not a true workaholic: I take as much time off as I can, as much as my business permits. That is, I am not self-employed; I am employed by my business. It is an entity unto itself, and it sets the office hours for me, as it sets all the other conditions of my employment.

Confidentiality and Conflicts of Interest

One reason a reputation for integrity is so important is that your clients often find it necessary to make highly confidential information available to you. However, whether the information you have access to is confidential or not, it is essential that you always consider it to be so and treat it accordingly. It is quite possible – even likely – that you will at one time or another work for someone who is a direct or indirect competitor of another of your clients. It is essential that you do not permit yourself to have a conflict of interest: You must never discuss one client (or even a former employer) with another client. Compartmentalize each client and each project, and isolate it from all others. You may even be forced to turn down an assignment occasionally, as I must if two clients wish me to help them with proposals for the same contract.

. . . And about Your Competitors

Many years ago, I was representing a manufacturer of Magic Shower Doors in Miami. I approached a builder in North Miami Beach one day with the hope of winning a contract to sell and install my tub enclosures in his tract of homes.

"I'm using Abco doors now," he said. "What do you think of them?"

"Fine product," I said. "I know the owners. Nice fellows. But I'm here to talk about Magic doors."

"Good for you," said Mr. Builder. "If you had knocked Abco, I would have thrown you out of here. I hate salesmen who knock their competitors."

I made the sale. In fact, I did know the competitive product, and I could have made a good argument for the superiority of what I was selling. But it would have come across as knocking the other fellow, and that is always bad for sales. Rise above it, even if you have an unscrupulous or incompetent competitor or two, and focus on selling what you have to sell.

About Honest Advice

In consultations about marketing to the government, especially in writing proposals, a client sometimes wants me to evaluate a request for proposals and recommend a proposal strategy for them. That is usually followed by a request to help the client write the proposal. But sometimes I run into a situation in which it is my belief that the client has virtually no chance of winning the contract. Should I tell him or her so and lose the proposal-writing job?

Fortunately, I never have doubts about this: I have been hired to render an honest opinion, and I do render one, even if I lose the job. In fact, I may or may not get future business from the client, because the nature of what I do limits the amount of repeat business I am likely to get from any but the largest organizations, and the majority of my clients are small ones. However, I do get virtually all my clients today by word of mouth, and complete honesty in all dealings is essential to continuing to do so.

MORE TO COME

It would be nice if what I have said thus far were all there is to success in the consulting game. But there is more, of course, much more. And that is what the rest of this book is about.

FIND OUT WHAT
BUSINESS YOU ARE IN

Consulting may be a profession. It may even be an art. But to survive in it, much less prosper, make up your mind that it is a business. Even more important, find out *what* business it is. You may be surprised.

ARE YOU IN THE "ME, TOO" BUSINESS?

You are a consultant, and I am a consultant. We are both in business, but we are not in the same business. I don't know what your business is, but I do know what mine is: helping my clients win government contracts. That is what I am paid for, and I charge substantial fees for doing it.

I also sometimes train others in marketing to government agencies. This is done most often via the seminars I deliver to my clients and their employees. The seminars are in-house, custom presentations, under my usual fee arrangements. Much of my consulting, however, is a service of helping clients turn out effective proposals, usually in response to formal requests for proposals from government agencies. That is how I help them win contracts. So why do I not describe my business as writing proposals, helping clients write proposals, and teaching clients how to write proposals?

The truth is that I did at first conceive of and offer my service in those terms. I offered prospective clients a variety of services to help them turn out excellent proposals. Later, I decided—or perhaps I should

15

say, more accurately, that I *learned* or *realized*—that some clients might want to learn how to write their own proposals. Soon enough, I had to modify that vision also: I learned or realized that most of my prospects already know how to write proposals. They really do not need me for that. What most don't know is how to write *winning* proposals. They don't know most of the techniques and strategies of creating the programs and presentations that beat the competitors and win. In fact, to be brutally candid, most do not have the creative imagination necessary to invent and develop their own strategies, tactics, and techniques for winning proposals.

This shortcoming in their marketing via proposals is at least partly because they assign to proposal-writing chores staff members who are technical experts and business executives, but who are neither writers nor marketers. Proposal writing requires both kinds of skills to turn out the winners. Especially, it requires a knowledge of and talent for marketing, as much as it does technical, writing, and related abilities.

Proposal writing is hard work. It is a demanding job that requires lots of midnight oil. I have never finished writing a proposal without feeling weary and grateful that the job is at last over. I am good at it—my track record of turning out proposals that get the job is clear enough evidence of that—but I don't deceive myself: Proposal writing per se is not my business. It is what I must do to achieve my real business objective of helping my clients win contracts. It is necessary for me to be able to write and/or lead others in writing winning proposals, but that is incidental to what I do as a consultant. That is not why clients retain me and not what they pay me for. I am paid to help clients get the *results* they want: contract awards. That is their only reason for hiring me and paying me a good bit more than they pay any but their top executives.

8

Find out what the "carrot" is that is tempting marketing prospects to hire you. What success of theirs are you helping *them* to achieve? That is what you are being paid for—not, strictly speaking, for what you do. When you answer this question, set your rates accordingly.

Does making that distinction seem to be splitting hairs? Pedantic? Academic? Pettifogging? It is not. It is an important distinction to make for at least two reasons:

1. The client is intelligent enough to understand that skill in proposal writing is the key to how I get the results for which he or she pays me, but it is the contract that draws the client into buying my services. It is important, in a marketing sense, to emphasize that winning the contract is your reward; it is why the client retains you and your service. Make no mistake about this truism of marketing: All customers are moved by emotion, not reason. Reason is what most customers use to rationalize their buying decisions because they are intelligent enough to know that they must be rational in their buying.

2. You must remind yourself, as well as your client, what it is that you charge your rates for, not only because it is a stimulus and an inspiration to you in devising the right marketing strategies and sales arguments, but also because it helps you perceive realistically what it is that you do for your money – what it is that motivates the client and persuades him or her to pay your outrageous hourly or daily rate. It helps you keep your feet on the ground and evaluate the effectiveness of what you do and what you must argue to prospective clients if you are to sell them. (It wouldn't matter how clever a writer I were if I won no contracts, and I must never lose sight of that. My clients don't really give a damn how good a writer I am, how well their proposals are written, or how close we come to a win. They care only whether we did or did not win: everything else is irrelevant.)

Reminding yourself what it is that you charge your rates for will also give you a realistic basis for setting those rates. They ought to be based on a variety of factors, including the following:

- Just how specialized am I (are my services)? This must be judged on the basis of how rare your skills are, how difficult it is to find others who do what you do, at least locally, how available they are, and other measures bearing on the question.
- What is the market for what I do? That is, what do others offering a competitive service charge *in this area?*
- What advantages, if any, does a client's retaining my services offer over the client's retaining the services of others?
- How well known am I in this community?

9

Evaluate your marketability and the basis for charging fees on a number of factors, including how rare your skills are, competitors' fees, your special qualities vis-a-vis competitors, and how well known you are in your community.

Consider that, were I just another proposal writer, I would be in the "me, too" business–no better and no worse, no more and no less valuable, than any self-employed writer who knows merely how to organize and assemble a proposal. Such proposal writers are, in fact, free-lance writers, not consultants. In that capacity, I would not be worth even one-half the fee I now command as a marketing consultant specializing in government contracts.

Until I learned that basic truth, my direct mail and other marketing campaigns did not generate a satisfactory response. I did some business, of course, but not the amount that I wanted and thought that I should be able to win. I did not yet realize it, but I was depending on my prospective clients to make the connection from expert proposal writing to contracts awarded (and this from clients who I knew did not understand the need for writing and marketing skills on their proposal-writing teams!). Expecting the client to make that connection is expecting them to do the selling job for you. It won't happen very often. Your business is to help the client achieve his or her end goal–the ultimate benefit the client seeks. Finally I grasped the truth: I had to get the attention of my own prospective clients by promising to help them win contracts and then explaining *why* they needed me and not just any old writer who knew how to put together a proposal. It made all the difference in the world. Clients began to respond. They wanted to know why I claimed to be the answer to their prayers. They began to see me as a consultant and not as a writer, and they began to pay me as a consultant and not as a writer. (Unfortunately, the business world regards a consultant as more important and worthy of higher fees than a scribe.)

This is not a lecture on how to write advertising copy and make presentations. It is a discussion of how you must think of what clients want and what you must do to attract and satisfy clients so that they will pay your rates. Still, you are a consultant and not a merchant. Clients expect you to help them solve their problems and satisfy their needs. They don't really care what it is that you do to satisfy their wants, at least not up front. Up front, they want to know that you understand what it is they want and are committed to getting it for them. Then and only then do they want to know how you go about it and what those credentials are that you have which ought to make them put their faith in you and your promises.

KEEP IT SIMPLE AND SPECIFIC

The problem with complex explanations is not that the average reader cannot understand them, but that the average reader does not want to and will not make the effort to decipher anything that requires a bit of cogitation. Mr., Mrs., and Miss Average Reader have been at work all day. They are tired. They don't care to exert effort. They will resist anything that demands effort. If you want them to read, understand, and react to anything you write and place before them, whether in an envelope, on a screen, or on a printed page, you'd better make it as simple as possible – that is, as easy to understand and react to as possible. That is all that advertising mavens are trying to tell you when they lecture you about selling the benefit – what the late Elmer Wheeler meant when he said, "Sell the sizzle, not the steak."

One problem with this strategy is that a great many professionals and business people who are not in the marketing and advertising world don't fully grasp the difference between the sizzle and the steak. Perhaps the following pairs of contrasts will help:

- A well-written proposal is not a benefit; the contract is a benefit.
- A better written computer program is not a benefit; time and money saved by a program that runs more quickly are benefits. Less time required to learn a program is a benefit.
- A more efficient office layout is not a benefit; time saved and money saved are benefits.

Years ago, when pharmacists truly compounded prescriptions written by physicians, the term *polypharmacal* was not unknown. It referred to the practice of some physicians to include a half dozen or more ingredients in a prescription in the hope that this would multiply the probability that at least one of the ingredients would do the job!

Many people define their businesses in this manner: They include promises of a multiplicity of functions and events in the hope that at least one of them will attract a client. Or they make things deliberately vague and general in the hope that the prospect will interpolate his or her own wants therein.

Both approaches avoid facing facts, and neither works well. When large corporations do many things, they create many organizational entities, each of which expresses its mission simply and specifically. General Electric Company has a Heavy Weapons Division, a Light Weapons Division, and other divisions, each clearly defined.

Note, too, the simplicity of their names. One government executive, reviewing brochures from a number of companies, remarked to me, with good-natured irony, but also with amused contempt, "The smaller the company, the bigger the name." Obviously, names that were thought by their authors to be impressive had the opposite effect, in this office at least.

10

Beware of vague or pretentious company names, advertising messages, and promotional materials. If you don't, you'll be scaring more business away by trying to sound impressive, rather than letting your simplicity and specificity speak for itself.

Much the same can be said for pompous statements of any kind, whether they are the chosen business names or the definitions of the business. There is a kind of nobility in a simple and specific name or definition that can be achieved in no other way. More important, there is power in a specific and easily understood image. IBM once represented its leading electric typewriters in such a manner that they were referred to as "IBMs," just as later a mainframe computer was "an IBM." Phonographs were once "Victrolas," which was an RCA trademark and not a true generic name. The companies in computer software development and related services often tend to somewhat cryptic and exotic names — American Eagle Software Integrators, Inc., Applied Axiomatics, Inc., and Authenticomm, Inc., are three I know of — but there are some relatively large companies in the field with unpretentious, easily understood names, such as Computer Sciences Corporation and Volt Information Sciences, Inc. I, for one, am far more impressed with these simple names that seem to radiate a quiet self-confidence, whereas those other, more elaborate and cryptic names seem to me to be shouting, trying to get attention.

ARE YOU REALLY A CONSULTANT? TWO NECESSARY QUALIFICATIONS

A discussion of who and what a consultant is has been taking place in CompuServe's consulting forum for the past few days. In part, this general discussion rises out of an earlier discussion of whether the specialist who hires him- or herself out as a temporary is a consultant. Opinions vary widely. One participant says that it is a matter of one's perception. Another counters that simply *saying* that you are a consultant does not make you one. Still others have their own standards by which they judge the legitimacy of anyone's claim to be a consultant.

This is not a new argument. It raged in government and even occupied a portion of the newspaper pages for a time during the Carter administration. It turned out that few others, in or out of government, agreed with administration officials (principally those of the Office of Management and Budget).

Obviously, I must define the term here for our own purposes of communication, and I deem the following to be a reasonable position to take in this matter. Consulting is two things. First, it is not a profession per se, but is a way of practicing your profession, whether you are a writer, a designer, a trainer, a computer systems analyst, an engineer, an accountant, a security expert, or some other kind of specialist. Second, it is a way of helping someone, a client, by doing what the client cannot do for him- or herself. That does not necessarily mean that the client does not know how to do the job; rather, it means that perhaps the client wants an outside, more objective opinion or that other problems require help of a specialized nature. To be a true consultant, you have to both practice your profession capably and do for clients what they cannot or do not want to do for themselves for whatever reason.

Your business as a consultant is the latter, but the definition of your business is a clear explanation of why the client needs you. That is, if you

11

More often than not, you'll have to sell (i.e., "create") the client's need for your services. Don't lose opportunities by thinking that clients already know why they need—or don't need—your help. Make your clients do the job of defining what your business means to them. All you have to do is learn to listen.

are an expert and consultant on security systems, someone who is conscious of a need for help in designing a security system (a *felt need*) may seek you out. But the bulk of your marketing must be to make others *aware* of their need for a security system (i.e., *create* a need) before you begin to sell the system. And the first step is to define what you do for the clients whom you have made aware of the need.

WHY DID YOU BECOME A CONSULTANT?

Have you thought about why you became a consultant? Did you think out just what it was you were going to accomplish and for whom? If you did, it was almost surely not in terms of whom you were going to help and how you were going to help them. You probably thought only in terms of what service you would sell and perhaps of who your clients were likely to be. You probably assumed that your clients would be those who knew they had a need for what you offered or who would recognize that need as soon as they learned of your offer. It doesn't work that way in life. Some people buy, but most have to be sold. If you waited for people to buy (i.e., feel their needs and react to those needs on their own initiative), you would soon be out of business. You have to sell people (i.e., "create" needs by making people aware of them and inducing them to buy). No, that is not a cynicism; it's a cold fact. You have to explain to prospective clients what their needs are. You don't do that by thinking of what you want to sell. You do that by thinking of what kinds of problems people have, whom among them you can help, and how you can help them – in effect, what benefits you can bring them. That is the purpose of consulting: helping those who need help. You therefore start a consulting practice by reasoning out who needs your help, what your help will do for them, and how you are going to let them know that you are ready, willing, and eager to help them.

How did I get so smart? The hard way, as most of us do: I made my share of mistakes, probably many more than my share, and I learned from them. I had a large advantage in that I did not shrink from recognizing my mistakes, or even my stupidities, for what they were. It is essential that you don't cringe at the thought of facing your own faults and failures. Being secure enough to be honest with yourself about such things is an immediate advantage over your competitors. It helps you overcome the myopia that handicaps so many of us.

WE ARE ALL MYOPIC

Nearsightedness is epidemic in the business world. If you are not sure just where you are going or ought to be going, you are not alone. A great many entrepreneurs – consultants and others – have that same problem. They can't make the fine discriminations between what they sell and what clients buy – and there is a difference: You want to sell your time, your knowledge, your experience, your skills. The client wants to buy the benefits of desired end results – problems solved, headaches eliminated, contracts won, or other targeted outcomes. Many people have trouble making these kinds of distinctions between what you want and what your clients and prospective clients want, and you must school yourself in doing so. It is analogous to the belief many have that learning how the government buys is learning how to sell to the government. Not so: How the government buys is one subject – the mechanics and procedures of the government procurement system; how to sell to the government is marketing, quite a different subject!

Many people in business display that kind of myopia when they are asked what business they are in. You can read here how a number of computer consultants responded when asked to describe their businesses. Here is the first one:

> *We're in the business of developing office automation software products, using OS/2 or DOS, for corporations for internal distribution or for vendors for commercial sale.*

This is a typical "me, too" description, not even as good as some others I have seen, because it is even more general, more vague, and more imitative than many other "me, too" company definitions. Have a look at several others:

> *I'm in the business of helping my customers plan, install, and support new chunks of technology as cleanly and as rapidly as possible, but with the least amount of negative effects on my customer's organization and personnel.*

This says even less than the first example. "Chunks of technology?" What does that mean? Is that how technology is packaged – in chunks? Or is this an effort to sound crisp and sophisticated? How about "the least amount of negative effects?" Is that what the consultant wishes to promise – that there will definitely be at least some "negative effects." But here is what another computer consultant promises:

> *I provide solutions for the mixed computer product environment, primarily to companies with dissimilar computer systems.*

There is a sensible idea here, but it's hidden behind deplorable expression that conceals it. Why didn't this consultant say something meaningful and in simple, clear language, such as "I organize your odd and assorted computers to work together as a single system?" That would have meant something. But have a look at this one:

> *I create and sell clever new arrangements of ones and zeros.*

This is a prime example of the worst curse of copywriting: the irresistible urge to be clever, even if it means making nonsensical statements and forgetting where you are supposed to be headed – to an argument promoting sales. This bit of cleverness is all the worse because it is coupled with the bad taste of ego stroking: The author could not resist adding the very word itself, so that you can be assured that the author is as clever in his work as he is in his writing.

There is one thing that is the same about each of these statements: They all describe what the consultant sells or wishes to sell. They all describe how the consultant views his or her service. None attempts to view the service from the client's viewpoint. The descriptions are of what the consultant wants to sell, rather than of what the typical client wants to buy. (What client wants to buy *any* "new arrangements of ones and zeros?")

These four statements are typical of the problems many independent consultants have. They haven't thought out clearly what they specialize in – that is, what *results* they specialize in getting for their clients. They fail to explain what it is they do or promise to do for their clients.

Frankly, your brochure would find a home promptly in my "circular file" if it came across my desk and was in the kind of language of the examples just presented. What these sets of words say to me in each case is that the author of them is not certain just what he or she can promise to do for me. Worse, the author evidently can't think clearly. You can only write what is in your head, so I must assume that muddy, unclear writing reflects muddy, unclear thinking. That's hardly what one wants in a consultant.

12

What does it mean when you are not sure enough of what your business is to state it in simple, unequivocal language? I have the notion that until you can state what your business is in terms that your prospective clients grasp immediately, not only do you not know what your business is, but you don't really have one. You appear to be floundering about searching for a business.

THE TWO KINDS OF CONSULTANTS

Harvey Mackay, in his *Swim with the Sharks without Being Eaten Alive* (Ballantine Books, New York, 1988) identifies two types of expert, one who tells you what he or she *thinks* is going to happen and the other who *makes* something happen. I think this applies as well to consultants, who are (or ought to be) also experts at whatever they do, but I would paraphrase the idea a bit: There is one type of consultant who counsels and advises only – that is, he or she tells the client how to make something happen – and there is another type who does whatever has to be done to help the client get the result the client wants. (Probably most consultants do both.) Now, there is a limited market for the first type of consultant; the medical field is one of the few places where this kind of consulting is fairly commonplace, although even here the consultant is often a surgeon or other specialist who provides medical procedures, as well as diagnostic opinions and recommendations for treatment. By and large, the second kind of consultant is more prevalent.

THE CLIENT CAN TELL YOU WHAT BUSINESS YOU ARE IN

One of the better ways to find out what business you are in is to ask your clients. You have to do this indirectly, however, because you are not the only one who has difficulties deciding just what your business is: Many clients have similar difficulties. Nonetheless, it is the client who decides what it is that he or she really wants you to do. If you doubt this, you have probably not yet had a great deal of consulting experience. Even face to face, doing your best to lead and guide the client in telling you all about his or her needs, you may find yourself frustrated in getting a clear picture.

One man I knew, Ralph W., an engineering executive in a small electronics company in which I worked many years ago, had a solution to this problem: Whatever you said to Ralph, whether it was information you volunteered or your response to some question he had asked, he paid close attention, looked thoughtful, and then said, "Let me understand you: You are saying . . ." (whereupon he repeated in his own words what you had just said, even if it was the one word, "Yes"). You were required to agree or disagree with Ralph's interpretation, and the exchange did not end until agreement was reached. It was rare that Ralph and anyone he talked to failed to understand each other!

Another place where it is easy to find confirmation of the difficulties clients have in explaining their needs is the statements of work included in their requests for proposals (RFPs). You will soon see how common it is for clients to be thoroughly confused or uncertain about their real needs. Such statements often ramble on about symptoms and concerns, without ever getting down to brass tacks. Always examine RFPs, in whatever form you get them, critically and with some skepticism. At least one-half of the "secret" of writing winning proposals and making winning presentations is in a complete and accurate understanding of the client's true need. Gaining that understanding is often quite difficult, even something of an art. Many government RFPs specifically require that the proposer present his or her own interpretation of the client's need, and an even tentative acceptance of the proposal can depend on the accuracy of that interpretation: When the client finds that the proposer has not exhibited a clear understanding of the client's need, the proposal is deemed nonresponsive and is disqualified from further consideration.

The "Ralph W. method" described here is a good one for spontaneous, face-to-face exchanges. For the problem with RFPs and their work statements, however, other solutions are usually required, according to the specific situation. Here is one example, a case where the successful proposer had to sort through—that is, analyze—the client's shortsighted and misstated ideas of the need, then had to redefine the need, and finally had to sell the redefinition to the client. (That means educating the client as tactfully as possible and selling your own definition or analysis of the client's need.)

The U.S. Postal Service (USPS), although a government corporation with its own standards and regulations, is like most other government agencies. Despite a huge number of employees—well in excess of a half-million, it was unable to get all of its work done. On one occasion, the

USPS computer systems division decided that it needed to augment its in-house staff of computer specialists with an ever-ready supply of consultants available whenever needed on a contract basis. (This is a rather common solution in government: In many cases the bulk of the staffs running government computers and supporting the computers with a variety of services are contractors, many working on site.) So the division announced an opportunity to compete for a task-order contract to provide short-term computer-specialist services when called for.

The USPS request for proposals (RFP) included a statement of work that specified separate lists of computer languages, types of software, machines (all mainframes), and computer-linked occupational specialties (programmers, systems analysts, designers, etc.). Each list was about eight to ten items long. As a basic requirement, the statement of work stipulated that the successful contractor had to be someone who had enough specialists on staff to provide, on demand, individuals representing any combination of knowledge, experience, and capability drawn from the lists.

With so many items on each list, the possible combinations represented a need for a rather large and unusually diversified staff of computer specialists, a requirement that would be difficult for any but the largest firms to meet.

One proposer responded by first presenting an interpretation of the requirement that was somewhat different than the one stated by the USPS. The proposer stated in its proposal that what the Postal Service needed was the immediate availability of a pool of experts such as that described, regardless of where they came from or how they got there. That is, said the proposer, the real requirement was that the contractor be able to produce any required consultant, whether that individual was on its permanent staff or not. Thus, having all the specialists be a part of the permanent in-house staff was not truly an absolute necessity. The proposal then went on to present ample evidence that the proposer could meet the need as a result of having a huge roster of computer specialists to support its normal business of supplying technical and professional temporaries. In fact, said the proposer, it offered greater reliability because its computerized roster of available specialists, most of them independent consultants who hired out often as temporaries, was far larger and more diversified than anyone's staff of permanent employees.

The proposal was successful. It satisfied the client (the USPS) that its need had been restated and clarified successfully, and the proposer was awarded a contract for the specified services.

13

Always be capable of *redefining* your business, because every job carries different needs and benefits with it. Always be specific about what you are selling *now* to "this" particular client, even if you've worked with the client many times before.

THE MOST IMPORTANT DEFINITION
OF YOUR BUSINESS

The firm that won the USPS contract redefined its business in terms of the USPS's expressed need: The proposer's business now was the satisfaction of all USPS needs for computer specialists to carry out all tasks that might arise. But that is the nature of custom work, is it not? For general purposes—for example, for marketing and promotion generally—you must be able to furnish a description of your business that is specific in what you normally achieve for a client as a direct result of what you do. But you are a consultant, doing custom work, often addressing new and different problems than any you have ever addressed before. In doing custom work, you often must write a proposal or make a presentation, even if it is only an informal letter or a simple presentation across a desk in someone's office. You must explain to the client just how you will solve the problem and satisfy the need that he or she is concerned about. In giving your explanation, you are actually *redefining your business* by defining it for that one application. In fact, since most of us rarely, if ever, are faced with exactly the same problem a second time, we are constantly redefining our businesses. Or at least, we should be. The best definition of your business is not what you do for *all* clients, but what you are going to do for *the particular client whose business you are after at the moment*. At that moment, what is important is not "what I do for all my clients and will do for you," but "what I do that will solve your present problem and satisfy your present need." At that moment, that is all the client cares about. Don't distract him or her with other matters: Everything else is irrelevant for now. Focus all your knowledge, skills, and imagination on this, the client's, problem.

There is a method for defining your business that is very useful, if you keep an open mind and pay close attention. The following is not a digression, but a tip that ought to help you discipline your analytical ability in a beneficial way. In fact, it is a handy tool for many kinds of analyses and diagnoses.

A TRICK TO ACHIEVE OBJECTIVITY

During World War II, there were shortages of materials typical of major wars. All sorts of substitutions were made. Thick copper bus bars in many plants were replaced for the duration of the war with silver bus bars, costly though silver was, because copper was in short supply and in demand for military needs. Plastics were substituted for metals in many places, and everyone's ingenuity was strained to make do with less satisfactory substitutions for all the materials that we were used to having in abundance. Despite these shortages and substitutions, an executive at the General Electric Company took note of a strange phenomenon: Frequently, the substitute material was not only more readily available than the original material, but it was cheaper and better than the original! There was nothing more to do about it at the time, other than to remember it, but the executive did remember it. He stored it in the back of his mind until the war had ended, and then he did something about it: He authorized GE engineer Lawrence Miles to investigate the phenomenon of improving products while reducing costs, and/or adding utility. The result of Miles's work done as a consequence of that order was what is now known as *value engineering*, or "VE," also called value analysis and value management as a result of extending the method into other areas of application.

We are now going to look at and borrow a simple, but effective, diagnostic tool from value engineering. Never fear: This is not going to be a dreary technical lecture. We shall borrow from only one phase of value engineering, the study phase. And even then, we are going to review, not the entire phase, but only the first steps that are used to identify an item properly. In these steps, there is a neat trick that has many other useful applications.

WHAT DOES IT DO?

Value engineering seeks answers to a series of questions referring to the item being studied. The first question is "What is it?" The objective is simply to make a firm, unequivocal, and rational identification of the item in the simplest language possible. More important, however, is the second question asked of the item, which is "What does it do?" There, the need for objectivity, clarity, and precision is even more essential in value engineering.

The strategy of value engineering depends not only on objectivity, but also on the idea of *functionality,* as exhibited in the functional analysis that answers the second question. *Functionality* is a basic and integral thread that runs throughout the value engineering process and tends to dominate it. Fortunately, grasping the concept comes easily to engineers. Unfortunately, it does not come easily to many others and has thus been something of an obstacle in transferring the idea of value engineering to other activities where it could be beneficial.

Most things have more than one function, but most usually have only one *basic* or *main* function. A wristwatch is a familiar item that most of us own and wear. What is its main or basic function? If you said "to tell time," go to the foot of the class. I have a novel alarm clock that has a speaker and a mechanical voice that literally tells the time, but my wristwatch merely *indicates* the time. It is I who tells the time.

"What's the difference?" you ask. "*Tell, indicate.* It's just semantics."

Well, yes, but semantics, contrary to popular opinion, is the study of the relationship between symbols and what they refer to and is an exact science. Semantics requires precision in thinking, also necessary in value engineering and in defining your business to your prospective clients. Our words reflect what we think and how we think. (What else can they reflect?) We must therefore choose and use words as precisely and as literally as possible. What does it do? Indicates time. Verb and noun, and nothing else. Not "time of day" or "A.M. and P.M.," but single verb and single noun: indicates time.

That's a basic rule: verb and noun. It is imposed to enforce objectivity and to eliminate, as far as possible, all emotional, subjective influences and other bars to clarity in answering the question, "What does it do?" No adjectives and no adverbs; just verb and noun. Sometimes you must add a word to qualify the verb or noun, a compound verb or noun if and when it is necessary, but only when absolutely necessary.

14

> Use the principles of value engineering to be objective and precise in analyzing your business. The verb-noun rule is an invaluable diagnostic tool in leading you toward specificity and in defining your practice.

There is a great deal more to value engineering than that, of course, but we need no more. We borrowed what we needed: the verb-noun rule. We can apply it as a diagnostic or troubleshooting tool to help us analyze what we do for clients. It can tell us what is wrong with our initial business description and put us on the right track. Let's start with my own case. What do I do for my clients? Win contracts. That is it, the verb and noun. Oh, yes, they are government contracts, and I don't literally win them myself; my client does. I help my client win contracts. Still, when I have reduced what I do *for my clients* to a single verb and single noun, I have made a great deal of progress in getting rid of all that excess baggage of adjectives and adverbs, all that excess of superlatives, all that hype, and all those other hanger-on words that add no truly essential meaning and that often obscure whatever significant meaning there is to begin with. I now have defined the essence of what I do for my clients. It is a sound base on which I can now build.

Let's look again at those four examples of business descriptions that we examined and discussed earlier:

> *We're in the business of developing office automation software products, using OS/2 or DOS, for corporations for internal distribution or for vendors for commercial sale.*
>
> *I'm in the business of helping my customers plan, install, and support new chunks of technology as cleanly and as rapidly as possible, but with the least amount of negative effects on my customer's organization and personnel.*
>
> *I provide solutions for the mixed computer product environment, primarily to companies with dissimilar computer systems.*
>
> *I create and sell clever new arrangements of ones and zeros.*

Try reducing each of these statements to a single-verb, single-noun expression, and see what you get. Let's try our hand with the first one: *develop software.*

That doesn't say very much does it? Let's expand it a bit, just to study it: *develop office automation software.* There is that compound noun I mentioned. Unfortunately, it doesn't say much either, although it does say essentially as much as the original statement did. Everything following the words "office automation software" in the original statement is superfluous. It is information that is useful somewhere, but not here. It does not contribute to a definition of the business you are in. The original definition does not answer the question you must assume the client has: What are you going to *do* for me—that is, what are you going to do for me that I can't get from any of your competitors? (Of course, you will claim that your service or product is better than that of your competitors, but the client will want some evidence to back that claim.) Whether you work with DOS, OS/2, or some other operating system software is irrelevant, for the moment, even if the client does know the difference between them. (He or she may or may not even know what you are talking about here.) Also irrelevant for now is what kinds of clients you perceive that you work with. (It is probably irrelevant in general: Would you turn away a client who is not a software vendor and who does not intend to distribute the program internally?)

Perhaps you can see that the verb-noun rule is a good diagnostic tool: Its use can reveal weaknesses in your description of your job by stripping away all those words that conceal, rather than reveal, what you do, and it can also help you find the right words.

Decide what your service or product does that furnishes an important benefit to the client. In this case, what benefit does automating his or her office produce? I suggest that it *increases efficiency* or, better yet, *cuts costs.* (Note the verb-noun combinations.) You may be able to find many other benefits, such as *reduces labor dependence.* (Note the compound noun here.) In expanding this idea into a presentation, you would explain that, by reducing the client's dependence on skilled labor, you reduce the labor costs of the office. But the point is that you have forced yourself to think out in detail how what you do benefits your clients by building your business definition around one simple central idea. (For example, we increase your office efficiency or save you money or make you more profitable by developing custom office automation software for you.)

Try the same thing on the other statements as an exercise, and see where it takes you. (Frankly, I have no idea as to what you can do with the "ones and zeros" definition. I wouldn't even try to find a verb-noun combination that would help me analyze the meaning of that. It might be a good idea to trot out later in a brochure or presentation, but it is definitely not a good lead-off idea.)

BEATING MURPHY'S LAW

My wife is a worrier. She always expects the worst to happen. I am an optimist. I expect that everything will work out. If it doesn't, I will make it work out. I am always sure that I can. Still, I plan and prepare for disasters. Optimism is the way to go, but there is no use in being a fanatic about it.

THE BEGINNER'S LUCK
BOOBY TRAP

David Moskowitz, an independent computer consultant in the Norristown suburb of metropolitan Philadelphia, is one of many independent consultants who have reported and commented on the misfortune of winning a first client and contract too easily. That is a fairly common phenomenon, but it is not the only kind of beginner's luck that turns out not to be the good fortune it seems at first to be, but too often proves to be a concealed petard, a booby trap that blows up in your face later. Here are a few specific examples of beginner's (bad) luck that you may be unfortunate enough to encounter:

- Your first contract was verbal, following casual, unhurried negotiations. You and your first client came to an agreement quickly and easily, sealed your bargain with a firm handshake, and all went well, with no challenges or disagreements.

- Your first client was easy to negotiate with, understood your need to cover your overhead, as well as draw a salary, and agreed to your stated rate with little discussion.

- Your first client added a few items to the requirements you set forth during the course of the project. You mentioned that this would add costs, but the client assured you that you would not get hurt by the changes and agreed readily to an adjustment in price that was highly satisfactory to you.

- Your first client paid your bill promptly when you presented it at the completion of the project.

These are all examples of Murphy's law in reverse: Instead of everything going wrong, everything goes right—the first time. Murphy would smile knowingly, however, if he were to read this. He would know that exceptions are not a reversal of his law. They are just diversions that will make the eventual truth of the law all the more apparent. In fact, they *are* Murphy's law in the truest sense: You are being lured to the precipice, and made ready for the fall.

15

Don't let your guard down because of beginner's luck. Easy negotiations, a gentleman's agreement that is honored, or the quick payment of your bill will be the exception rather than the rule. Always keep Murphy's law in mind, and plan accordingly.

Suggest that these outcomes are normal to most experienced consultants, and they will smile and ask you if you believe in the tooth fairy, too. Such early experiences are comparable to that of the individual who hits a small jackpot on a first or second try at the one-armed bandits of Las Vegas. Nothing will convince that individual that he or she does not have a magic touch and can win really big money by continuing on and depending on that magic touch. Nothing but the real disaster of putting all the winnings back in an effort to win even more brings truth and disillusionment.

APPROACH WITH CAUTION ANYTHING THAT
COMES TOO EASILY

The truth is that you win most clients and contracts only after arduous and energetic marketing in which you make many tries for each. (You do very well to bat even .250 in marketing.) Clients often speak with a forked tongue, so that verbal contracts are, as Sam Goldwyn was alleged to have said, not worth the paper they are written on, smiles and firm handshakes notwithstanding. Clients may smile and chat pleasantly with you, but they will fight you tooth and nail to get your best price, often by inviting opposing bids, proposals, and presentations from tough competitors. They will pick your brains for a free analysis of their problems. They will change requirements after you have signed the contract and work is under way, but they will try to avoid renegotiating the original price, despite the added work and expense to you. They take as long as they can to pay your bill, and sometimes you have to resort to stringent collection action to get paid at all.

Discouraging? Truth often is, but it shouldn't prevent you from taking the proper measures – countermeasures, that is.

THE COUNTERMEASURES

The first and most important countermeasure to Murphy's law is to recognize it. Agree that it is a reality and accept it: Don't become a cynic or a complete skeptic, but do become a realist. Recognize that clients are individuals, business people who are trying to follow the classical formula for business success: Buy low and sell high. Some of them will do this honestly and legitimately; others will not. The latter will be dishonest and careless about legitimacy, as long as it is in their interest. They will exploit you and take advantage of you if they can, and some of them are quite skilled at doing that. Here are some of the propositions I have been offered by prospective clients who wanted me to write proposals for them:

- I will pay you if I win the contract.
- I will give you a large part of the job as a subcontract.
- We will be partners in the proposal and the contract.
- I will recommend you to all my friends and get you lots of work.

Did I fall for any of these? Of course, I did. How do you think I got my experience? (It was Wilson Mizner who was credited with saying that "Experience is the name people put to their mistakes.") I prefer to regard my mistakes as inevitable and necessary, an education that never comes without cost and is usually worth whatever you pay for it – if you are wise enough to benefit from it. However, you don't have to make all the mistakes personally: You can learn from others' mistakes too, mine in this case, for most of whatever wisdom I have is really 20/20 hindsight, of course.

MARKETING: WHEN TO DO IT

From a marketing viewpoint, consulting is not like selling Fuller brushes or Avon cosmetics. It is not a "one call" business: You don't go out knocking on doors at 9:00 A.M. and return with a few orders at the end of the day. Almost without exception, winning a new client and a contract is an extended proposition. It takes many days and many calls and is likely to consume many weeks or even months of effort. Sometimes I have run into that unexpected stroke of pure luck, such as a client who decided immediately to hire me on the strength of my great persuasive powers or, more likely, because he could not afford to spend any more time finding someone acceptable. Even then, it generally took up to three weeks of administrative paperwork and other delays before I could begin work. That is part of marketing, too. On the other hand, some of my contracts resulted from marketing work I had done several *years* earlier – general marketing work, PR, image-building work, not in pursuit of any specific client or contract. Here is one case:

A presentation I had made in Harrisburg, Pennsylvania, to a convention of mail order dealers, circa 1979, brought me a contract with the Salvation Army in Jacksonville, Florida, circa 1984. An official of the Salvation Army had been present at the Pennsylvania convention and remembered me several years later when his organization wanted help in writing a formal proposal. That kind of thing is not especially unusual; it has happened a number of times. Sometimes you reap harvests from seeds you didn't even know you had planted. Marketing professional services effectively and efficiently is not a once-in-a-while activity; it has to be a permanent, ongoing function that you pursue at every opportunity. But you don't wait for serendipity; you must *make* opportunities to elevate your visibility. Never put off marketing until you "have the time," or you will have nothing but time: You will have no clients and no contracts. Set aside time to market even when you are at your busiest. All successful businesses do. That is principally why they are successful.

If you are a consultant, all your activities, especially your public appearances, are important elements of your marketing, even if you don't realize it. Therefore, belong to as many organizations as you can, and make time to be active at meetings, conferences, conventions, and other events. Learn to be a public speaker, serve on committees, write papers and articles, and participate in every way possible, but especially in those activities that raise your visibility to the maximum. Many of these activities are referred to as *networking*, but they come down to becoming well known and well respected as an expert in whatever field you specialize and consult in.

16

Make networking an important part of your activities as a consultant. Join both job-related and civic organizations, attend conventions, serve on committees, and speak at meetings. All these will increase your visibility and make you well known as an expert in your field. That attracts new clients.

NEGOTIATIONS AND CONTRACTS

When it comes to negotiation and contracts, never mind smiles, firm handshakes, and verbal agreements: They are only the preliminaries to real negotiations and contracts. Get your agreement down on paper. It need not be a formal contract drawn up by lawyers, and, in fact, it usually should not be. (Certain prospective clients will break deals if a lawyer goes overboard with too many whereases, too many clauses, and too many pages requiring signatures and seals.) A letter of agreement, a memorandum of understanding, a purchase order, or a letter accepting a proposal is usually adequate for all but major projects. Be sure, however, that your client's signature is inscribed somewhere in such manner as to indicate clearly his or her agreement to the terms.

Be sure that the agreement is specific – that it includes both qualitative and quantitative commitments by the two parties. Have it say not only *what* you will do, but *how much* of it you will do. That can be an agreed-upon estimate of hours, days, pages, lines of code, number of

17

In general, avoid having lawyers draw up contracts with clients—but always get something in writing nonetheless. The challenge is being as specific as possible in the units of work you'll be providing, based on what you and the client think needs doing.

drawings, square feet of coverage, inches of tape, or whatever units are appropriate to quantify the work or end product, but this estimate must be there if you want to be covered should the client dispute whether you have performed as agreed upon and whether you are entitled to be paid. If you believe it impractical to specify these estimates to the nth degree, you can insert a figure with a tolerance—for example, ± 10 percent. (Even here, however, if you leave room for dispute, you will encounter dispute.)

Clients often fail to specify what they want even qualitatively, much less quantitatively. And that kind of deficiency is usually equally apparent in their formal requests for proposals. It may or may not be an oversight on the client's part, but it probably reflects the client's inability to provide a detailed specification of need (as observed in the previous chapter).

An example of what can happen because of a lack of specificity is offered in a recent procurement by the IRS of 50,000 AT&T personal computers for $1.43 billion. Originally, the IRS chose AT&T's proposal as the winning one, although IBM had offered to fill the IRS requirement for $708 million, and Lockheed had proposed to furnish the computers for $900 million. The reason that the bids were so disparate, explained an IRS spokesman when questioned, was because the IRS bid solicitation was vague in describing the need and the problem the IRS had: old-model computers, poor interoffice communications, and a lingering large residue of paper records. The IRS had a panel of experts go over the three proposals, and the panel decided that the AT&T computers were the best buy for the government, despite the higher costs.

The IRS case is a classic one, proving again that price is not always the chief determinant of the winning proposal. (In fact, it is rarely the chief determinant, unless the proposals are judged to be equal in technical and other merits.) Nor is that situation peculiar to the government by any means. The Borders super-bookstore is invariably busier by far than the competitive super-bookstore of a prominent chain less than a half-mile from it, despite the greater discounts offered by the chain book-store. This is because many customers assess *value,* rather than cost, when considering purchases. (Bear that in mind when writing a proposal or making a presentation: Explain the value of what you propose.)

Thus, vagueness may be a glaring fault in a procurement, but it is probably unavoidable in most cases, because the client either is unable to provide more details or prefers to give you the maximum opportunity to propose those details. In any case, you cannot afford to ignore this lack; it is essential that you do something about it. In fact, it is not necessarily a fault or failure on the part of the client: There is a clear implication in the lack of a detailed specification in a request for pro-posals that you are expected, as a proposer, to propose a set of specifica-tions. The truly wise client requesting proposals tries to encourage each proposer to offer his or her own ideas so that the client has the oppor-tunity to evaluate and compare the technical merits of the various proposals. You must infer that as the client's intent, whether the client did or did not mean to imply it. Nor is a lack of specificity by the client necessarily a disadvantage to you or a problem for you in writing a proposal: Quite the contrary, it is really an opportunity for you to show how you excel over your competitors. It is an advantage if you use it well.

We will discuss this at greater length in a moment, but first, observe that there is another course of action you might be tempted to follow, as so many are: You can point out the problem to the client and request clarification or specifications. That is the first course of action that occurs to many consultants. But is it the logical thing to do? You may think it is. However, let's consider it and examine the pros and cons. Maybe there are some aspects to the question that are not immediately apparent.

Asking for Clarification

When we are confronted with a request that is less than clear, most of us almost instinctively ask the client questions: How long should this man-ual be, Mr. Client? Do you want all windows and doors secured or just the doors secured, Madame Client? Should I include the cost of preparing new drawings, or will you update them? Will I have to travel to Guam to interview the engineers, or will someone here be able to answer all my questions? In what form do you want the program and in how many copies? Should the package include a lecture guide or just lesson plans?

These are typical questions that occur to proposers when they perceive gaps in statements of work. Proposers ask these questions at preproposal conferences and in telephone calls to clients. The Federal Aviation Administration once requested proposals and quotations to prepare an annual report on the year's safety engineering. The contractor was expected to have 500 copies printed with about 75 color illustrations, but the client, the FAA, did not furnish an estimate of the size of the report or the source of the color photographs. Nor did the client specify inks, papers, and type for the printed report. In a similar vein, the Bureau of Naval Personnel requested that a security training manual be written for junior officers, but gave not even a clue as to how the manual would be designed, what it would include other than Naval security regulations, or how big it would be. Aberrations? No; these are typical problems, and they are not peculiar to government agencies. I have encountered the same kinds of problems when responding to requests from International Telephone and Telegraph (ITT), American Telephone & Telegraph (AT&T), Control Data Corporation, and numerous other business organizations.

This kind of vagueness is to be expected from organizations seeking expert help. It occurs because they don't have the answers for which they seek the help of consultants. The client who wants a manual written or a computer program designed may know absolutely nothing about writing or computer programming. It is implicit in the arrangement that you, the consultant expert, can or should be able to furnish the answers. But how? Let's look at a possible scenario (abridged to essentials):

> YOU: *You don't specify the size or content of the training manual, Mr. Client. Can you give me some idea of how many pages you think you will need, as well as some other specifics?*
> CLIENT: *I really don't know, Mr. Consultant. I hadn't thought about it. I guess I have to ask my staff what they think and get back to you.*

What the client does then is consult with others, in or out of his or her own organization, and come up with some estimates. Those figures are then used to clarify the client's statement of work, whether it is part of a formal request for proposals or only an informal request for quotations. In either case, it is improved information furnished to any other consultant the client is talking to. The client may, in fact, be answering questions that have not occurred to your competitors, thus furnishing

NEGOTIATIONS AND CONTRACTS

41

18

In a competitive situation, be wary of asking too many questions if you feel the client is vague. In writing a proposal or pitching your work, you may clarify the client's thinking in ways your competitors haven't. By settling too many questions on the phone with the client, you may be inadvertently bolstering the causes of your rivals, who may be updated by the client after your call.

them with information that they would not otherwise have had. Not exactly to your benefit, is it?

Giving the Store Away

Of course, there are hazards in being too forthcoming with free information: The client may be only picking your brains with no intention of letting a contract to you or to anyone else, or the client may decide after getting your information that there is no need to award a contract. You need to demonstrate that you are capable and know what you are talking about, but telling too much may be self-defeating.

A certain prominent aerospace company called on me once in connection with services for the Postal Service for which they had a contractual obligation. They were uncertain as to what to provide to satisfy the obligation. Someone on staff there knew that I had had considerable experience doing contract work for the Postal Service and suggested calling on me. I met with the company's people, several of whom I knew from earlier business dealings, and we discussed their need. Since I had done considerable work for this aerospace firm a few years earlier and enjoyed cordial relationships with its staff, I had no reason to have any misgivings about speaking openly and frankly with them. It was a mistake, however, for my trust was misplaced: After getting my detailed proposal, with my $14,000 estimate for doing the job, they hired someone as their direct employee at a $12,000 salary and assigned him to carry out the program I had so naively designed for them in my proposal, in effect donating it to them at no cost.

Fortunately, incidents such as this are relatively rare, but they are certainly not unknown. They are a definite hazard, at least in doing business in the private sector, and are something to guard against as best you can. They always remind me of what the referee says to the two prizefighters before the bout begins: "Protect yourself at all times." That is one way to interpret Murphy's law. Try not only to withhold a few critical pieces of information, but try also to make it clear to the client in some indirect way that they are being withheld.

The client may choose to discuss the specifics with you when you point out the lack of precision in the specifications of the RFP and statement of work. In your innocence, assuming that the client is talking to you and you only about this project, you offer your own opinions and estimates, as I so trustingly did. You think you are solidifying your position here, but you may simply be setting up the same result as in the scenario described. You are probably helping the client at your expense or, possibly, helping your competitors more than yourself. It certainly does not hurt to ask the client whether the procurement is to be competitive or negotiated with a selected source. If you get an evasive answer or a refusal to answer, be guarded in what you reveal without a contract and payment.

Ask Questions

That brings up another point: Many of us are overly reluctant to ask hard business questions. Perhaps we are afraid of being offensive or appearing to be without tact. Perhaps we have a great fear of rejection, such as a direct refusal to answer would constitute. These fears are unfounded. Clients seeking services from consultants must expect to be questioned, and they do. You must ask questions about the business side of a prospective relationship, as well as about the technical side. Perhaps you don't have to ask every question directly; often, you can infer answers from other, indirectly related discussions. But you should not remain in the dark about important matters such as whether you'll be competing against others, what role cost will play in the decision to hire a contractor, and the like. You can always find tactful ways to ask questions, no matter what the questions are. Of course, different situations call for entirely different questions, and you must ask those that are appropriate to the situation.

A caution is in order, however: You ask questions for your own benefit, not for that of anyone else. Ask questions only if there is no indirect way of getting the information, for the answers to the questions are likely to reach the ears of your competitors: You must assume that the client will be prompted by your questions to make the answers part of the work statement or the information released to all prospective vendors.

19

When relevant to a prospective contract or project in which you are interested, seek answers to some typical business questions, such as:

- Is this to be a competitive or selected-source procurement?
- Will this procurement be by sealed bids or by proposals?
- Will you explain the criteria by which you will evaluate proposals?
- How important will price be in making a choice?
- What type of contract do you contemplate awarding?
- May bidders propose an alternative type of contract?
- Will there be negotiations—for example, best and final sessons—with all bidders who are in the competitive range?
- Will you accept alternative proposals?
- Will you make payments based on the progress of the work?

Admittedly, it can be a bit tricky to discuss the client's need without giving away the very thing you sell, your expert knowledge. You need to have some fallback positions to protect yourself. Let us suppose that you have unavoidably been forced to point out to the client that it is impossible to price the job on even the broadest terms without a reasonably accurate specification of the work. Suppose the client then asks you for a casual estimate of numbers of pages, lines of code, numbers of security checkpoints, or other such data. How do you avoid providing this information without sounding evasive or defiant?

At this point, you explain the difficulty:

Madame Client, all I could give you now would be an almost wild guess. It wouldn't be very helpful. In fact, it could be harmful and mislead both of us. It will require a good bit of time to study this and develop estimates. If you definitely plan to have this work done, I will be happy to study the need and prepare a specific proposal for you with estimates I have carefully worked out.

That puts the ball back in the client's court, while also qualifying the client—verifying that the client has a serious intent to retain someone.

As we go on to discuss the alternative to giving the store away, you will see the significance of the preceding explanation more clearly. There is a paradox here, however: I am enjoining you against gratuitously aiding the client in clarifying the requirements of the job, while earlier I enjoined you against signing a contract that did not include a clear specification of the work to be done or product to be delivered. The solution to this anomaly is what we must discuss next.

20

When initiating a response of any kind to a client's initiative, you can assume that:

- The client will eagerly pick your brains to the extent that you allow it.
- The client will invite (or has invited) competitive bids or proposals.
- The client does not know any more about his or her needs than is stated in the RFP.
- Your competitors are as smart and as competent as you are.
- What you give away now you can't get paid for later.
- Even worse, what you give away now may be a fatal mistake.

The Alternative to Asking Questions

At some point, you must offer your own clarification of the work to be done or the products to be delivered. It would be reckless to agree to a contract without such specifications being clearly established. The point is not *whether* to do so, but *when* and *under what circumstances* to do so. The circumstances to be sought are these:

- It is clear that the client is committed to awarding a contract to someone to have the work done.
- You are beyond the initial, exploratory stages and into the response stage, where you are to bid, make a quotation, or (preferably) submit a proposal to the client. You and, presumably, your competitors who are also in pursuit of the contract are through discussing the client's wants and are now engaged in furnishing responses in whatever form they are required to take.
- At this point, the client is not in a position to furnish clarifications to other prospective consultants seeking the contract. He or she is waiting for your response. What should that response be?

RESPONSE ALTERNATIVES

In most cases, the best marketing and contracting vehicle, from both the client's view and your view, is a proposal. That is especially the case when there are missing or unclear specifications in the RFP. It is in the proposal that you address the problem of missing details. There are three ways to do so:

1. You may suggest a two-phase project, the first phase being one in which you will explore the client's need and prepare a detailed specification. Then you will discuss the detailed specification with the client and use it as the basis for proceeding with the second phase of the project, whatever that will be. (It has been my experience that many clients like this approach.)

2. You may propose the specifications you believe most appropriate for the client's need, with a rationale to back them up, and a tactful suggestion that you will be happy to discuss the specifications.

3. In some cases, it makes good sense to suggest one or more alternatives or a discussion and negotiation based on your proposed specifications. Many clients prefer this more direct approach. I prefer it whenever I can make it appear to be the logical thing to do, because it virtually compels the client to hold discussions with you, exploring the various alternatives. It also provides the best base for negotiations.

21

Minimize the possibility that the information in your proposal will be appropriated without remuneration for your efforts. This can be done by informing the client that your proposal is copyrighted and that the information it contains is proprietary.

Of course, there is always the hazard that the client may cancel the procurement and use your detailed proposal as the basis for a new request for proposals or use one of the other alternatives described earlier. I have known this to happen occasionally, but not very often. You can minimize this hazard by placing prominent notices in your proposal and in your letter of transmittal specifying that your proposal is copyrighted, that it contains proprietary information that you developed at your own expense, and that it may not be disclosed outside the client's environment or for any purpose other than negotiating a contract and performing the work described. (In government procurements, the request for proposal will furnish suggested language for accomplishing this.)

These approaches work well when the client wants a response in the form of a proposal and usually result in the client inviting you to discuss your proposal, which is pretty much tantamount to preliminary contract negotiations. However, it is rather difficult to implement any of these strategies in a quotation or bid, which is little more than prices asked for specified work. Still, the client who is unaware of missing information in his or her statement of work is unlikely to recognize that it is missing and may ask for a bid or quotation. That does not mean that you may not volunteer a proposal, at least when marketing in the government sector. It also does not mean that you must offer a formal and full-blown proposal. You may, in fact, offer a quasi-proposal in a letter that qualifies your bid or quotation, explaining why it is necessary and offering to discuss the matter across the table. If successful, that will virtually constitute prenegotiation. At least, it will put you ahead of any competitor who handled the problem with less finesse.

WHERE ELSE CAN MURPHY STRIKE?

Now you know the most sensitive areas in which you must be prepared to handle the inevitable problems that will be yours – the many places and ways that things can go wrong, as Murphy predicted. You are not home free yet; Murphy's law permeates everywhere and can strike at any time and in any place without warning – wherever it can create the greatest difficulties for you.

Take those situations in which you are forced to rely upon others for critically important functions to get the job done. There are more than a few examples.

Moonlight Help

You are overloaded and facing a deadline. You hire a moonlight worker to help you with your work. You run into one of the following glitches:

- The moonlighter suddenly decides that he or she has to get more money than you had agreed upon and won't go on with the job unless you agree to renegotiate your agreement.
- The moonlighter gets sick or decides against working nights and just stops showing up.
- The moonlighter's work is not what you had been led to expect and is unacceptable. (But the moonlighter still insists on being paid, and you know of no way to avoid paying for unusable work.)

Vendors and Suppliers

You are forced to rely on an outside supplier – for example, a printer – to get a report or manual printed in time. You run into problems remarkably similar to those in the case of the moonlight worker:

- The printer gave you an estimate, but suddenly decides that she seriously underestimated the job and elevates her price sharply.
- The printer had assured you that she would meet your deadline, but now decides that she has more urgent work, and yours has to wait. Possibly you can bribe her with a large premium for overtime, however.
- The printer calls and tells you that her key equipment is down or her workers are out sick, and she can't make the deadline.

Internal Breakdowns

Your own equipment – for example, your computer or printer – breaks down, it's late on Friday, you planned to work over the weekend, and you can't find anyone who can repair your equipment before next week.

Are all these examples exaggerated? No, not at all. Things like them have happened to me. I expect them to happen again because I know they will. The laws of disaster enunciated by Murphy are immutable. But they can be beaten. They can be beaten by advance preparation – by knowing that they will happen and by being prepared to counter them.

Take the case of moonlighters, for example. Moonlighters can be a problem. They get tired of working nights after putting in a normal day's work, and they tend to lose their enthusiasm for earning some extra money. After all, they reason, it *is* just extra money. That doesn't mean

22

If you must use the services of a moonlighter, be sure that the person is dedicated enough to do the job even when he or she is tired or over-worked. As backup insurance, retain another moonlighter in case the first one reneges on the agreement.

you should never use moonlighters. Many are dedicated and will see you through any job they agree to do, even if they are tired and wish they hadn't accepted the job in the first place. But you need to be sure that you have that kind of moonlighter. To protect myself, I would normally have at least one other moonlighter lined up, just in case.

There is another alternative that also works in many cases. One moonlight worker tried to hold me up for substantial advances on a book he was about halfway through. Knowing him by now, I feared that if I agreed to this, he would never get the book done. I therefore refused to pay him beyond what his completed work was worth. I offered, instead, to pay him chapter by chapter, as I accepted each chapter. He refused and threatened to abandon the job altogether. I responded that he would then be in breach of contract, but I would accept that if it was his wish. He hesitated and then asked challengingly how I would get the book done. I said I would work nights and finish it myself.

He seemed stunned. "You know the subject that well?" he said. (It was a technical work.)

I assured him that I did.

He caved in, accepted my terms, and went on to finish the job.

In another project, I needed 250 copies of a rather thick manual that had a firm deadline. My regular printer complained that I did not allow him enough time to do the job. I thanked him courteously, and the following conversation took place:

ME: "I guess I will have to make other arrangements."

HE: "What do you mean, 'other arrangements?' If I can't do the job on your schedule, no one else can."

ME: "I suppose you are right, but I have to try. There certainly are enough printers in the area. One of them must be hungry enough to do what I want."

HE: "Well, wait a minute. Let me see if I can't squeeze your job in somehow."

Of course, he did the job for me and on the schedule I asked for.

The moral of this little anecdote is that you should never allow yourself to be at another's mercy, but more important yet, even if you do, never allow that person to *think* that you are at his or her mercy.

Of course, you can't or shouldn't bluff; you do have to be prepared to follow through. I could, indeed, have finished that book, had it been necessary, although I would certainly have not relished the job. In the case of the printing job, I was sure that with enough telephone calls, I would find a printer who would work around the clock, if necessary, to get my job done. And whenever I hired a moonlighter, I usually had a roster of several others I could call on if necessary. The same thing is true for equipment repair: I know of a number of small repair shops where I can get emergency service if and when I need it. Or, if necessary, I can get access to others' equipment.

23

Whenever you are dependent on anything that is not totally under your direct control, have at least one alternative prepared. Doing this has saved my schedule and my reputation many times. On one occasion, I was in the print shop personally helping the printer assemble, bind, and package copies of a report that absolutely had to be in the mail and postmarked before midnight!

A Few Miscellaneous Areas

The laws of disaster are insidious and strike where and when least expected, in relatively minor areas, as well as in more important ones. When you hung out your consultant's shingle, what kind of stationery did you buy? Was it that most expensive stuff, with gold leaf and embossed initials on costly parchmentlike paper? And did you buy a lifetime supply because it was a lot cheaper in quantity? (Printing is one area where economy of scale is a fact.)

If you did all that, the laws are likely to strike you in any of several ways:

- The Postal Service changes your zip code.
- The telephone company changes your area code or exchange.
- Some circumstance forces you to move.

- You decide to change your company name or some other important copy.
- You change your specialty.

24

If you must have that unnecessarily expensive stationery, wait until your practice stabilizes and settles down. Or at least make the initial quantity you buy a modest one. Wait until you are reasonably sure that you will be able to make use of that stationery as stationery, rather than as scratch pads, before you buy that lifetime supply.

A great deal of expensive stationery is used every day as scrap paper for notes and informal memos. The chances are very great that you will make many changes in the first year – even in the first few months – that you are in business. Many, and probably most, entrepreneurs wind up in a business that is considerably different than that in which they started or intended to be in. I had no thought of becoming a consultant when I began an independent free-lance writing/government contracting venture, much less of being a newsletter publisher and a mail order entrepreneur! Consulting is especially experimental in the early months – and for some, even years – of practice. Most of us know the general field in which we will work, but we have to learn by experience just what specialties within that field will prove to be right for us. Even then, we undergo growth and change, which we must contend with.

Thus, go slowly in buying expensive equipment and stationery. Wait until you know for sure just how much you will use a fax machine before you decide how expensive a machine you need. Besides, prices of computers, fax machines, printers, and many other kinds of equipment will come down if you wait until you truly *need* the items.

I am thoroughly stabilized and settled now, after a great many years, but I still have envelopes preprinted only with my name and address, and I am going to discontinue those and print my own in the future. With a laser printer, I create my own letterhead whenever I write a letter. (See Figure 2-1.) I keep it simple (I equate "simple" with "classy"), and yet it looks professional enough, I believe. I could be much more elaborate if I chose to; a modern laser printer enables one to do that. But I like the simple approach, and I keep a supply of good-quality writing

HERMAN HOLTZ
P.O. Box 1731   Wheaton, MD 20915-1731
301 649-2499   Fax 301 649-5745

HERMAN HOLTZ
HRH Communications, Inc.
P.O. Box 1731   Wheaton, MD 20915-1731
301 649-2499   Fax 301 649-5745

Figure 2-1.   Spontaneously generated letterheads

paper on hand for correspondence. In fact, since I am incorporated as "HRH Communications, Inc.," I maintain computer files to create more than one letterhead, as the figure shows. Given the equipment I now enjoy in my office, I could even do the same for my business envelopes, but it seems more convenient to have them preprinted.

I also print my own labels, envelopes, and other items I use regularly. The cost differential is enormous: Number 10 envelopes that I can buy blank for less than $10 per 1,000 cost nearly $40 per 1,000 if I have them printed. Shipping labels that cost me about the same price per 1,000 when printed cost me about $13 per 1,000 when I buy them blank and do my own printing. I can do the envelopes with my word processor: I have a template that automatically prints a return address when I address the envelope, so there is no extra work. I create the labels with a label-printing software program. (See Figure 2-2.)

Obviously, you do not get two- or three-color printing, nor do you get embossing and gold leaf on your stationery, when you use these

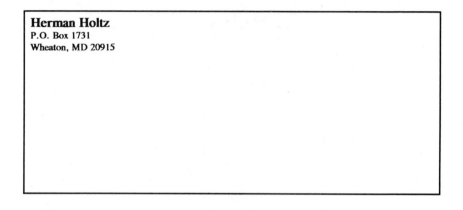

Figure 2-2.   "Homemade" envelopes and labels

methods for getting things done. So far, however, my simple utilitarian stationery has not deterred major companies from doing business with me.

What you have read so far is prologue. The stress was first on the basis for establishing a firm marketing foundation and then on major pitfalls, with some general guidance in avoiding them. From here on, we shall focus on positive activities to place the firmest possible base under your consulting practice. You will be confronted with a large number and wide variety of business possibilities that can lead you to as broad a diversification of your practice as you wish.

25

Do you really need a prestigious address in an expensive office building? Are you sure that you cannot work at home with equal effectiveness and an equally prestigious business image? If you don't normally have clients visiting you, what is the point of an impressive (and expensive) office?

At one point, you were urged to determine just what business you are in. In the pages to come, we will pursue that further, but not in the general philosophical terms of the first chapter. Rather, we will consider the how-to-do-it aspects of the various business possibilities open to you, which you may fairly regard as different kinds of business available to you. We begin this inquiry in the next chapter.

CHAPTER 3

SOME NEGLECTED METHODS OF MARKETING

Some of the most effective marketing ideas are not very well known, because none of us are eager to share our best ideas with our competitors. At the same time, they are not truly dark secrets or difficult to learn and put to work in your own behalf.

ABOUT THE "SECRET OF SUCCESS"

A number of years ago, the popular magazine *Reader's Digest* carried a line of wisdom that said, "The secret of success is hard work, which is probably why it remains a secret." Very likely, that is one of the reasons that many methods of marketing remain relatively unknown: They require energy and dedication to be used effectively.

All marketing is work, although it is true enough that some methods involve greater effort than do others. Thus, some of the marketing methods and measures you will read about in this chapter require a great deal of effort, as compared with other methods. A large part of the reason for the popularity of print and broadcast advertising is that it is essentially a passive method: As an advertiser, you don't have to do very much but sit back and wait for orders—if they come. Sometimes they don't, and we call that a recession. I make no apology for suggesting that you work hard to win your clients and their projects: Hard work alone is enough of a marketing strategy to beat a great many of your competitors. Even so, you may find that some of these "hard" methods of marketing are really fun.

26

Know the difference between passive and aggressive networking. If you're relying on the former, you're probably on thin ice. To make networking work as a marketing strategy, it must be part of an intense, focused campaign.

NETWORKING: WHAT IS IT?

If you listen carefully, you will hear the word *networking* used frequently in connection with marketing, especially with marketing a service. To those not intimately acquainted with the idea, it is usually taken to refer simply to marketing via referrals (called "contacts") à la the "old boy network." We all do some of this kind of marketing, consciously or unconsciously, via friends, relatives, personal acquaintances, and business acquaintances. We get occasional business as well from these kinds of sources. Those who specialize in writing and lecturing on the subject are likely to refer to this type of networking as "passive networking." That means that you are not marketing aggressively via contacts and, hence, not networking effectively, or at least, not networking as effectively as you could be. Instead, you are waiting patiently for business to come from such contacts, rather than going after the business that is presumably to be had as a result of the contacts. Those who are experts in this kind of marketing say that in passive networking we use only a fraction of the potential of the methodology of networking. If we wish to succeed, they maintain, we should make networking a highly organized effort, founded on a well-structured basis and with a deliberate methodology. They tend to perceive organized, calculated networking in much the same manner as a chain letter is perceived, where each recipient knows many more recipients, each of whom, in turn, knows many more, so that the number of people in the chain rapidly approaches an astronomical figure.

But of course, there is much more to the idea than that. The people we know who may favor us with business directly or furnish us leads to business are called *contacts*. If we were to classify our contacts, we would call friends, relatives, and business acquaintances with whom we maintain close relationships "strong contacts." Strong contacts are those individuals with whom you are exceptionally friendly or have such a close connection that they especially want to be helpful to you and see you as successful as possible. They will therefore strive to steer business leads to you. Personal and business acquaintances who are not especially close to you are called "casual contacts." They are well disposed toward you, or at least are not hostile to you, but they have no special reason to go out of their way to help you. Their chief value to you lies in the fact that they know who you are, what you do, and how you may be useful to them or others when the occasion calls for it.

CREATING CONTACTS

Contacts are made in many ways. Some people utilize their educational background informally as a networking resource by joining alumni clubs. Others join associations of other kinds, such as professional societies, industrial associations, business clubs, and fraternal orders, at least partially for the same purpose. Obviously, joining organizations helps in creating business contacts. However, most of the people you become acquainted with in this manner are of limited utility in networking because they are chance acquaintances. Any business you get through a chance acquaintance is a chance occurrence. For maximum effectiveness, networking cannot be left to chance, any more than you can leave anything else to chance if you want results. Instead, you must build an organized network over which you gain some control.

We can learn a lot in this regard from history. Early networking, although not known by that name and still a more or less informal process, is manifest in such organizations as the Lions Club, Rotary Club, Kiwanis, and other groups. In fact, what is now called networking was the specific aim of the founder of the Rotary in 1905, Chicago lawyer Paul Harris. The point was to bring together individuals (men, originally, before women entered the business world in significant numbers and brought about appropriate changes) from various fields to create an informal system of referrals among the members of the organization.

Modern networking does not require the agency of a formal organization designed expressly for that purpose. Instead, an informal or ad hoc group can be formed, or networking can be made a function of any existing group of people with some common marketing need and purpose. For example, networking may be instituted as a function of your local association of independent writers, consultants, or other independent careerists of one kind or another. Or it may be initiated in an association connected with some specific industry, profession, or community services – indeed, in practically any kind of organization, as long as it includes a sufficient number of members who are interested in and whose businesses are suitable subjects for network marketing. You may in fact find it expedient to expand your networking activities by belonging to more than one business, professional, or other association. Quite possibly no single group will serve all your marketing needs.

If you belong to an association or club and it does not currently support networking activities, you might want to start the ball rolling in that direction. On the other hand, if you do not currently belong to such a group and there is none readily available to you, or if the one you belong to resists starting a networking activity, you can still proceed on your own. Most people in any business or profession are interested in increasing their marketing effectiveness, but those operating as independent practitioners have a special interest in the subject. Usually, they must handle their own marketing and can handle only one job at a time. Under that condition, a more or less steady source of new projects is a necessity. These people know that word of mouth – referral – is the most effective marketing method to maintain a *flow* of new business. They know that they can devote only some relatively small portion of their time to marketing if they are to have enough billable time to be successful. It is thus usually not difficult to recruit a few other practitioners to join with you in forming a new networking group.

RECRUITING NETWORKING ASSOCIATES

There are several ways to recruit other independent practitioners to join with you in creating a new network. Note that the others need not be in the same field as you; in fact, it is best if none of you is directly competitive with anyone else – that is, you may be in the same field, but in different specialties in that field, so that you are not direct competitors for the same clients and contracts. Here are some suggestions for recruiting people for a networking group:

- Place classified advertisements in periodicals – newspapers, magazines, trade journals, and other sources. Preferably, these periodicals should appeal and be distributed to a broad audience of independent practitioners, rather than to the public at large or to a highly specialized audience.

- Use direct mail: Send a letter explaining your ideas to a suitable mailing list of independent practitioners. Just make sure that everyone on the list lives within easy reach of you and each other.

- Conduct a telephone campaign: Call as many of your friends and acquaintances as you can reach, and ask them to pass the word to their friends and acquaintances, as a special networking method.

- Post notices on electronic bulletin boards in conferences frequented by independent practitioners.

- Post notices on physical bulletin boards in libraries, universities, and other locations.

- Send notices out for publication – for example, write and send out a press release to local newspapers and newsletters.

27

In recruiting independent practitioners to join you in forming a new network, strive to gather a group of practitioners that are in different fields or, at least, in different specialties in the same field. That way, you avoid competing with each other for business. To recruit independent professionals, you can place classified advertisements in the media, use direct mail, conduct a telephone campaign, and post notices on bulletin boards, among other things.

When forming a networking group, explain briefly what your purpose is in such a manner as to make it clear that the respondent is likely to benefit. (For example, in an advertisement, you might say, "Win clients and business through low-cost, cooperative method of networking with others. Call/write _____ for details.") When there is no room to explain at length – for instance, in a classified notice in a periodical – use some appeal to persuade the reader to call or write you, and you can then explain your ideas via telephone or letter. Your immediate goal is to organize an initial meeting to establish a group. The appeal to persuade the reader to respond need not be elaborate; it may be merely the promise of some kind of information, together with a hint of what that information is. If you can manage only a poster or a small sign and need copy even briefer than that for an advertisement, try "FREE HELP IN MARKETING. CALL/WRITE FOR DETAILS."

ORGANIZING A NETWORKING GROUP

To be effective, a networking group probably ought to have at least 20, but not more than 40, members. Too few limits the number of useful contacts, while too many makes the meetings and functions unwieldy and even unmanageable. Should your group grow too large, you will probably do well to split into two or more groups, each operating separately, although you may establish some kind of linkage between them.

The first step is to organize an initial meeting, or mixer. (Networking involves holding such mixers frequently.) This is true whether you have assembled a group of beginning networkers within some organization or pulled together an ad hoc group of prospective networkers from wherever you could find them.

One way of starting is to get the new group together in some meeting place, introduce yourself and your subject briefly, and get acquainted with each other informally. I suggest opening with something along these lines:

> *Good evening. I am Joe Organizer, and we are here tonight to talk about a method of marketing that will help each of us get business by helping each other. It's called networking, and it has been used with great success by others. But there are a few things to do before we get into a serious discussion. Let's first make out your name tags. Print your name large enough to be read easily by others, and also write in your business name or some indication of the kind of thing you do. After you have done that, let's mingle for a half-hour or so and get acquainted with each other. Then we will get down to business.*

Once the ice is broken and people have had enough time to mingle, begin explaining how the networking idea works. To do this, you will need to know about and use some networking tools.

NETWORKING TOOLS

The most essential tools for networking are:

- Business cards in abundant quantity.
- Badges with names, companies, and types of business printed clearly on them.
- Brochures and other literature about your business.
- Blank slips and pens to write leads on.

Depending on the kind of business you operate, you may need special literature, samples, models, or other marketing aids to help others understand just what you do and how it helps clients. If so, these are also part of your basic networking tool kit.

Keep plenty of your business cards with you at all times – in your wallet, your purse, your pockets, and/or your briefcase. It's an excellent idea to keep a backup supply in your automobile also. Business cards are an essential; you should hand them out freely.

Wearing a badge is important so that others you meet have no difficulty in learning, at a glance, not only your name, but also the name of your company, or the business you are in if your company name does not define it. Check with your stationer. You can find a good-quality badge with enough room to print your name and other relevant information in large enough letters to be easily visible, even in a dimly lighted room. (For serious networking, which means doing it frequently and for extended periods, you should have a permanent name badge, formally printed in large type.)

28

Print two brochures for your personal marketing efforts. A small brochure printed on an 8½- × 11-inch sheet and folded twice will fit conveniently in your pocket or purse so you can have a few with you at all times and give them out freely. The person you give it to can slip it into his or her pocket or purse, so that it does not become burdensome to carry. On the other hand, only a large brochure (printed on an 11- × 17-inch or larger sheet and folded to 8½- × 11-inch final size) affords you room to do a proper presentation. You use it after you've made the first contact, to follow up by mailing it out or carrying it along on subsequent one-on-one visits or business lunches.

You need to have a brochure that describes your business at some length and in terms that anyone can understand. The focus should be on benefits – on what your service does for your clients. As a matter of fact, I believe that you really need two brochures, a small one for convenience and a large one for more concerted marketing efforts.

Also, carry a supply of 3 × 5 cards, slips of paper, or a small note pad on which to make notes and write sales leads for yourself and others. The notes you make are one of the main elements of networking; they are a primary means of handing out leads to others and getting leads from others.

NETWORKING AS AN INDIRECT MEANS OF MAKING COLD CALLS

The oldest and most reliable means of getting business is calling directly on prospective clients and soliciting their business – making cold calls. It works, and it works well when it is done properly. That means when it is done steadily, with the clear understanding that cold calling is similar to all kinds of selling in that it is a "numbers game." That is, if you make enough calls every day, you will "strike oil" every once in a while and close a sale or find a prospect with whom you will eventually close a sale. The experienced salesperson who makes calls every day is always conscious of that ratio of calls to sales or leads and thus manages to endure the inevitable rejections by rationalizing that each call, even if it results in a rejection, is a step closer to the next sale.

Unfortunately, most of us dread cold calling, despite that rationalization, because the many rejections are often rude and mean spirited. It takes a rather special kind of person to do cold calling willingly and cheerfully. Thus, most of us don't do it, even though we know that it works for the persistent caller. However, we can think of networking as a special means of making cold calls, a way that eliminates their worst elements because you make the "calls" in a congenial atmosphere, without the stress of direct and immediate rejection. Think of it that way as you consider the following points.

THE MAJOR POINTS OF NETWORKING

- Networking is not a passive way to market; it is an active and aggressive approach. You must be energetic in pursuing it. Go to as many mixers as possible, and make it your business to meet *everyone* there. Don't spend more than about 10 minutes with each person, on average, to allow yourself time to meet everyone, but make that 10 minutes count. Make sure that the other person knows exactly what you do and that you know exactly what he or she does. Remember what business you are in.

- Be sure that everyone gets one of your cards and even several, if they are willing to pass them on to others at other functions. Be sure, too, to have some kind of brochure to hand out, while you explain what you do.

- Be interested in the other party. Be sure that you know the person's name, have his or her business card and brochure, and understand the business the individual is in. Networking is casting bread on the water: You must give to get. Ceaseless activity in both directions – seeking leads for yourself and leads to pass out to others – pays off because it must. Nothing is quite as powerful as persistence and determination; they are omnipotent.

- Learn to be a good listener. Ask the right questions, involving who, what, when, where, why, and how. When you learn of a problem or need someone has, make a note of it and suggest someone or bear it in mind as a lead you can pass on.

- Carry your networking tools with you at all times, and be prepared to network at all times and on all appropriate occasions. Attend as many such occasions as possible: Belong to relevant associations, go to meetings, and attend conventions, symposia, and other such events.

- Follow up meetings with people by sending notes to them, calling them by telephone, and getting together with them for lunch or some other occasion. Remember that networking does not normally produce sales; it produces *leads,* and a lead is something that has value only if you follow it up.

You can get more information about networking by writing

Consultants National Resource Center
P.O. Box 430
Clear Spring, MD 21722-0430
ATTENTION: J. Stephen Lanning
or call 301-791-9332.

WRITING PROPOSALS: IS IT A HIGH-RISK GAME?

Unfortunately, many consultants and other professionals shrink from writing proposals. For some, a general dislike of writing is responsible for their reluctance. For others, it is a distinct lack of faith in the proposal as a marketing tool. Some suspect that it takes great writing skill to excel at proposal competitions. Others mistrust the entire process, suspecting that a request for proposals (an RFP) is a subtle means of steering awards to favored candidates. Those who believe and propagate such myths are fond of assuring themselves and others that all proposals are fixed in advance, and the honest newcomer or outsider has absolutely no chance of winning.

Another objection is that a proposal is hard work and requires a serious commitment of time, effort, and often even substantial out-of-pocket costs. Yet another is that these drawbacks must be faced in an atmosphere of uncertainty, almost like a lottery. Many consultants also voice the objection that there is a great risk involved, in that the consultant is expected almost to give the store away by making a free analysis of the client's problem and designing a plan that a less than scrupulously honest client may seize and then have executed by someone else, perhaps him- or herself.

As a consequence of all these objections, many consultants write proposals – if they ever do – reluctantly and only when a client or prospective client issues an RFP and there is some special reason to commit the effort necessary to respond to it.

That is a mistake, however. The proposal is so important a marketing tool in providing custom services, as consultants inevitably do, that you are seriously handicapped when you do not have a well-developed proposal-writing skill. Many of the problems that consultants cite as their reasons for being reluctant to write proposals certainly exist. However, many of the objections they cite are nonetheless rationalizations, arising out of the consultant's unwillingness to learn how to write an effective proposal.

So important is the proposal as a marketing tool, that you should follow up any initial discussion with a potential client who describes a specific need or problem by offering to submit a proposal. (In fact, I myself don't just offer to submit one; I *promise* to send it on.) I find that clients rarely demur when you make an offer such as the following:

"Mrs. Prospective Client, that is an interesting problem, and I have a few ideas that ought to interest you. I'll set them down in a simple letter proposal and send it on to you. That will give you time and opportunity

---
29

Don't fall into the trap of avoiding proposal writing until it's "absolutely necessary" for an RFP. Instead, you should *create* opportunities to submit proposals without being asked. A well-thought-out proposal package is a mighty powerful follow-up to a contact. Such "unsolicited" proposals may be one of your best marketing tools.

---

to study them and even talk them over with others in your organization. You can expect the letter in a day or two."

Before going into just what ought to be included in a proposal, formal or informal, let us take a brief peek into a typical RFP and see what we are likely to find there.

THE RFP PACKAGE

A formal request for proposals must by its nature include at least the following:

- A cover letter introducing the RFP as such. The letter usually identifies both the proposed project in general terms and the requester, states the deadline – when and where the proposal is to be delivered and in what quantity – and defines the type of contract the client will offer, either one with a firm fixed price or some other variety, such as a labor-hour or time-and-materials contract.

- Some document specifying what information is to be in the proposal. (This could be included in the statement of work, but usually is separate.) The document may also stipulate a proposal format and other conditions, such as the cost information required.

- A statement of work. This is the heart of the RFP. It describes what is to be done, nominally in sufficient detail to constitute a specification. Unfortunately, many statements of work fall short in this respect by being quite a bit less than specific or complete.

Other documents may be included in the proposal, according to who the issuer is and the requirements. There might, for example, be standard "boilerplate" about the procurement regulations and policies of the client and the forms to be completed.

There is an abundance of mythology about proposals. Let us examine some of the myths, debunk the common mythology, and present the truths of marketing via proposals.

THE PROS OF MARKETING VIA PROPOSALS

- In many, if not most, situations, the proposal is the most effective marketing tool you can bring to bear when competing for a specific project. The proposal gives you more time and greater opportunity to do a thorough needs analysis, think everything out, gather adequate market intelligence, develop a specific marketing strategy, and prepare a reasoned plan to win the contract.

- The proposal is a means for presenting your technical plan and sales arguments without interruption, in carefully chosen language, with any illustrations you believe necessary. (Remember the admonitions about defining your business in terms of what you *do* for your clients when you work up your sales arguments!)

- The proposal gives you the opportunity to stipulate your own terms and requirements (indirectly and tactfully, of course), cover vague or unspecific areas of the RFP without alerting competitors, anticipate objections and respond to them before the client voices them, present detailed rationales, and offer alternatives.

- In a proposal, you are in complete control of the presentation. You cannot be summarily interrupted with objections or questions. The reader must hear you out.

- The client can read and reread your proposed program as often as he or she wishes, have others review it, meet with others to discuss it, and finally, ask you to sit down and discuss it.

- The proposal becomes a part of any contract by reference and, if you use it properly, enables you to solve a common problem of unclear, inadequate, or completely missing specifications. (Keep this in mind; there will be more on this later.)

- Used wisely, the proposal can become a strategic tool for greatly increasing the probability of persuading the client to request your presence for a discussion of your ideas. That is a positive step toward negotiations and a contract.

By way of contrast, it is difficult to do most of these things effectively with a "dog and pony show" kind of presentation, even with hardcopy handouts. There, the client can interrupt your presentation, break your train of thought and line of argument, and prevent you from having complete control of the presentation.

THE CONS OF MARKETING VIA PROPOSALS

Obviously, there are drawbacks in marketing via proposals. It would be dishonest to suggest otherwise. Here are the main ones commonly encountered:

- Proposal writing is time consuming and hard work, often against difficult schedules (when done to a client's mandated deadlines) and often involving considerable expense.
- The information you need to write a proposal—relevant marketing intelligence—is often quite difficult to get, and what you do get is inadequate, compelling you to make your best "guesstimates" and develop your technical plans and sales arguments with your fingers crossed.
- There is the risk that you are providing the client, free of charge, with information for which you are normally paid, after which the client may use your plan to do the work him- or herself or have someone else do it at a lower cost. (In other words, you are permitting your brains to be picked.)

TYPICAL PROBLEMS WITH THE RFP

Probably nowhere is it more true that "there are no problems, but only opportunities" than in the case of proposals. The most common such problem is a vague or poorly written RFP, especially its statement of work.

The statement of work purportedly explains the client's problem, need, and/or requirement and presents a specification of what is to be done or produced. Unfortunately, relatively few statements of work do a really good job of this. Many display some or all of the following faults:

- The statement of the problem, need, or requirement is at best ambiguous.
- Instead of the problem itself, the client identifies one or more symptoms of the problem.
- The client appears to have drawn a totally erroneous conclusion from the evidence presented in the statement.
- The statement is completely lacking in specifications, making it almost impossible to offer a specific responsive program and equally impossible to project probable costs and a price.
- The client has included unrealistic schedule requirements.
- The client specifies an obsolete, inefficient, or otherwise unwise standard or methodology for doing the job.

30

Don't automatically turn away from a muddled RFP. You usually have far less competition when you respond to a vague RFP than when you respond to that occasional crystal-clear, well-written one. That is because everyone finds it easy to respond to the latter kind of RFP. A great many contenders drop out of the running in responding to a vague RFP. Some are truly at a loss to know how to begin to respond, while others see that responding requires a great deal of effort, which they don't care to make. If you don't shrink from the job of responding, that alone greatly elevates your chances of winning.

THE MAJOR HAZARD

The major hazard in proposal writing lies in accepting an RFP with problems such as those described and responding to it as though the problems were not there. There are competitors who will do that, with their fingers crossed. They are the spectators applauding the new clothes of the unclad emperor as he strides majestically along the boulevard. Can you – should you – be the child who exclaims that the emperor has no clothes? No, of course not. That could only get your head chopped off. You must simply ignore the emperor's condition and design for him even prettier clothes befitting his majesty. Or is there some midcourse, some way of telling the truth without giving offense? Is that the secret of many successful proposals?

Believe the Client

Apparently, some respondents studying a vague RFP believe that the client is playing games, since they have been heard to mutter to themselves, as they pore over the statement of work, "I wonder what he really wants here." Evidently, it does not occur to them that the client is being totally honest and sincere: What the client presents in the RFP and statement of work is all that he or she really knows about the problem. The client may be wrong – dead wrong – but is not necessarily deliberately deceiving you. It would not be in his or her interest to do so, ordinarily. Yes, there is that occasional exception when the client is steering the RFP toward a favored supplier and misleading others deliberately. Even that, however, is generally a sin of omission: The RFP is not lying, but merely withholding some information.

Many who read an RFP that is vague believe that the paucity of directly useful information is a signal that the contract is "wired" for a favored supplier who is the only one who knows what the client really wants. That may be the case, but when it is, it is the exception. There are better and easier ways to wire a procurement if the client wishes to do so.

I generally find it sensible to believe the client. If the RFP is bad enough that I must make an intensive study to interpret his or her need, I believe that the client is crying, "Help!" I believe that the client wants me to do everything necessary to identify or define the need and propose a solution. The client expects me to be completely explicit (I am, after all, the expert, am I not?) and provide every detail, including specifications that furnish a complete definition of what I promise to do and what I shall deliver.

In my view, therefore, to respond by telling the client that the RFP is too vague and that I must get his or her answers to many questions before I can proceed and write a proposal is a confession of my inability to do the job required.

True or not, logically justified or not, from the marketing viewpoint, that is the most helpful position to take. You will then provide a *responsive* proposal, whereas many others will not respond directly or will provide nonresponsive proposals.

══ 31 ══

Remember these guidelines when taking your best shot at a vague RFP:

- Make your best estimate of the client's need.
- Devise the *minimum* (least costly) solution that you believe will meet the client's need, and propose it as just that.
- Offer one or more alternative solutions that offer more than the minimum.
- Price each alternative solution separately.

It is quite likely that when you do these, you will be asked by the client to visit, formally or informally, to answer questions and discuss your proposal. (I have known it to work out that way again and again.)

GATHERING MARKET INTELLIGENCE

Of course, responding to a vague RFP does not mean that you stab blindly and guess what the client really needs. You need something more than pure wild guesswork to guide your hand. You need market intelligence. Decisions are based on information, and the quality of a decision owes its merit or lack of it to the volume, accuracy, and value of the information on which it is based.

There are two kinds of market intelligence: intelligence about the market generally, usually resulting from general market research, and intelligence about a specific client and his or her specific need of the moment. In responding to an RFP with a proposal—even an informal letter proposal of just a few pages—it is necessary to know more than what the words of the RFP and statement of work convey, especially when they convey far too little. It is necessary to research the specific client and his or her need.

Getting the kind of information generally referred to as market intelligence delivers two benefits to you. First, it helps you write the most responsive proposal, and in many cases in which the RFP is completely inadequate, it is often an absolute necessity if you are to respond. Aside from that, however, knowing more than your competitors do about the client and the requirement puts you into the strongest competitive position. When a client invites competitive proposals, he or she often shuts off access to more information once the RFP is issued, except possibly for a preproposal conference, at which all competitors are in attendance. It is then often not advisable to ask too many questions directly, because too many times you manage to give away information to competitors that they otherwise would not get. Hence, even if the client is willing to be questioned, it is advisable to gather information independently if that is at all possible.

There are routine or general sources of information, and there are special sources of information. The routine or general sources include these:

- The client's own literature – brochures, annual reports, and other such items.
- What has been written and published about the client. (Check library sources, including public data bases.)
- "Common knowledge" about the client. Ask your own staff, friends, and business acquaintances. Quite often, you will be surprised at the wealth of information that is available on the grapevine.
- Careful study of the RFP, including the statement of work. The common jest, "When all else fails, read the instructions," applies here: Often, you will find the information you want between the lines. It can easily escape you on a first or even second or third reading. You must *study* the RFP and do so thoroughly.

These sources, together with what you already know out of your own expert knowledge and what you believe you can infer with confidence, may be enough. If they are not, there are some special measures available if the procurement is large enough to justify going to the trouble and expense.

One method that has been used successfully is advertising in help-wanted columns, with a "blind" advertisement (using a box number for responses) requesting resumes. The copy is slanted as much as possible

---

32

When dealing with a major proposal, or one of a technical nature, a particularly crafty means of achieving intelligence is to place a classified ad that will draw resumes from your potential client's staff. The information you uncover may put you ahead of your competitors, but be careful to keep the names and information you obtain strictly confidential.

to encourage responses from the staff of the client. Studying the resumes of employees and former employees of the client can provide a great deal of helpful information about the client's interests and situation. But there are other instances in which such a strategy can produce beneficial results for you:

- On one occasion, a project was to be run in another city and employ several people to be hired locally there. Running help-wanted advertisements and interviewing a few respondents in that city furnished information about local salaries and provided resumes for the proposal, as well as a staff to do the job.

- The method has been used successfully to gather intelligence about a competitor, drawing resumes from the competitor's staff and allowing a number of them to be interviewed.

- In one case in which a massive and ongoing project had been operated by the same contractor for several years, the successful proposer ran a help-wanted campaign to attract people who formerly or currently worked on the project. The campaign produced a mass of information about the incumbent contractor and the project, along with invaluable information about its problems.

Having someone apply to the client or to a competitor for a position is yet another way to get information if your investigator is clever enough to ask the right questions during an interview, even one with a personnel manager.

A SPECIAL PROBLEM OR TWO

An especially difficult problem is that of the wrongheaded client who "knows" things that are not so or who has just enough knowledge to be dangerous. Some clients fitting this description will specify an unrealistic or obsolete methodology for doing a job in an RFP and do so in such terms that you know immediately that it would be unwise to oppose them directly.

Now, the problem can be handled, but it must be done quite tactfully. Your proposal must not appear to confront the client, of course. One way to handle this problem is to prepare a proposal that solemnly offers to do just what the client has all but mandated, but then offer alternatives, pointing tactfully to their advantages. Then, when the client invites you to discuss your proposal, as he or she is most likely to do, you can evaluate the client's real reaction to your proposal and evaluate how best to proceed in converting the client to your viewpoint without provoking a confrontation.

A variant of this situation is the client who is somewhat wrongheaded about what experience and other qualifications are necessary to do the job. Such clients sometimes demand specialized experience that does not appear to you to be at all relevant to the job. The reaction of many consultants is an instant conviction or at least a heavy suspicion that the contract is wired for some favored consultant to whom the RFP was tailored. That may or may not be, but even if it is, the fact that an RFP was issued indicates that, for whatever reason – a legal requirement in the case of a government procurement, or company policy and regulations in the case of a private corporation – there must be an appearance of open competition. If the RFP is indeed wired, it means that someone is trying to defeat the regulations. But then, that means that the RFP may be able to be unwired, and that happens often enough: No wiring scheme is foolproof. In most cases, if you believe that you can write a strong proposal, it pays to go ahead. Again, believe the client: Believe that the competition is open. This is the healthy attitude, the one that produces winning proposals.

PROPOSAL FORMATS

An RFP may or may not mandate a format. If it does, the following general format is usually entirely satisfactory (be sure, however, that your proposal includes all the information the RFP has listed as required of the proposal):

- *Introductory section.* State who and what you are, your interest in the procurement, and your understanding of the requirement.
- *Technical discussion.* Discuss the requirement, the pros and cons of various approaches to satisfying it, and what is needed to do the job properly. End the section with a logical technical and sales argument for your approach, and introduces the next section.
- *Proposed program.* Present the specifics of the approach you have just argued for in the previous section. Include infor-

mation about the project organization and management, deliverables, schedules, specifications, and other details of what you will commit to doing.

- *Qualifications.* Discuss the experience and other qualifications of your organization, including its facilities, resources, and the like.
- *Front matter.* Insert a table of contents, an executive summary, and possibly a foreword or preface of some kind at the front of the proposal. If you wish, you may include appendices at the back.

When an RFP is informal or does not mandate a format, a letter may serve as a proposal. The letter should contain the essential information found in a formal proposal, even though it is not formally organized into chapters and front matter. The philosophy of the presentation is also the same as that of the formal proposal.

CAPABILITY BROCHURES

A publication commonly referred to as a *capability brochure* or *capability statement* is a useful document in marketing one's technical and professional services. Such a document is used widely by those who pursue contracts and are likely to write proposals. The capability brochure resembles a proposal, albeit on a most generalized basis.

33

When the opportunity arises, use a capability brochure to market your services. Distribute the brochure to clients who are likely to solicit competitive bids or proposals, and carry it with you in a binder or manila folder for those occasions upon which you can leave it in a prospective client's office when the need arises.

Unlike the general advertising brochure, capability brochures normally are not printed in large quantity for mass distribution. Instead, they are distributed to those who are likely to solicit competitive bids or proposals and who collect lists of qualified contenders. Government agencies planning a future procurement, for example, often issue an open invitation to all to submit such a brochure as an application to be placed on the bidders' list for the contemplated procurement. The agency then reviews the brochure to judge whether the submitter is qualified to compete for the procurement.

The capability brochure, therefore, need consist only of a few pages of typed copy explaining your company, what you do, for what kinds of clients you normally do it, for whom you have done it in the past, the facilities and other resources you have to offer, and your technical and professional qualifications. You can enclose it in an ordinary report binder, or in a manila folder if you prefer. Make up a small supply of capability brochures, and carry them with you as a "leave behind" when the occasion justifies it.

THE GOVERNMENT MARKETS

Of some 15 million businesses in the United States, fewer than two percent, or about 250,000, do business regularly with the thousands of governments and their hundreds of thousands of agencies. Probably, never were more opportunities lost to more entrepreneurs than in the failure of independent consultants to address these beckoning markets.

38,777 GOVERNMENTS

The U.S. Census Bureau reports that there are 38,777 governments in the United States. They are broken down as follows:

- Federal government: 1
- State governments: 50
- Counties: 3,042
- Municipalities: 18,862
- Townships: 16,822

Actually, the Census Bureau lists these as "government entities" and also includes under that designation 15,174 local school districts and 35,962 special districts, adding up to a grand total of 79,913 such entities. The powers of these entities include the power to buy goods and services, of course, and all buy from individual, independent entrepreneurs, as well as from larger organizations of all kinds.

THE MODUS OPERANDI
OF GOVERNMENT PURCHASING

In the federal government procurement system, purchasing and supply are greatly decentralized: Most of the thousands of federal departments, administrations, bureaus, commissions, offices, and other agencies can and do the bulk of their purchasing independently through their own contracting officers. In fact, the larger agencies usually have regional offices (generally 6 to 10 in number, although some agencies have fewer), and in most of these, each has its own contracting officer. Thus, purchasing by the federal government alone is astronomical, amounting to millions of contracts annually and a procurement budget well in excess of $200 billion.

34

It would be a grave mistake for an independent consultant not to at least consider government markets in his or her business plans. The federal government alone contracts out $200 billion worth of procurements each year. The common conception among most consultants that government procurements are "too complicated" works in your favor. Once you know the rules, you will leave most of the competition behind.

This is not to say that there is no centralized procurement in the federal government; in fact, several organizations oversee the function on the federal level. The General Services Administration (GSA) operates the Federal Supply Service (FSS), with its stores that are available to everyone in the federal system, to many government agencies at state and local levels, and even to some prime contractors. (Large cost-plus contracts often permit the contractor to buy supplies and equipment at the FSS stores, where prices are generally lower than those at the usual commercial sources.) The Department of Defense operates the Defense Logistics Agency as a centralized procurement and supply source for military organizations. The Department of Veterans Affairs is a central purchasing agent for its many offices, hospitals, and domiciliaries. The U.S. Postal Service also handles procurements centrally for many of its needs. These are exceptions, however: Most federal government procurement is done individually by each agency through its own contracting office and procurement staff. State and local governments, on the other hand, tend strongly to go the other way and do the bulk of their purchasing via centralized purchasing and supply departments or divisions located in state capitals, county seats, and city or town halls. There are some exceptions, under which some of the agencies within the state or local government are permitted to buy at least certain goods and services independently. Fortunately, consulting is one of the kinds of services most frequently found to be among the exceptions.

Broadly speaking, most governments' procurement systems resemble each other and tend to emulate that of the federal government in many ways, because most are based on a set of principles and practices set forth in what is known as the Uniform Procurement Code, created by the American Bar Association. Thus, what I will say about federal procurement is generally applicable to state and local government procurement, too, except as otherwise noted.

THE STARTLING STATISTICS

The statistics of government markets are staggering. The U.S. government has more than 34,000 offices throughout the nation, occupying more than 433 million square feet. The federal government owns more than 405,000 buildings, costing well over $200 billion (undoubtedly valued at several times this figure today), and pays out more than $2 billion (again, a figure that has undoubtedly been swelled by inflation) in annual rents for other offices. Yet even these figures are dwarfed by the aggregate figures of state and local government operations.

Obviously, it takes a lot of people to buy this much and more in goods and services for the governments, spending about $2 billion each and every day of the year. More than 130,000 federal employees are employed full time in procurement functions, and an even larger number are employed in state and local government procurement. You can imagine (or maybe, better, you can't!) the number of contracts awarded to satisfy government requirements for hundreds of billions of dollars' worth of goods and services every year.

Much federal procurement is noncompetitive by necessity. If, for example, a major aircraft manufacturer develops a special aircraft or aircraft system for the Department of Defense, it makes sense to negotiate directly with that firm for a production contract. There are also many other situations that justify negotiating contracts without competition.

Nonetheless, the size and complexity of the federal market for consulting and related expert services make the number of competitive contracts awarded significant. The following table is illustrative (note that consultant services are listed separately, but the figure is highly misleading, as the bulk of the expert services procured are not listed as consultant services per se):

Competitive Federal Government Procurements

Number of procurements:	797,416
Negotiated procurements:	348,676
Small-business set-asides:	233,279
Fixed-price contracts:	336,932
Research and development contracts:	32,997
Automated data-processing services:	8,213
Automated data-processing equipment purchases:	19,075
Consultant services per se:	1,491

The federal government has divided its needs for goods and services into approximately 100 "supply groups," of which 19 are for services. Following are the official listings, plus descriptions of those services that are consultative in nature, even if not so specified in their title or designation. These are the headings under which requirements are advertised in *Commerce Business Daily*, the federal daily publication that announces contract opportunities. Each published notice explains the requirement briefly and advises the reader where and how to get the solicitation, known colloquially as the "bid package" or "bid set," which provides the details and instructions necessary for submitting a bid or proposal. Note that many of the descriptions and definitions overlap each other, but that is the nature of much government work. The descriptions are based on what has typically appeared under the categories listed. Some of the services under category X may appear bizarre—for example, renting mules and handlers and rounding up wild horses—but they have appeared at one time or another under that category.

A: Experimental, Developmental, Test, and Research Work

Medical, scientific, or social research, especially advanced and sophisticated projects, studies, surveys, laboratory developments, feasibility studies, design and development, modeling, and educational research.

H: Expert and Consultant Services

Engineering and technical services, research and development, surveys, technical writing, economic analyses, and management consulting.

L: Technical Representative Services

Engineering and technical services, especially field engineering/maintenance of sophisticated equipment and field support of technical training.

R: Architect-Engineer Services

Design commissions, civil engineering, geological studies, surveys and mapping, preparation of plans and drawings, archaeological surveys and studies.

T: Photographic, Mapping, Printing, and Publication Services

Primarily printing, but includes topographic surveys and photogrammetry, technical writing, mailing and addressing, photos (ground and aerial), typesetting, copy preparation, and various related functions.

U: Training Services

Development of training materials (manuals, audiovisuals, and the like) and presentation of courses.

X: Miscellaneous

Anything that does not appear to fit into other categories—for example, teleprocessing, rental of mules and handlers, rounding up wild horses, bagging groceries, and supplying sports officials.

Requesters in government agencies thus have a rather wide range of categories under which to list their requirements. Hence, it is not surprising that many notices appear under categories that they do not seem to fit very well. For that reason, it is necessary to scan all the possible categories when studying the publication in its hard copy or public data-base version. Moreover, it is necessary to keep an eye on what would normally be irrelevant categories: Some notices manage to migrate to irrelevant categories, through whatever are the vagaries of Murphy's law when it makes mischief in typesetting and printing.

35

The extensive number of categories of procurement listed in *Commerce Business Daily* often create special opportunities for consultants. A notice calling for bids or proposals for a consulting service may easily wind up in a category reserved for products. As a result, the response to the bid or proposal may be sparse, and the competition minimal for anyone who happens to find the notice! It is wise, therefore, to scan the entire issue of the publication daily, for a gem of a procurement may be found by this means.

The categories for products, as distinct from those for services, are identified by number, rather than by letter, from 10 to 99. A few of these are also relevant to contracting opportunities for consultants. For example, category 69 is for training aids and devices and is normally cited when buying audiovisual materials, test materials and devices, language laboratories, and other equipment. But sometimes, requirements for designing and creating training materials appear under that category also.

Similarly, category 70 is for general purpose automated data-processing equipment, software, supplies, and support equipment, but sometimes requesters use that category to hire consultants for various computer services. And there is a miscellaneous supply category, number 99, that is used to announce requirements for goods that do not fit into any of the other categories.

State and local governments generally use a system closely resembling that of the federal government and often surprisingly close to the federal system in size and diversity, as well, for everything except military goods.

HOW GOVERNMENTS BUY

Most of our governments buy according to the general pattern known as the Uniform Procurement Code of the American Bar Association, mentioned earlier. In general, contracts are designated either firm, fixed price, or based on reimbursement of costs, but each of these has hybrid forms, often of a task-order variety, which are of the "indefinite quantity" or "annual supply" type (in other words, the government doesn't know exactly what or how much of a given item it will need), with fixed rates or unit prices.

The names by which these contracts are known vary, although the general conditions of each are the same. Some names you may encounter are:

- T&M, or time and material.
- BOA, or basic ordering agreement.
- TA, or task order contract.
- Indefinite quantity contract.
- Annual supply contract.

In the federal system, there are also some 300 annual supply contracts negotiated every year by the Federal Supply Service of the General Services Administration. (Usually, these are referred to as "the Federal Supply Schedules.") Here, again, the unit prices are fixed, but there is no guarantee of work. Instead, you, what you offer, and the prices or rates agreed on become catalog items that you distribute throughout the system. You mail the information to the Federal Supply Service, which will put it on a list letting everyone entitled to use the "GSA Stores" know what and how to order from you via a government purchase order. The contract you then negotiate will specify the maximum size of order that may be placed via the purchase order, which may be less than or more than the statutory $25,000 limit placed on orders under the federal Small Purchases Act.

All state and local governments have their own small-purchase acts, which usually prescribe a much lower maximum than does the federal act. Often, the limit is as low as $500.

Technical Evaluation

There is an old jest stating that no one wants to fly in an airplane built by the low bidder. It is that consideration – that in many kinds of procurements there can be an enormously wide variation in quality of the product or service delivered – that bars using the sealed bid as the sole procurement method. Contracting officials would by far prefer using sealed bids, which mandate awards to the lowest bidders, as the most economical and most expeditious way of purchasing goods and services. However, the method is practicable only where there is assurance that the product or service will be the same, regardless of the contractor. Thus, the sealed bid is useful only in buying highly standardized commodities or in cases where the requester can specify precisely and in great and readily verifiable detail what is required. In many types of procurement, such as developing new products, solving various problems, or providing most kinds of custom services, these conditions cannot be met. Hence, the proposal method, now known as "competitive proposals" and formerly as "negotiated procurement," is employed whenever what is to be procured is not a standard commodity or cannot be specified in complete, precise, and easily verifiable detail. In effect, the government is freed from any obligation to accept the low bid, and acceptance is based on which proposal offers the greatest value or most desirable solution, with price a secondary factor.

In practice, the method requires two proposals: a technical proposal and a cost proposal. The two must be physically separate documents, and no cost information is to be included in the technical proposal. A team of competent experts (usually on staff, but sometimes outside consultants hired for the purpose) evaluates each proposal for its technical quality and awards it points of merit. The team is barred from seeing the cost proposal until the evaluation is done, to ensure an objective technical evaluation.

This method of procurement is the one most used to award contracts for expert and consultative services of all kinds. Thus, the consultant who would pursue and win government contracts must learn to write persuasive proposals.

Special Preferences

State and local laws often grant preferences to local businesses, many times in the form of extra points awarded in technical evaluations. Preference may also be granted to small business, to businesses owned by members of disadvantaged minorities, or to businesses owned by women. The federal government and many state governments run such socioeconomic programs.

GETTING STARTED

There are several ways to do your research and find both individual opportunities and a pattern of market activity that will best serve your needs. Initially you will want to pursue *all* the methods, at least until you reach a point where you have a satisfactory pattern or routine established.

Reading *Commerce Business Daily* is a primary means for uncovering business opportunities in the federal government market. Synopses of all current procurements sought by the various agencies, with an indication of where and how to request the complete solicitation, are printed. The solicitation consists of the necessary forms, the statement of work, and the instructions for writing a proposal or making a bid.

36

Subscribing to *Commerce Business Daily* is a must if you want to expand your practice into government markets. The periodical may be ordered from the Superintendent of Documents, Government Printing Office, Washington, DC 20407. It is also available as a public data base, CBD ONLINE, on the CompuServe system. When online, you need not download the entire issue each day, but may download only those categories that interest you. You may even have the service do a search and select only those synopses that respond to whatever keywords you select.

In addition, you can determine what government facilities exist within whatever you consider to be your local service area and visit each personally. Call on the contracting officer, and seek his or her assistance in determining what the typical procurements of that office are. Ask for a blank Standard Form 129, "Application for Bidders List." Try to learn the names of individuals who are likely to be requesters in that office for the services you provide. Many contracting officers are both friendly and knowledgeable in this respect and will furnish useful information if approached properly.

Fill out Form 129 and make a number of copies. Then, file a copy with every contracting office that you believe is likely to have procurements that interest you. Stay in touch with the contracting officials, and try to become acquainted with the people who request the services you provide. In particular, find out what their typical problems and needs are.

If you are willing to travel and do business outside your local area, mail copies of Form 129 to other government offices. By monitoring the *Commerce Business Daily,* you will learn what agencies are most likely to be good prospects for you. Study the publication not only to learn of specific business opportunities, but also to detect trends and market areas. When a government agency is funded to undertake a new program

══ **37** ══

Study *Commerce Business Daily* to determine which government agencies are likely to have business for you. Observe in particular the funding of new programs. These almost invariably require much outside consulting help.

it needs a great deal of assistance from business organizations in the private sector, and many contracts result. For example, the creation of the Office of Economic Opportunity and the establishment of the Postal Service Training and Development Institute were two events that created years of work for a great many consultants. And on a smaller scale, when the Consumer Product Safety Commission started a campaign to educate the public about certain product-related hazards, consultative help was needed. *Commerce Business Daily* is a place to learn about these emerging markets and special-niche markets.

Check contracting offices regularly. The larger ones often have bid rooms, where notices of current requirements are posted on bulletin boards. Even the smallest contracting office has a file of such notices available for your inspection – you need only ask for it. After a while, you will know what the best pattern is for your purposes – that is, what offices to call on and how frequently to do so.

State and local governments do not have an equivalent of the *Commerce Business Daily,* although the state of Maryland lists major procurements in the *Maryland Register,* its equivalent of the *Federal Register.* Many state and local governments publish their requirements in an English-language classified advertising section under the heading "Bids and Proposals," although frequently they also use display advertising to invite bids and proposals for major programs. In most cases, the state and local statutes governing procurement require that the notices be so advertised. This is, of course, in addition to the practice of sending out solicitation packages to those listed on the appropriate bidders lists.

Be aware that getting your name added to the appropriate bidders lists does not ensure that you will get a copy of all relevant solicitations, for at least two reasons:

- Contracting officers read Form 129 for the appropriate bidders list and try to determine for which forms the solicitation is appropriate. They may or may not make the proper match-up, so you may not be singled out as an eligible bidder for the procurement,

- Many of the bidders lists are quite extensive, having perhaps 50 to 100 names on them. The contracting official will usually send out about 10 or 20 copies of the solicitation. When the list of names is long, the contracting officer is likely to rotate the names, so that you may get a copy of every third or fourth solicitation, rather than of every one. You would then have to specifically request each solicitation that is of interest to see them all and have a chance to respond to all of them. Thus, you ought not to depend on any single method for monitoring the market if you want to make yourself aware of every opportunity. You must employ a number of monitoring methods, and even then you may miss a few procurements.

38

If you want to keep your name on contract officers' bidders lists, then, when you get a solicitation and decide not to respond to it, send the contracting office a "no bid"—a note that explains that you are not responding to the solicitation for some reason, but do want your name kept on the bidders list. Otherwise, if you fail to respond to several solicitations, the contracting official will decide that you are no longer interested and will drop your name from the bidders list.

GETTING MORE INFORMATION

In the federal government, procurement is controlled by what purports to be a uniform set of regulations, the federal acquisition regulations. These were compiled from several earlier sets of regulations and a miscellany of notes, memoranda, and acts. The result is more a collection than a system: There are so many regulations and they are so diverse, that any contracting official who is really trying can find legal justification for almost anything he or she wants to do. Ergo, don't assume that what is law or policy in one agency is equally potent or unequivocal in another agency; it probably is not. For example, most contracting officials will invite the originator of a request to suggest some candidates to which he or she would like solicitations sent to invite their bids and proposals, but the contracting official at the Department of Labor had the opposite view: He absolutely barred requesters from suggesting such candidates and requesting that copies of the bid set be sent to them. I learned of opportunities in the Department of Labor because an acquaintance there for whom I had done some work in the past telephoned and informed me that he was issuing an RFP and would like me to respond to it. But he pointed out that I myself would have to request a copy of the RFP if I wanted to respond to it.

The law permits an agency to use a purchase order and a simplified procurement process, instead of a formal contract, for purchases up to and including $24,999.99. But the law does not *require* the agency to do so. Accordingly, some contracting officers place a lower ceiling on small purchases by establishing an internal policy to that effect and require formal contracting for those purchases above the ceiling figure, even when the purchase is for something well under $25,000. Eventually, you get to know the policies of the agencies that interest you, but it is always a good idea to ask about them anyway. Contracting officers often will not volunteer the information, but they will furnish it when asked.

Most of the major federal agencies – the full-fledged departments, for example – publish a brochure or manual explaining their typical procurement needs, policies, and practices, along with more or less universal "boilerplate" on government contracting processes in general. A letter requesting information about the agency's procurement will usually bring a package of literature offering perhaps more than you ever wanted to know about contracting with the government. And very much the same situation applies to state and local governments: Many offer surprisingly thick packages of guidelines and other literature, rivaling that of the largest federal agencies and presenting an astonishingly large and diversified list of their own agencies and supply groups. California's supply group numbers, for example, closely resemble those of the federal government.

BUSINESS SERVICE CENTERS

Another way to get an armful of helpful literature explaining the federal procurement system and guiding you in the pursuit of government business is to call on any nearby General Services Administration (GSA) Business Service Center. There, you can discuss marketing with a counselor who can answer your questions and give you literature relevant to the subject. GSA Business Service Centers are located at the following addresses:

Boston:	McCormack P.O. Bldg. and Courthouse, Boston, MA 02109
New York:	26 Federal Plaza, Rm 19–130, New York, NY 10007
Philadelphia:	600 Arch Street, Philadelphia, PA 19106
Washington:	7th & D Streets, S.W., Washington, DC 20407
Atlanta:	1776 Peachtree Street, N.W., Atlanta, GA 30309
Chicago:	230 S. Dearborn Street, Chicago, IL 60604
Kansas City:	1500 E. Bannister Road, Kansas City, MO 64131
Fort Worth:	819 Taylor Street, Fort Worth, TX 76102
Denver:	Bldg. 41, Denver Federal Center, Denver, CO 80225
Los Angeles:	300 N. Los Angeles Street, Los Angeles, CA 90012
San Francisco:	525 Market Street, San Francisco, CA 94105
Auburn:	GSA Center, Auburn, WA 98002

If it is not a practical measure for you to call personally on one of these centers, write to the Denver facility and request information on contracting with the government. You can also call on or write to any of the following for guidance and informative literature, seeking out or addressing the contracting officer or public information officer in each case:

SMALL BUSINESS ADMINISTRATION
1441 L Street, N.W.
Washington, DC 20416

GENERAL SERVICES ADMINISTRATION
18th & F Streets, N.W.
Washington, DC 20405

DEPARTMENT OF ENERGY
1000 Independence Avenue, S.W.
Washington, DC 20585

DEPARTMENT OF THE INTERIOR
18th & C Streets, N.W.
Washington, DC 20240

NASA HQ CONTRACTS DIVISION
200 Maryland Avenue, S.W.
Washington, DC 20546

DEPARTMENT OF DEFENSE
The Pentagon
Washington, DC 20301

DEPARTMENT OF COMMERCE
14th & Constitution Avenue, N.W.
Washington, DC 20230

GENERAL SERVICES ADMINISTRATION
Denver Federal Center
Denver, CO 80225

ENVIRONMENTAL PROTECTION
AGENCY
401 M Street, S.W.
Washington, DC 20460

DEPARTMENT OF TRANSPORTATION
400 7th Street, S.W.
Washington, DC 20591

DEPARTMENT OF LABOR
200 Constitution Avenue, N.W.
Washington, DC 20210

DIRECTORATE FOR SMALL BUSINESS
AND ECONOMIC UTILIZATION POLICY
The Pentagon, Room 2A340
Washington, DC 20301

39

Lists of contracts awarded, found in *Commerce Business Daily,* are an excellent source of subcontracts. Many corporations subcontract significant portions of the work they contract for, and in numerous cases the bids or proposals are competitive. Peruse regularly the lists of contracts awarded, and keep your eye peeled for subcontracting opportunities.

SUBCONTRACTING

Commerce Business Daily carries lengthy lists of contracts awarded, usually at least once or twice each week. These awards are for prime contracts, and the notice describes briefly the nature of the contract, as well as the awardee and other data. The notices represent an excellent list of prospects for subcontracting, from which many sales leads may be generated. Even the largest and most diverse corporations subcontract a great deal of the work they contract for. In just one major procurement, for example, RCA awarded 360 subcontracts to a record-breaking $1 billion-plus U.S. Air Force contract. In many cases— especially where the prime contract is of the cost-reimbursement variety, there is a stipulation that the contractor must utilize competitive bids or proposals in selecting subcontractors for awards larger than those considered to be small purchases. Even when there is no such stipulation, the contractor often follows federal procurement methods in awarding subcontracts.

40

When doing business with governments, the terms *consultant* and *consulting* should be avoided as much as possible. In many cases, the use of these words automatically puts a cap on the allowable rate. For example, a given agency may have decided, as a matter of policy, that a consultant merits a maximum of $250 a day. It then does not matter what you do or how well you do it; the agency will not pay more than $250 per day. To avoid this kind of entrapment, it is far better to quote a price on any other basis. This might be a "for the job" price, or it can be a price on the basis of an hourly rate or a price for producing an end product, such as a manual, report, program, or tape. It can even be a price "for expert services," since that is a general term without the bias so often attached to the idea of consulting.

41

The *technical or program strategy* is the strategy of a better and more attractive program design. It is based on either or both of two elements: greater benefits delivered to the client because your design is superior and the avoidance of some disaster that would occur if the key points of your design were lacking. (The latter, an appeal to fear, is also a competitive strategy, pointing out the hazards of accepting competitive designs.) Ideally, the technical or program strategy ought to be based on an outstanding feature or characteristic that dominates the program design with a most important benefit offered the client.

STRATEGIES FOR SELLING TO THE GOVERNMENT

Most of the foregoing information focused on how government purchasing works. This is not exactly the same subject as how to sell to governments. Governments use competition in buying as a basic strategy for getting optimum prices and quality. Contractors selling to governments, on the other hand, focus on outwitting and outselling their competitors as one of several strategies in winning government contracts. What competitors tend to lose sight of, however, are the emotions, often veiled, on both sides. The following tips offer different strategies that have worked in selling products or services to government agencies. When angling for a government contract, keep in mind that there are other strategies besides simply "blowing the other guy out of the water." Consider the following approaches, and decide which is best for your immediate need:

The two basic appeals in all sales strategies are to acquisitiveness and fear. Clients are motivated, as we all are, both by the prospect of gaining something and by the fear of losing something. Most advertising and sales approaches are based on the promise that the person will gain something – a benefit of some sort. Your strategy could prove that your

---
42

The *cost strategy* makes your cost a key point; indeed, it even makes you appear to be the low bidder. (Yes, there are some situations in which you can appear to be the low bidder, even when you are not.) For example, when the client has asked you to price each item in a "laundry list" of services, you may underprice those services that you have good reason to believe will rarely, if ever, be ordered. The risk is small, and it is a strategy that has worked in many cases.

═══ **43** ═══

The *presentation strategy* sells your proposal in a classic "dog and pony show." Getting attention is an important part of selling, and the most attractive offer will not be appreciated by the client and win the contract if the client is not made fully aware of the offer and its superiority over other proposals. It is thus often necessary to develop a dramatic, high-impact presentation to be absolutely sure that you have the client's attention and that he or she is completely aware of the full significance of your offer. Preferably, this strategy is based on some outstanding feature of your program design or cost, which it dramatizes appropriately.

approach to the problem is by far the best, the most reliable, the most economical, or the most whatever for which you can present credible arguments. That assumes, of course, that you have gauged accurately in selecting your benefits as those that the client will recognize and agree are benefits that are important to him or her: It's no advantage to offer a benefit the client doesn't care about.

The appeal to fear is quite a powerful strategy, too. Insurance and security systems are usually sold with that in mind. One such appeal is to something known as a worry item, which has become a central item in

═══ **44** ═══

The *competitive strategy* shows yourself and your program to be superior to all competitors and their programs. There are many ways of doing this without deliberately knocking your competitors. (Doing that is most inadvisable, because it may easily backfire.) One way is the earlier suggested appeal to fear. But there are other methods of suggesting the superiority of your own talents, skills, resources, and approach so that the client is induced to compare them with those of competitors and find yours to be superior.

═══ **45** ═══

The *capture strategy* is just a general term for the main strategy, the one you expect to be decisive in capturing the contract. It may, and probably will, be one of the preceding strategies, but that will be a matter of judgment: You will have to decide which of them is of the greatest importance to the client. That doesn't mean that the other strategies are not important, too, but they will be subordinated to the main strategy, which will dominate your approach.

proposal writing. A worry item is any item that appears to be of special concern to the client – for example, cost, schedule, or reliability. Ideally, it is a worry of which the client is intensely conscious. Often, you can read the worry item or items quite clearly in the RFP and statement of work. The client either states his or her chief concern quite plainly or places so much stress on one aspect or another of the procurement that the main concern is readily apparent. Your own strategy ought then to be built around this concern, addressing it as a main feature of your proposal.

46

Even when writing a proposal to a government agency, don't forget the client's emotions. Identifying a client's worry item is always a valuable exercise that allows you to target your benefits directly at the client's fears. You get extra points if you create a worry item and then devise the means of avoiding it.

Unfortunately, worry items are not always readily apparent. Sometimes you must study an RFP carefully, closely, and at great length to read *between* the lines in quest of the worry items. And sometimes they are not there at all: The client simply is not conscious of any items of special concern and has no specific worries. In that case, the approach is to *give* the client something to worry about – *to create a worry item*. That is, you must make a thorough analysis of the requirement, to determine whether there are potential hazards of which you ought to make the client aware – the danger of runaway costs, a hazard to the schedule, a hazard to reliability, or some other hazard. The objective is to make the client aware of those hazards and of your plans to prevent them from realizing themselves in the program you propose. Here is an example of how that can be done:

A client issued an RFP in which he asked for something to be done on a virtually impossible schedule, calling for the development of a complete training plan in about two weeks. The successful proposer pointed out the normally insurmountable problem involved in doing this, but he showed the client how he could overcome this problem because he was aware of it in advance and had material on the shelf that could be modified easily to be a precise fit for the client's need. Because of this good fortune and his resourcefulness, only he could *guarantee* absolutely to meet the client's schedule.

USING PR PROFITABLY

"PR" is the popular shorthand for *public relations,* the primary objective of which is publicity—free advertising. High visibility with a favorable image helps greatly in winning clients and contracts. The news release and product release are classic PR tools, but there are many other methods. Writing and speaking are also effective ways to promote your image. Even better is getting yourself written about and interviewed on radio and TV talk shows.

THE PUBLIC MAN AND WOMAN

Many ordinary lay people shrink almost instinctively from appearing in the spotlight. Most of us would rather not draw attention to ourselves publicly. We don't really want to be on public display, scrutinized minutely by everyone. We are acutely aware of every minor defect we have, real or imagined, and we are sure that everyone is staring intently at our imperfect noses and listening critically to hear our less than ideal speaking voices. But if simply appearing in public is a formidable prospect, being the sole focus of attention is an even more dreadful, knee-watering, butterflies-in-the-stomach prospect. We wonder at those who can mount the dais and speak for hours calmly and with obvious ease. How do they do it? Perhaps that is one reason that so few independent consultants take full advantage of the powerful weapon of PR to win clients and contracts: It means coming out from under the cloak of anonymity, a frightening prospect.

47

Make formulating a PR strategy one of your top priorities. Achieving publicity, through press releases, published articles, media interviews, and public speaking, can be more potent than passive advertising, because it builds your professional image in a real-world context and is not a financial drain.

On the other hand, while public speaking and public appearances generally are among the more effective PR measures, not all PR requires you to stand on a platform before an audience and appear to be completely comfortable and at ease. There are other forms of PR, forms that are far less stressful, yet equally useful in developing a productive professional image. We shall examine some of these in this chapter.

THE PRESS RELEASE

The most widely used and best known tool of PR is the press release (see Figure 5-1), which usually has the following components:

1. Identification as a release by a bold header such as RELEASE, NEWS RELEASE, PRESS RELEASE, PRODUCT RELEASE, or PUBLICITY RELEASE.

2. Identification of the source, either on a special form (used by those who issue releases on a regular basis) or on regular letterhead.

3. Dateline, that is, city of origin and date.

4. Double- or triple-spaced copy.

5. Single-sided copy.

6. Headline. This is optional: Some advocate against it, some for it. I am for it, to capture the editor's interest and help him or her grasp the essence of the story immediately. The argument some make against using a headline is that editors prefer to write their own headlines, which is true enough, but irrelevant: The editor is always completely free to change the original headline or anything else he or she wishes to edit and will very likely do so, regardless of what you do. Don't think of the headline as something directed to the reader of your release. Think of it rather as a quick summary of the

---

HRH COMMUNICATIONS, INC.
P.O. Box 1731   Wheaton, MD 20915
Fax: (301) 649-5745   Voice: (301) 649-2499Z

NEWS   6/28/92

For Immediate Release   Contact:
                                               Herman Holtz
                                               (301) 460-0000

HOW TO SELL TO THE $200 BILLION GOVERNMENT MARKET

Information Now Available in Audiocassettes

Business people have complained for years about the difficulty of getting

information and guidance in selling to the U.S. Government, despite the literature

on the subject published by the government. Written literature has not proved

very helpful to the newcomer to this market.

Now, for the first time, complete information and instruction package on

selling to the government is available in convenient audiocassette form. The set

includes four 1-hour cassettes and a 65-page directory of government purchasing

offices, with a summary of the Federal Acquisition Regulations (FAR).

The package was developed over the past year by a special team of government-

market experts, who interviewed dozens of government purchasing officials and

reviewed over 12,000 pages of official documents to distill this 4-hour program.

The program incorporates the latest information available. An explanatory

brochure explaining the program is available from HRH Communications, Inc.

###

Figure 5-1.   Typical news release.

---

release, intended to help the editor grasp the message instan-
taneously. Busy editors appreciate anything that spares them
excessive reading and saves their time.

7.   Whom to contact. Give a name and number to call to follow
up ideas, ask questions, request photos, validate facts, clarify

points, or otherwise pursue more information, and perhaps even to get "the story behind the story." (In some cases, a release can turn into or result in a feature story.)

8.   Editorial guidance. Write "More" at the bottom of each page to let the editor know that there is more copy and "End," "###," or "-30-" at the bottom of the last page to signify the end of the story.

9.   Time frame. Say "For immediate release" or "embargoed until" some specified date. (The latter is used in case the release is to be published as a report following a speech, convention, or some other occasion.

10. Photograph, when appropriate. For example, a release heralding a new product may need an accompanying photograph to be presented adequately.

What Does a Release Do for You?

There are at least two things a release does for you:

1.   It provides publicity with your name displayed prominently. (Write the release so that your name is an inextricable element of it.)

2.   It can be designed and employed in such a manner that it provides specific sales leads. Keep both of these features in mind as you read on and encounter further examples (besides Figure 5-1) of press releases.

The Most Common Mistakes

There are several common mistakes that are made in preparing releases. Some of the more serious ones are the following:

* Offering copy that is not newsworthy in any real sense of the word (i.e., copy that is transparently pure hype).
* Providing single-spaced instead of double- or triple-spaced copy.
* Providing copy on both sides of the paper instead of on one side only.
* Giving no contact name.

- Failing to provide an embargo date when the release mentions some event that has not yet taken place.

- Presenting an unclear message without any real point (e.g., using evasive language or hazy expressions).

48

Avoid the more serious common mistakes people make in writing press releases: copy that is not newsworthy, single spaced, on both sides of the paper, without a contact name, or with a pointless or unclear message.

In addition to avoiding the preceding mistakes, be sure that what you report are facts and are in good taste. If you make a mistake that causes an editor to commit some faux pas and be embarrassed thereby, you will probably kill your chances of ever having that editor consider using your releases again. It is therefore especially important to be careful about accuracy: your relationships with editors are at stake, and that is an important factor in conducting PR successfully. On the other hand, if you write a good press release, editors will gain confidence in you and select and use your releases more readily.

USING HEADLINES AND SUBHEADS

Editors of periodicals—especially newspapers—have daily and often hourly deadlines and, consequently, are busy people. Usually, they are all but swamped with releases arriving in the morning mail. If your release is less than crystal clear and not very easy to read, an editor is likely to discard it impatiently, rather than spend time trying to make sense of it, for he or she has a great many others to read. That is one cogent reason for having a headline, and it offers a clue as to what the headline ought to say: It ought to summarize the main message of the release. That is what the headline in Figure 5-1 does, and that is also why a subhead is used there to augment and expand the message. The editor can grasp the essence of the message immediately, which speaks well for the release and gives the editor reason to believe that it may be worthwhile to take a minute or two to read it. (You would be surprised how nearly illiterate some releases appear to be!)

Aside from being clear, a headline ought always to be a grabber in terms of attention-getting, interest-arousing substance. It ought to *demand* attention and arouse interest immediately. One way to have done that with Figure 5-1 would have been to use the following headline and subhead:

THE U.S. GOVERNMENT PAID ME $6,000
TO ANSWER THEIR MAIL
Guidance on Selling Your Services
to Government Agencies
Now Available on Audiocassettes

This kind of headline, used as a lead, requires an immediate follow-up to expand on it, which you can do with a subhead, as shown, or with the first sentence of the release. The subhead is the more direct way of doing the job, complementing and expanding on the headline, while also serving to introduce the body of the release. The subhead thus acts as a bridge, making the transition from the headline to the text, which proceeds directly from the established theme to explain the headline. (With this new headline and subhead, the first paragraph of the release in Figure 5-1 would have been considerably different than that shown.)

49

Take advantage of the fact that a surprisingly large number of press releases do not use a headline, much less a subhead. Therefore, your use of these features makes your release somewhat distinctive, improving its chances for demanding and getting attention and, thus, leading to a contract.

A FEW DOS AND DON'TS

One of the more common mistakes in using press releases effectively has to do with where to send them. It is poor practice generally to address a release to a large publication or other medium (e.g., a radio or TV newsroom) without specifying a destination within the organization, such as an editor or, at least, a department. (An exception to this is the case of a small publishing house, where the release could not possibly get lost.) Remember that in large organizations, mail addressed to the organization generally, rather than to an individual, is usually opened in the mail room, where someone – usually a mail clerk – attempts to judge the proper destination within the organization. On a large newspaper or magazine, your undirected release is likely to wind up on a managing editor's or city editor's desk, but it could wind up on the sports desk or even the circulation manager's desk if you have not specified otherwise. That individual then may or may not spend time reading the release and deciding where it ought to go. In fact, the most likely scenario is that he or she will be too busy to worry about it and just drop it casually into the "circular file" without further thought. Even if the individual decides to pass it on to someone else, it is still likely to wind up in the wrong place and eventually find its way into that famous "circular file" anyway.

On the other hand, even if you do manage to get your release to the appropriate editor, columnist, or other party, it is still necessary that the release be of interest to that person. That is, you should not ordinarily write a release and then decide where to send it (a typical error of the uninitiated), but you should follow the reverse pattern, along the following lines:

1. Decide whom – what reader, viewer or prospect – you want to reach.

2. Decide what kinds of media – which periodicals, which columnists, which radio or TV programs, and so on – are most suitable for reaching your audience.

3. Decide what subject and what angle or aspect of the subject would interest the editor, columnist, or producer of the organization you are sending the release to.

FINDING TOPICS TO WRITE ABOUT

The most difficult part of writing releases for many consultants is finding something to write about that is newsworthy. Especially difficult for those who are not professional writers is finding a string of new ideas on which to base a series of releases, since a single release rarely does the job that a stream of releases does: There is definitely a cumulative effect in a continuous effort, resulting in a synergy in which the total effect of the series is greater than the simple sum of the releases.

Obviously, your press releases are not going to be newsworthy in the sense that front-page stories in the newspaper, usually called "hard news," are. Still, they are newsworthy simply in that they offer new, interesting information. Always remember that a press release should come across not as a marketing tool, but as a genuinely helpful vehicle of information. Keep your focus on who, what, where, and why – from the media's point of view.

50

Use information such as the following in press releases:

- Announcement of a new product you have developed or for which you are a distributor or an agent.
- Announcement of your practice when you hang out your shingle.
- Announcement of a new service you offer.
- Announcement of a major contract award from a prominent local company or government agency.
- Announcement of some new development in your field that the periodical might otherwise not learn of or cover.
- Announcement of a free seminar, report, or brochure you offer on any subject of interest. (This can be a never-ending source of material on which to base your releases.)

Keep in mind the range of possible destinations for your release, depending on its content – the science editor, financial or business news editor, state desk, city desk, sports editor, new product editor, and so forth.

SLANTING YOUR RELEASE

Slanting copy is a simple concept. It means writing the release in such a way as to address the direct and specific interests of a given audience. Suppose, for example, that you provide computer services – say, programming design and related functions – and are preparing a release to help make yourself and your practice more widely known. Suppose further that you wish to publicize your offer of a free demonstration and how-to-do-it seminar as a means of attracting prospective clients and developing sales leads. There are several possibilities open to you. Your release will have to suggest some particular program or kind of coverage that you will be demonstrating and explaining. If your specialties include data-base applications for inventory control and management, accounting systems, purchasing control, and other business systems, you will have to decide which application is most likely to attract the prospects you want – those you think are most likely to become clients. An inventory program is going to attract only business people for whom inventory control and management are important – an owner of a supermarket or a manufacturer, for example. It certainly is not likely to appeal to the owner of a small restaurant or newsstand; their business interests and needs do not run heavily to computer systems!

You could, of course, present a program covering data-base management generally, with a few examples. But if data-base management per se, rather than a given application, is your focus, you will probably attract dbm personnel primarily, rather than other kinds of executives. This is a form of slanting, too, of course.

What emerges from this example is that you can create more than one version of a release (or a seminar or brochure), so that you can attract many people having far different special interests. But you must also think in terms of the periodicals and other media toward which you slant your material. What you might consider one and the same thing may vary from one publication to another. Thus, what one newspaper calls the financial editor another may title the business editor, although the dullest mail room clerk may be able to interpret your wishes and direct your release to the right editors.

A special problem presents itself in sending releases to columnists. Normally, columnists should be addressed by name, and since many are syndicated and are not on the staff of the individual periodical carrying the column, you must either determine what the columnist's mailing address is or send your release in care of the periodical.

Not everything can be slanted effectively. For example, it would be difficult to slant a release for a male audience explaining how crocheting is making a strong comeback, because few men are likely to take up crocheting. On the other hand, relatively few women are enthusiastic about fly fishing, so an article or release on this topic might be slanted to fly fishermen with different interests – some like to tie their own flies, while others prefer to buy them ready made and will try every new one they can find. What they each have in common, however, is an interest in fly fishing. (In fact, perhaps the most common factor among fly fishermen is their almost legendary zeal, which borders on fanaticism, according to all reports.) Now, difficult as it may be, it is still entirely possible to slant material on fly fishing to women who have no direct interest in fishing at all if you address the wives and sweethearts of fly fishermen with an appeal to buy fly-fishing gear, accessories, or related publications as gifts to the zealots who happen to be the husbands and sweethearts they love.

Be sure of your facts, however, for it is easy to be mistaken about this. You might think, for example, that few women are fans of wrestling, but a visit to any arena featuring wrestling matches will reveal how many women are highly enthusiastic about watching this entertainment represented as a sport. In fact, advertising of cosmetics, weight loss programs, and other items of special interest to women are among the frequent commercials that accompany televised wrestling. These certainly reveal who the wrestling audiences are.

Many products lend themselves to multiple uses and users, and each potential use and user suggests the keys to a slant. In writing releases to publicize my own services and publications on marketing to government agencies, I found many ways to slant them to different audiences. The two most obvious and most basic slanting opportunities for me were these:

1. To companies already doing business with the government, the theme was how to do more business with the government.

2. To companies who had done little or no business with the government, the theme here was how to break into the government market most effectively.

51

Probably the most well-known way to use press releases is to mail them out to editors of periodicals and, in many cases, to columnists who write for periodicals. However, you can enclose one with any promotional mailing you send out, and even that hardly exhausts the possibilities. For example, you can distribute releases at business meetings, at seminars, at conventions, in hospitality suites, and wherever there is a literature table or rack.

But there are many other possibilities: In my case, I could slant releases to small businesses generally, to minority-owned businesses, to very small businesses such as free-lancing individuals, to businesses selected by the nature of what they sell, to businesses selected by the nature of the kinds of customers they pursue, to businesses in selected geographical areas, and to an even greater number of possibilities than these. With an active imagination and a bit of introspection on possible uses and users, slanting is usually not especially difficult.

52

The idea of using press releases to invite people to call or write for a brochure or free report of interest is an idea that can be used in many ways to generate sales leads. The key is simply finding the link between the reader's interest and what you wish to publicize: Not many people will write or call for a brochure that, as far as they know or as your announcement suggests, is simply advertising for your practice, but they will call or write to request a brochure or report that offers them specific benefits. Design such a brochure or report to appeal to those who would be good prospects for your services. Note that there is little point in offering calendars and lists of emergency telephone numbers in a press release. Those kinds of items have their uses, but they rarely fit the promotional plans or goals of a consultant.

WHERE TO SEND RELEASES

Newspapers and popular magazines are obvious targets for press releases. Bear in mind, however, that you are not trying to reach the casual reader; you are trying to reach readers who are prospective clients. If you are addressing releases to a general newspaper, you want to reach the proper editor or department. Normally, you will not be trying to reach the city desk; the city editor is concerned with real news, hard news. But there are other editors and desks that may be right for you: the financial or business editor, a health editor, an entertainment editor, a literary editor, an education editor, and various other special editors. A large city newspaper is very much like an assortment of periodicals, each addressed to the interest of a different reader. (This is especially the case with newspapers that have Sunday editions.)

The same thing is true of magazines: Most have various departments and editors, each with special interests; such as reviews of new products and notices of personnel changes.

Probably the trade press and special-interest newsletters will be of the greatest attraction to you. Make it your business to find out about and compile a list of the trade journals read by those you want to reach – the individuals most likely to be good prospects for you. Go to your public library and ask the librarian for help. He or she will direct you to several guides that list and describe a wide variety of periodicals and newsletters. You will probably be quite surprised at the large number and diversity of trade publications the library has. There are many thousands of them because most industries have several trade periodicals.

Nor should you neglect the news departments of your local radio and TV stations. They may also help you reach prospective clients. Executives driving to and from work often listen to the news on radio stations and watch the evening news on TV at home.

53

One of the best targets for a press release is the huge number of newsletters published in the United States. Even conservative estimates put the number at 30,000, and some experts place it as high as 100,000. It was always my experience that newsletters would make use of good news releases, and I took advantage of this as often as possible, especially to attract registrants for my seminars. In fact, were I forced to use only one kind of medium, I would probably opt for newsletters for most applications.

GETTING PUBLISHED

Getting your name before that part of the public or business community that will provide you with most of the prospects for what you sell is an important objective of PR. Press releases are one excellent way of reaching this segment, as long as you are successful in having them published and in otherwise getting them into the hands of prospective clients. However, there are other ways of accomplishing the same purpose, ways that may be easier and possibly less costly in terms of your time and money. They are not necessarily to be used in place of releases; rather, they should be used in addition to releases, for maximum benefit.

One important such way is getting published—writing articles that will appear in either the general media or the trade media. In some ways, articles can be even more effective than press releases: Being published in the journals of your field carries with it a certain prestige, an aura of professionalism, that writing press releases cannot approach. And being published frequently enough that your name becomes a familiar one confers a rather special status on you: When your name has become familiar, it is automatically invoked when a potential client is in need of the kind of service you provide. Whether merited or not, the frequent appearance of your name in print as an author tends to make you an authority in the minds of many.

54

Does getting published sound too ambitious for you? I hope I can convince you otherwise in these pages. But at the very least, consider writing a letter to the editor to some journals in your field. Even that can be effective in drawing attention to what you do and what you have to offer your clients.

Every industry and trade has its special publications, or *trade journals.* Some are slick-paper magazines that are as costly, as thick, and as artistic as the most costly, the thickest, and the most artistic general-interest magazines that appear on the newsstands in bookstores, super-markets, and drugstores. Many are tabloids printed on light pulp paper (newsprint), although some tabloids are inked on slick paper. (*Meeting News*, published by Miller Freeman, Inc., of New York, is an excellent example.) Then there are the newsletters, also mentioned as targets for press releases. They range from single sheets of two sides, through that most populous field of four- and eight-page newsletters, to publications whose publishers have not yet decided whether their products are newsletters or magazines. With most trades and industries spawning such a large number and diversity of publications, there is little reason for your name to fail to make at least an occasional appearance in their pages as a byline under the title of an article about your profession.

The chief obstacle to this for most consultants is not writing ability: You do not need to be Henry James or Ayn Rand; you need only to be able to be explicit and address the objective of the piece in an organized manner. Most individuals who are competent enough to be consultants are at least that competent in writing skills, and you surely are. Despite that, a great many who are highly intelligent and highly competent in their technical and professional fields are reluctant to write, and that is itself a great obstacle you must overcome if it stands in your way. Unfortunately, some have a fear of writing almost as great as the fear of public speaking so many have, some have a sense of inadequacy as writers that is almost surely unmerited and unjustified, and some simply have a distaste for writing, probably because writing is hard work. It would be foolish to deny that, of course, but where is any success achieved without hard work?

Still another obstacle is a lack or perceived lack of creative imagination – difficulty in finding adequate subjects about which to write. That is a completely different skill. It goes much further into the heart of what writing is about. However, there are ways to address the problem of finding ideas and subjects about which to write, which we shall discuss shortly. But first let us consider the other problem mentioned.

OVERCOMING THE FEAR OF OR DISTASTE FOR WRITING

In at least some cases, and probably many more than you would suppose, the distaste for writing is rooted in a doubt that you can write well enough to be published. And true enough, to those who have never written anything much longer than a page or two, it may seem a rather formidable task to plan out and write something that will run to thousands of words and many pages. However, it has been my experience that difficulty in *research* – gathering and, especially, *organizing* information – is often the root cause of what we might call poor or bad writing, rather than difficulty in constructing sentences and stringing them together to form paragraphs.

55

If you have an almost instinctive bias against writing, make up your mind that, first of all, you do not address a writing task as a job to be done in a single sitting or as a single chore. In the same manner in which you plan a cross-country trip with daily destinations and overnight stops, you plan a writing task by subdividing it into its major elements and then subdividing those into their own subordinate elements. The process is known as *outlining* and is something we've all learned from grade school on.

Link the difficulty in research to the resistance of the beginning writer to the almost inevitable and necessary task of rewriting at least the first draft, and the major difficulties are identified. Those not accustomed to writing and those with a prior bias against or distaste for writing resist rewriting, although for most of us rewriting is the key to good writing. Even geniuses rarely produce truly good first draft; the professional writing attitude is to recognize that fact.

Remember that all writing has a beginning, a middle, and an end, of which it is often said that we introduce the subject, present the information, and summarize what we've written, respectively. While this is rather general guidance and not of a great deal of help, if you work at a computer keyboard, as any modern writer should, you can invoke an outlining software program to see what it means.

FINDING IDEAS FOR ARTICLES

Overcoming the other obstacle mentioned, getting ideas for articles, can be likened to priming the pump: You must input some ideas to start your brain working. One way to do this is to read what others have written and consciously see what new ideas such reading can foster and stimulate. Ask yourself a few provocative questions as you read the most recent editions of some journals. The following are good thought starters:

- Is this really the latest news about the subject? Are there some newer developments?
- What other applications might there be?
- Is this article complete? Does it cover the subject? What else ought the reader learn about it?
- Does the material evoke memories of some interesting case histories or anecdotes?
- What is the probable future of this field? This specialty?
- Is there some fascinating history behind this story?
- What are 5 or 10 significant points readers ought to know about this subject?
- What are the hazards of this material?
- What are the advantages and disadvantages of the material? The pros and cons? Is there another way of doing this story?

As an example, the most recent edition of a magazine for home-based small business has an article on the self-publishing of books. What ideas does this suggest to me immediately? Here are a few:

- An article on self-publishing monographs, rather than books.
- A special or innovative way of marketing self-published books, a way not covered in the article.
- A conventional means for marketing books not known to most of those not engaged professionally in book publishing.
- A reference work explaining a few mechanics of production and listing suppliers – printers, binders, typesetters, illustrators, and others – and distributors – wholesalers and large publishing houses that will distribute books for small publishers.
- What types of books are best suited to self-publishing for whatever reason? Is there an article idea buried in that question?
- What shortcuts are available to the self-publisher? What equipment will pay for itself quickly?
- A collection of success stories.

The list can go on and on. In the beginning, you read the material with these things in mind and you make a conscious search for ideas. After a time, you begin to condition your subconscious mind and you no longer need consciously search for ideas: Your subconscious does it for you, suggesting ideas spontaneously.

FINDING IDEAS FOR BOOKS

As do professionals in other fields, many consultants write books about their field. Authoring a book confers a special kind of prestige on the consultant qua author. It is an accomplishment that has a value all its own. I can testify to more than one case where one of my books inspired a client to seek me out.

56

Books have an almost magical way of moving you and your credentials to the top of the pack. There is nothing more impressive than responding to a stone-faced prospect with: "Let me send you a copy of my book." An excellent volume that offers an easy-to-follow book-publishing strategy is the recently published *Publish and Flourish – a Consultant's Guide* (John Wiley & Sons, 1992). Written by Garry Schaeffer and Tony Allessandra, the book can be ordered by calling 1-800-CALL-WILEY.

Getting ideas for books is not much different than getting ideas for articles. Frequently, in reading an article or a chapter in someone's book (even in one of my own books), it becomes apparent to me that the article or the chapter barely penetrates the surface of the subject, and the coverage could and should be expanded to book length. That alone has been the seed that spawned some of my own books, as it has for other authors.

There is a great market for business and professional books. You can, of course, publish your work, but you can also seek to interest one of the commercial book publishers in publishing your book. The commercial book publisher is in a far better position to handle the entire task, including distribution through the proper channels.

PUBLISHING IDEAS FOR SELF-STARTERS

To get started publishing, consider writing a brochure to draw inquiries and build sales leads – for example, a "Free Checklist of Ideas for Writing and Publishing a Book" or "Seven Tips for Finding the Best Accounting Software." It doesn't cost much to do this. Unless you need very large quantities of such items, you can even turn copies out in your own office with your own copier or laser printer. Even if you have the items printed outside by a print shop, you can probably do your own typesetting, layout, and general copy preparation yourself.

One way of getting published is to publish your own newsletter. The physical production of a newsletter is really not at all difficult, especially with the modern equipment just referred to and the abundance of computer software designed for such work. Nor need it afford any other kind of a burden, since it is under your total control. Chapter 6 presents ideas on how to turn a newsletter into a profit center, and not just a publicity vehicle.

GETTING YOURSELF WRITTEN ABOUT

In many respects, the best PR is getting yourself written about. The average reader accepts stories about various individuals in the professional, business, and entertainment worlds as spontaneously generated events. Readers have no idea how most of these stories have been carefully engineered, usually by highly paid PR experts. Still, you don't have to be an expert or even hire one to get yourself written about. Often, being aggressive is enough.

A while ago, some friends of mine offered to persuade a certain business-news reporter of their acquaintance to do a story about me in the newspaper for which he worked. I waited patiently for many weeks, while my friends assured me that they were working on the problem, but nothing happened. Finally, I decided to take the project over: I wrote a letter to the reporter, without mentioning our mutual friends, explained what I did that I thought was newsworthy (I helped people write proposals and win government contracts), and suggested that he might want to cover this. Not long after, he showed up in my office with a photographer and wrote a quite nice story that appeared in the newspaper's business pages a few days later.

That story inspired journalist Peter Williams to interview me for another story on government purchasing that he was doing for a magazine. It also led to other stories in newspapers and magazines, as well as to several consulting assignments. All of this coverage turned out to be invaluable in my career, and it all stemmed from one letter. If you do "pitch" yourself to a business writer, read the person's by-line for a few weeks to get a feel for his or her preferred angles. Then convince the writer you fit right in with those angles.

57

Don't be reluctant to sound your own horn. It sounds as loudly as when others sound it for you. You can get yourself written about, as I have done so many times. Most of us do newsworthy things or offer newsworthy services. They don't all merit newspaper coverage, but there are thousands upon thousands of newsletters, magazines, and other periodicals covering newsworthy events and subjects. You can be one of those subjects if not one of the events.

PUBLIC SPEAKING

Public speaking is one of the leading PR activities. The fear of it that so many have is legendary, as noted earlier. In fact, even those who are veterans of public speaking and who appear to be completely at ease on the platform are not always so: Many have confessed to having butterflies and watery knees every time they mount the dais.

I have found a few devices that help overcome or at least neutralize this fear to some extent. One is to break into public speaking gradually, under the far lower stress of being a member of a panel. There, you are normally seated at a table, flanked by at least two other individuals, and often more than two, so some attention is focused on you, but not all of it. A few sessions in that mode will help you gain a bit of confidence and build up your "platform comfort."

58

If at all possible, condition yourself to public speaking by starting with appearances under circumstances and conditions that produce the lowest stress. Here they are, in order of priority, from lowest to highest:

- Speaking while seated at a table with others.
- Speaking while seated at a table alone.
- Making a brief address as one of many speakers.
- Speaking from behind a lectern.
- Speaking with self-contained aids, such as movies and other audiovisuals, in a darkened room.
- Speaking with accessory aids, such as posters, slides, and overheads.

From that beginning, allow yourself to graduate to solo performances. Ideally, your next appearances will be brief ones of 15 to 30 minutes. (Even those can seem to be an eternity, until you become accustomed to being a center of attention in a large room.) Try to arrange to be a guest speaker at occasions—seminars, perhaps—where there are several speakers. Or seek out your local Toastmasters chapter for camaraderie and valuable experience as you get into the swing of things.

Ultimately, with practice, you will either overcome your fears or learn to cope successfully with them. Coping with fears is not quite as ideal a solution as overcoming them is, but it will serve the need quite well.

SUMMARY

The foregoing is not, of course, the definitive discussion of PR for consultants. Others have written entire volumes on PR and still not said all that can be said on the subject. By all means, seek out more information and additional ideas on how you can use PR to enhance your own practice.

CHAPTER 6

ALTERNATIVE METHODS OF CONSULTING

We tend always to think of consulting as a face-to-face and one-on-one service. You, the consultant, sit down with the client, you learn what the client's problems and needs are, you analyze the situation, and you develop a solution and provide it, often with personal counseling. Sometimes the problem is such that you can virtually reach into your briefcase and pull out a perfect solution. But of course it rarely works that way: Not every consulting problem lends itself to a straightforward, classical approach such as this. Sometimes you need to struggle to find a suitable answer, and that often proves to be too much for the client. Because of this, we need alternatives.

THE BASIC ECONOMICS OF CONSULTING

As independent consultants, especially when launched into new ventures, we do not always understand even the most basic economics of consulting. Many of us – particularly those least experienced in the day-to-day realities of a business – tend to become entranced by the prospect of earning $200 a day. To many, that appears to be a handsome income. It adds up to $52,000 a year, even without working overtime and weekends for expanded rates, and so appears quite munificent to anyone who has worked for considerably less as someone's employee. It could easily produce $75,000 to $100,000 per year, with overtime, couldn't it? Little do many of us realize, however, that in the beginning, that $200 per day will result in a substandard wage for our profession.

Ironically, we often lose potential contracts because many prospective clients find that a cost of even $200 a day, much less the more common higher rates, is too much for them. Some object under the delusion that our rate, whatever it is, is exorbitant; others truly cannot afford even $200 a day for our normal face-to-face, one-on-one service. Realistically, few among us can afford to work for even $200 or $300 per day, much less, lower fees than that. Consider the harsh realities: Allow six weeks for lost days—sick leave, vacation, and holidays—and that leaves only 46 weeks, or $46,000 annually. But that amount assumes that we can bill a full eight hours a day every day and does not allow for nonbillable time— the approximately one-third of our time spent in marketing and general administrative work. So we really earn a net of only $30,682 per year— hardly enough to go skiing in Aspen or winter on the Riviera!

In actuality, $200 a day is coolie wages for a skilled consultant. A far more realistic daily rate is an absolute minimum of $300, giving a probable annual income of $46,000. And remember that even this amount means zero profit for the firm. The consultant is, or at least should regard him- or herself as, an employee drawing a salary, which is a cost to the firm, and not profit. The firm ought to have some profit on which to grow and build a reserve to cover future needs—slow periods, purchases of new and improved equipment, tax increases, assessments, and other unexpected costs.

In reality, especially in the economy that exists at the time of this writing—namely, inflated costs and a broad range of high taxes—a full-fledged, competent consultant ought logically to be able to charge and be paid a daily fee of $500 or more. (The overall average is much higher than that.) Such an amount would enable the consultant to pay him- or herself a reasonably adequate salary, while building that reserve of dollars that is necessary to make the practice a viable business enterprise. But today's economy is also recessionary—at the moment, at least—with a great many businesses cutting back sharply on expenditures, even as individuals work to pare their costs.

GROUP CONSULTING

Thus, while $300–$500 a day may represent a reasonable return on investment for you, it also represents an intolerably high cost to a great many prospective clients. Many small businesses cannot afford the several thousand dollars of consulting services they need to solve their problems any more than you can afford to give away your time and knowledge at less than minimal standards. The result is an apparent impasse, but fortunately, there is a workable answer: Just as many therapists offer group therapy to patients who cannot afford individual therapy, it is possible for you to offer group consulting to clients who cannot or do not wish to pay your individual consulting rates. In short, the "flip side" of direct, face-to-face consulting services is group consulting, with the obvious advantages of much lower cost to the client and an expanded market for you.

59

Group consulting offers you an expanded market—the opportunity to accommodate many more clients, earn a great deal more money, and place your consulting practice on a much more secure basis than through individual consulting. You can deliver group consulting via a number of vehicles, including lectures, seminars, workshops, training classes, audiotapes, videotapes, and publications of various kinds, such as newsletters and manuals.

The basic vehicles for group consulting are all those media and methods with which you can address and help many people with a single presentation. As in group therapy, each individual pays a fee that is only a fraction of that which individual therapy would cost. As the practitioner, you do not suffer, because the total income from any session or single presentation is as great as or greater than the income you would enjoy from counseling a single client at your daily or hourly rate. The economics of such group-based presentations are quite different from those of providing consulting to individual clients at a fixed daily or hourly rate. There, you have assured yourself of a fixed fee for each hour or day of your service. In group presentations, there is some risk involved—too few participants means working for fewer dollars than your normal rate—but there is also the balancing factor of the possibility that you will attract enough participants to earn more than your daily rate.

There are many ways to offer group consulting. You can lecture or run courses and seminars at local universities and junior colleges, in your own offices, via seminar-production companies, on a custom basis for organizations, under the sponsorship of various organizations, and by your own production. Each of these means can be an income-producing center in itself, but most of the activities mutually support and reinforce each other. For example, a newsletter of your own is one means of delivering services to a great many participants, but it is also an excellent advertising and sales medium for selling other products and services. Group consulting can be presented via audiotapes and printed materials – newsletters, special reports, manuals, and books. The sale of such items is often combined with lectures and seminars to conduct "back-of-the-room" sales. That is, the lecture or seminar serves as a medium for such sales. In fact, it is a popular income producer for professional speakers.

NEEDS SATISFIED BY GROUP CONSULTING

A great many people perceive consulting as concerned primarily with solving problems for clients. Whether that is true or not depends on how one defines the word *problem*. A problem may be perceived as purely technical, beyond the skills of the client, and needing expert services to be solved. An example is a computer system that is producing erratic results, the cause and resolution of which are entirely beyond the skills of the client and the client's staff. But often, the client knows how to solve the problem but hasn't the time to do it, necessitating the services of a consultant by default, so to speak. There are many kinds of problems that require a solution, for example:

- Analyzing and defining a need.
- Designing a system.
- Developing a system.
- Debugging a system.
- Improving a system.
- Installing a system.
- Training a staff.
- Making recommendations.
- Augmenting a staff.
- Counseling the client.
- Writing specifications.

These are necessarily general classifications and few in number. They may apply in dozens of different ways, however, for different consultants and different projects. A system may be a computer program, an office system, an inventory system, a marketing system, a security system, a communications system, or any other kind of system. Staff training may be general training in some field, such as how to write a proposal or how to operate a personal computer, or it may be specific training in operating or maintaining a system you have designed and installed in a turnkey contract. One contract may call on you strictly to counsel a client, while another may require you to conduct lengthy troubleshooting, analysis, design, and implementation.

Not all client needs lend themselves to group consultation. If a problem or need is unique and peculiar to the individual client, the only solution is likely to be that one-on-one, individual consulting service in the classic consulting model. When, for example, a client has computer software problems, such as that of a program taking far longer to run than it ought to, the solution must be undertaken on an individual basis. However, when the client wants to, say, have a staff trained in direct marketing, a seminar, workshop, or other training program is appropriate, and that it need not be an in-house program if there is a need for training only a few people.

SEMINARS AND WORKSHOPS

Seminars and workshops (I use the terms almost interchangeably) are excellent vehicles for group consulting when training or solving a set of problems common to a group is the need. The cost to the client is relatively small, and the profit potential for you is quite large. In today's market, the fees for attending a seminar or workshop usually range from $200 to $300 per person per day, so a seminar or workshop that draws 40 people produces a gross income of between $8,000 and $12,000 a day.

60

Seminars and workshops offer another avenue for consulting. Their small cost to the client and potentially large return to you make them almost ideal vehicles for group consulting. Gear them toward groups that are in need of training or toward individuals that, as a group, have a problem in common.

Of course, there are expenses. You will have to spend time and money to rent a room (usually a hotel meeting room), develop the materials to be used, advertise to induce people to register, and perhaps pay some help if you need help to run the session. If you have coffee and soft drinks available as refreshments (these are almost standard fare at seminars), you will also have that expense. Then you will have the expense of renting a slide or overhead projector if you don't bring your own (which is usually the case). Finally, there are production and promotion expenses, unless you do these jobs yourself. Thus, you will spend the equivalent of several days of your time doing some of the work or paying for help and services.

Locale

The most common place for conducting a seminar or workshop is a meeting room in a local hotel or motel. Such rooms vary in capacity from a low of about 25 to a high of hundreds of people. In most modern hotels, a series of meeting rooms is arranged side by side, with folding doors separating them, so that several rooms can be combined into one when necessary. And most hotels also have one or more ballrooms or auditoriums for conventions and other large-scale gatherings. You generally rent meeting rooms by the day, and you must usually arrange for their use weeks in advance, but that is a variable factor, too: I have found that hotels in downtown business areas can usually accommodate you easily and on short notice for weekend events. Hotels in suburban areas, however, are often booked for weekends many months in advance for social events of many kinds. In any case, you must ensure the availability of the meeting room in advance.

Advertising and Marketing

Seminars to which the general public is invited are usually announced via print advertising in newspapers. Seminars and workshops for specialists are usually advertised most effectively via direct mail, with brochures. (Some presenters also run print advertising in the relevant trade press.)

The most widely used method is the self-mailer, a four- or six- page 8½ × 11-inch brochure that is mailed flat at bulk mail rates (see Figure 6-1). However, bulk mail being what it is, much of the mailing is immediately discarded as junk mail by the addressee. For this reason, you must mail large quantities of these brochures—usually 25,000 or more—to get enough response for your needs.

United
Business
Institute

presents a marketing seminar

Secrets of Success in Winning Consulting Contracts with Federal, State, and Local Government Agencies

- **How government agencies buy**
- **How to sell to government agencies**
- **Finding the contract opportunities**
- **Writing winning proposals**
- **Beating the competition (under the new Competition in Contracting Law**
- **Benefiting from government budget cutbacks**
- **And many, many more insider tips and secrets**

Personally conducted by Herman Holtz,
  author of the best-selling book:
  "How to Succeed as an Independent Consultant"
Washington, D.C. **May 7, 1986**

Figure 6–1. Front panel of conventional large brochure.

The brochure typically contains descriptive text, describes the presenter or presenters, and includes an outline of the material to be presented. (See Figures 6–2 and 6–3.) But you needn't feel compelled to be bound by the traditional format and mailing practice of brochures. I tried a different idea that, as far as I know, no one else has used. I prepared a brochure that was printed on an 8½ × 11-inch sheet folded to fit into an

How to Win Government Consulting Contracts

You can earn substantial dollars consulting with the federal, state and local governments. Government personnel cutbacks are creating a greater demand for consultants than ever before.

Key Benefits of Attendance:

- Hear one of the nation's most successful consultants tell you how to turn your present knowledge and experience into marketable skills.
- How government cutbacks benefit you.
- Find out how to penetrate the $200 billion market of federal contracts and billions of dollars in industrial and professional services.
- Get the facts from Herman on how to win contracts—he has won over $260 million in federal contracts alone.
- Learn how to write proposals that win.
- Find out why it is now easier for you as a consultant to penetrate the federal contracts market and win. The new law, "Competition in Federal Contracts Act," went into effect on April 1, 1985.
- Learn how to market your services with confidence.
- How to locate government markets.
- Understand the key to mastering sales and marketing skills.
- Leave armed with the tools you need to get started immediately—the knowledge and a seminar handbook, personally developed by Mr. Holtz.

"*A large portion of those who enter into consulting services as a profession do not survive the first year, the chief reason being the failure to market their services effectively.*"—*Herman Holtz.*

The above quote is but a sample of the straight talk you will hear from Herman Holtz at this seminar. You will learn how to market your skills effectively and much more. That's why you can't afford to miss this opportunity to consult for a full day with Herman Holtz.

- How to turn your talents to profits
- How to inventory your technical assets and your talents
- How to cash in on trends
- Where the money is today

Some Previous Participants

Alcoa	Kenton
Bethlehem Steel	General Kinetics
Sikorsky Aircraft	Pitney Bowes
General Research	DSI Computer Services
Western Union	Dynamic Data Processing
Computer Sciences Corporation	Digital
Memorex	Marriott
Boeing Computer Services	Owens Corning Fiberglass
Bionetics	Sperry
Burroughs	Tele Sec Temporary Personnel
Raven Data Processing	AT&T
Finalco	Techplan
Tracor	Control Data Corporation
Watkins-Johnson	Color-Ad
Genasys Corporation	Systematic General
Illinois State OMBE	Scientific Applications
Flow General	The Maxima Corporation
Rolm Corporation	Battelle Memorial Institute

Seminar Leader

This seminar is personally conducted by Herman Holtz, the author of the best-selling book: "How to Succeed as an Independent Consultant."

Instructor
Herman Holtz

- Consultant
- Lecturer
- Author
- Seminar Leader
- Winner of over $260 million in government contracts

Herman Holtz can point to specifics—about $260 million—of success in marketing through his own direct efforts as a proposal specialist, director of marketing, and general manager of various organizations, and as a consultant to many companies. He has been employed by such major corporations as RCA, GE, and Philco-Ford, and has served many others—IBM, Control Data Corporation and Dun & Bradstreet, for example—as a consultant. As an independent consultant, he also lectures and conducts seminars on marketing, proposal writing, and a number of other subjects about which he has written extensively. And because of the great success of his book, *How to Succeed as an Independent Consultant,* he has been invited to speak frequently on that subject, as well as to continue to write on the subject of consulting.

Herman Holtz is an independent consultant in Washington, DC and the author of several books including:

How to Succeed as an Independent Consultant, John Wiley & Sons, 1983.
Government Contracts: Proposalmanship and Winning Strategies, Plenum, 1979.
The $100 Billion Market: How to do Business with the U.S. Government, AMACOM (American Management Associations), 1980.
The Winning Proposal: How to Write It, McGraw-Hill, 1981.
Directory of Federal Purchasing Offices, John Wiley & Sons, 1982.
Profit from Your Money-Making Ideas: How to Build a New Business or Expand an Existing One, AMACOM, 1980.
Profit-Line Management: Managing a Growing Business Successfully, AMACOM, 1981.
The Secrets of Practical Marketing for Small Business, Prentice-Hall, 1982.
2001 Sources of Financing for Small Business, Arco, 1983.

Who Should Attend

Any man or woman with a marketable skill gained through education or experience—executives, managers, computer specialists, accountants, engineers, marketing reps, military, professors, grad students, entreprenuers, business planners, authors, real estate professionals, data processing specialists, computer scientists, lawyers, trainers, designers, personnel specialists, architects, psychologists, and anyone desiring to enter the consulting business.

Materials

Each participant will receive a personal copy of "Government Contracts—Proposalmanship," a seminar manual personally developed by Herman Holtz.

Figure 6–2.   Descriptive text of brochure.

ordinary number 10 business envelope. This small brochure included descriptive text in its six panels. (See Figure 6–4 for two of those panels.) However, I prepared a sales letter to introduce and accompany the small brochure. I mailed both first class in a regular business envelope without exterior "teaser" copy. Hence, the recipient would have no way of know-

SEMINAR OUTLINE

I. The $600 Billion Market
- Understanding the market.
- What governments buy.
- How to sell to governments; federal, state and local.

II. Locating Sales Opportunities
- How to uncover selling opportunities.
- Getting on the appropriate bidder's list.
- How to use the *Commerce Business Daily* as an effective marketing tool.
- How to use the Freedom of Information Act to market.

III. Understanding the Marketing Process
- The three elements of marketing successfully
- Are your technical skills enough?
- Mastering market skills
- The elements of selling: Promise and Proof
- Mastering selling skills

IV. How to Market Your Consulting Services
- Instill confidence
- Gain prestige and build a professional image
- Develop the all-important leads
- Following up leads correctly

V. How to Win Government Contracts
- Understanding the public sector market
- How to sell to governments
- How to uncover selling opportunities
- The New Competition Act and how to benefit from it
- How to get on and stay on the bidder's list

VI. How to Benefit from Government Cutbacks
- How to determine where personnel shortages are most severe
- How to locate funding set aside for consultant services
- How to capture your share of the market

VII. Proposal Strategy Development
- Why proposals?
- What is a proposal?
- What does the customer want?
- What must the proposal do?
- What makes a winner?
- Why strategy makes the difference.

VIII. Persuasive Proposal Writing
- What is persuasion?
- The art of persuasive writing.
- What makes others agree?
- What turns them on? And off?

IX. How to Write a Winning Proposal
- Writing to communicate.
- Writing to sell.
- Writing to arouse and sustain interest.
- Your proposal should promise desirable end-results.
- Your proposal should, preferably, be a unique claim, one your competition can't match.
- Your proposal must be able to prove its validity.

X. Formats and Proposal Content
- Recommended format.
- Front matter and other elements.
- How to use format for best results.

XI. Broadening the Base of Your Consulting Practice
- Expand your profit center
- Write to sell
- Publish newsletters, reports, books, tapes, etc.
- Public speaking for profit

XII. How to Price Your Consulting Services
- Understanding costs
- The elements of a cost proposal
- Construction of the quote

XIII. Using Cost in Marketing
- Using prices as market tools.
- Bid/no bid.
- Parametric cost estimates.

XIV. Negotiating Basic Rates
- Labor rates.
- Overhead costs.
- Putting costs where they will do the most good.
- Negotiating with the auditors.

XV. Open Discussion

REGISTRATION FORM

United Business Institute

HOW TO WIN GOVERNMENT CONSULTING CONTRACTS

Oxon Hill Center, Box 448, Oxon Hill, MD 20745
(202) 822-3100

To ensure participation in this exclusive seminar we urge you to register in advance. You may reserve your space(s) by telephone and confirm by returning the form below. List your name and other data in the space below and enclose remittance now or call 822-3100 for reservations. Late payment may be made at the door with firm reservations.

Name _____

Organization _____

Address _____

City _____ State _____ Zip _____

Telephone (_____) _____

Additional registrants from same organization:

Name _____

Name _____

Name _____

Name _____

Seminar Fee: $195.00 advance; $210.00 at door; $150.00 each additional registrant. Amount enclosed $ _____

☐ Check   ☐ Money Order   ☐ MasterCard   ☐ Visa   Card No. _____ Exp. Date _____

Planned Date of Attendance: _____

Figure 6–3.   Outline of presentation.

ing that the envelope contained a solicitation of any kind. I mailed the brochure and letter to only 1,000 names and addresses – although I had carefully selected these as being what I thought were the best possible prospects. Two weeks later I made a second, follow-up mailing to the same list. The mailing produced 54 paid registrations, fully justifying the

If you have the technical skills and even sales ability — it isn't enough to become a successful consultant. This one day seminar focuses on the marketing of your skills and developing other Profit Centers to keep your business growing.

Learn how to not only market your consulting services generally, but how to tap into the public sector markets on the federal, state and local levels. Learn first-hand how to create proposals, successful bids and contracts. Let Mr. Holtz show you how to expand your business into the profitable areas of WRITING, PUBLISHING, PUBLIC SPEAKING and other FREELANCE PROJECTS.

For the man or woman who's considering consulting professionally, or who's starting a practice and wants to develop it, HOW TO SUCCEED AS AN INDEPENDENT CONSULTANT is an A-Z seminar that will guide you to success.

Each participant in the seminar will receive a copy of Mr. Holtz's book: HOW TO SUCCEED AS AN INDEPENDENT CONSULTANT.

Instructor
HERMAN HOLTZ
- Consultant
- Lecturer
- Author
- Engineer
- Seminar Leader
- Winner of over $125 million in government contracts

Herman Holtz is an independent consultant in Washington, D.C. and the author of several books including:
- HOW TO SUCCEED AS AN INDEPENDENT CONSULTANT
- PROFIT FROM YOUR MONEY-MAKING IDEAS: How to build a new business or expand an existing one.
- DIRECTORY OF FEDERAL PURCHASING OFFICES: Where, What, How to Sell to the U.S. Government.
- GOVERNMENT CONTRACTS: Proposalmanship and Winning Strategies.
- THE WINNING PROPOSAL: How To Write It.

Mr. Holtz has been Director of Marketing at Volt Information Sciences, Inc. and Applied Science Associates, and has worked in various capacities as Editorial Director of the Educational Science Division, U.S. Industries. He has been a successful seminar leader in the marketing field in Washington, D.C.

SEMINAR OUTLINE

I. Introduction
   A. What Is a Consultant Today? Which Type of Consultant Are You? The Essential Elements of Consulting Services.
   B. Marketing as the Key to Consulting Success. Are Technical Skills Enough? Mastering Sales and Marketing Skills.

II. Understanding the Marketing Process
   A. The Three Elements of Marketing Successfully.
   B. The Elements of Selling: Promise and Proof.

III. Marketing Your Consulting Services Generally
   A. The Basic Need to Instill Confidence.
   B. How to Gain Prestige and Build a Professional Image.
   C. Developing the All-Important Leads.
   D. Following Up Leads Correctly.

IV. Marketing To The Public Sector
   A. Understanding Public Sector Markets.
   B. The Skill of Proposal Writing.

V. Broadening The Base of Your Consulting Practice.
   A. Expand Your Profit Centers.
   B. Writing: How To Write and Sell Successfully.
   C. Publishing: Including newsletters, reports, books, tapes.
   D. Public Speaking For Profit.

VI. Open Discussion.

Figure 6–4. Descriptive text and outline in small brochure.

methods chosen to get announcements out. (Of course, you must learn what methods work best for you.)

Prepare Presentation Materials

You probably will need some kind of visual presentation that is large enough for everyone to see simultaneously. Among the choices for this

61

When advertising a seminar via direct mail, include a provision for those who cannot attend or who choose not to attend by inviting them to suggest some convenient date and place for a future seminar or workshop or to request that their names be kept on your mailing list. This provides a valuable preferred mailing list for future events.

are posters, slides, and 8 × 10-inch transparencies. The last is the most practical choice for most presenters for several reasons: They are easy to prepare yourself via any laser printer or copier, overhead projectors are always available for rental, and the projected image can be as large as you wish, within the limits of the size of the screen (which is usually quite large). You will also find it convenient to have a blackboard or an easel and a large drawing pad available for spontaneous drawings.

Prepare Handouts or Manual

A large part of the appeal of a seminar or workshop is the promise of useful materials that the participant can carry away. It is always advisable to promise that handouts and some sort of manual or book will be given to each participant. In the case of my proposal writing/government marketing seminars, I prepare a substantial manual, designed with an extrawide right-hand margin so as to provide a column for notes on each page (see Figure 6–5). This is the centerpiece of my seminar, although handouts are in the portfolio given to each participant as he or she enters the room.

Administrative Details and Typical Problems

To advertise a workshop or seminar, you would normally send out literature with a registration form, requesting advance registration with payment to ensure seating, for it is possible to be oversubscribed. If that does happen and you know it early enough, you can usually arrange with the hotel to transfer you to a larger room. Most producers of seminars offer a lower fee for advance registration than for spontaneous registration at the door, to encourage early registration. In any case, you must handle the details of receiving registrations by mail, fax, and telephone and recording them properly.

Almost without exception, there are cancellations, late arrivals, and no-shows at every seminar. Most brochures include a provision for

---

I: AN INTRODUCTION TO PROPOSALMANSHIP
Proposals that say. "Me too," do not often win
contracts. The winning proposal is usually one
that says, "Here's why you need me. "

NOTES

WHAT IS A PROPOSAL?

A proposal is a sales presentation, and it is
essential that you recognize that as a first premise
upon which to base all your ideas about proposal
writing. Proposals do not win contracts by luck;
they win by determined and intelligent effort, and
by successful--which means persuasive--sales
strategies.

THE ESSENCE OF PROPOSALMANSHIP: STRATEGY

The essence of proposalmanship, the name
assigned to those proposal-writing methods and
philosophies advocated in these pages, is strategy.
Most of your competitors will deliver proposals
which demonstrate that they can do the job. But
the mere ability to do the job is not justification
for the award and will not win the contract; you
must somehow demonstrate that you can do the
job in a superior manner or otherwise give the
customer one or more *compelling reasons* to
select you as the winning proposer. Here are a
few of the general categories into which those
"compelling reasons" might fall:

   * Costs

Figure 6–5.   A seminar manual with margins for taking notes.

refunds only if the cancellation is made within some number of days
prior to the date of the seminar. Even then, many producers of seminars
deduct some portion of the advance payment as a "registration fee," the
remainder being an attendance fee. No-shows are generally denied refunds of any kind. Many producers exact a penalty for cancellations by

giving only a partial refund. A common practice is to charge two fees, one relatively small (e.g., $25), for registration, and the other for attendance. Thus, the attendance fee is refunded, but the registration fee is not.

62

If you present a seminar at regular intervals, one way to avoid refunds for cancellations is to use a method I invented: Promise that a rain check will be issued in the event of cancellation that is good for any future presentation of the seminar. My own experience has been that everyone finds this acceptable. As a result, I have been able to eliminate refunds entirely. Furthermore, the client does not risk losing any money if he or she registers and then is unable to attend—and my own cash flow is improved. I issue rain checks even to no-shows if requested; The complete elimination of refunds has enabled me to be generous.

Invariably, a few participants will arrive late to a seminar by 10 or 15 minutes. Accordingly, many presenters hold off starting for a few minutes, hoping that everyone will have appeared by that time. That is a bit unfair to those who were punctual, and it is a bit unfair to you also if you have a rather tightly structured schedule for your presentation. (In any event, it is difficult to stick strictly to a schedule in a seminar.) I have tried both starting immediately and waiting till all have arrived and finally settled on a compromise: I will wait just a few minutes—not more than five—and then I will begin. However, I try to arrange my material so that anyone who misses the first few minutes of it will not have suffered a serious loss. That is, I make the first few minutes a warm-up, getting acquainted with my audience and giving them a chance to get acquainted with me. I ask them to volunteer to tell all of us what kinds of businesses they are in, for example, and even to name their companies and make any remarks they wish to. It's a helpful preliminary for both the participants and the speaker.

A more serious problem is that of running seminars in other cities and arriving to find that the materials you shipped on ahead have not arrived. To forestall this eventuality, it is important to call ahead to the hotel before you leave, to verify that your materials have arrived while there is still time to track them down. If you are doing back-of-the-room sales (to be discussed in a later chapter), and the appropriate materials have not arrived, you will lose a significant amount of income.

Occasionally, you will encounter a kind of heckler. There are sometimes those in a seminar audience who wish everyone to know that they know more about the subject than the presenter does, or perhaps they simply have a great need to command attention every few minutes. Whichever the case, they tend to challenge the presenter or, at least, to offer their own comments frequently, which are not always relevant and do more to interrupt the presentation than to enhance it.

There are several ways to cope with this problem. One that veteran speaker Dottie Walters recommends is to thank the heckler for his or her contribution with a proviso, said with a grin: "Thank you very much, but I work alone."

Another counter is to thank the heckler and ask him or her to hold the comments for a later question-and-answer session or to say something along the lines of "Yes, that is an excellent point, but can you hold it for now because I will address that very point later."

In my own field, there are those who will assure everyone who is willing to listen that all government contracts are wired. Sometimes, someone who holds this view will challenge me. My response is along the lines, "Yes, indeed, there are a few contracts that are wired, and I congratulate you for being astute enough to detect that. But we are here to learn how to win them anyhow, so let us get on with that."

63

A profitable alternative to the full seminar is the miniseminar, which is focused sharply on a few well-defined topics or objectives. I have held these two- to three-hour sessions for 10 to 15 people in my offices on Saturday mornings, charging what was even then a rather modest fee—$25. If your offices are at home and unsuitable for the purpose, you can usually arrange to rent a room inexpensively somewhere.

A variant on this idea is to conduct two sessions, one in the morning and another in the afternoon, enabling yourself to register twice the number of attendees for a single day. (The total cost is only slightly greater for two sessions, and the income is, of course, doubled. Furthermore, you can sell books, tapes, or other materials at the miniseminar, making them just as profitable as at the full seminar.

The important thing is, of course, to never lose your aplomb. Always respond in a confident, poised way, regardless of what it is that you are saying. Be pleasant and completely courteous, but do speak directly and firmly. Let the other party know that he or she is merely holding things up with gratuitous remarks that offer nothing new and nothing that you would not be covering anyway. That gentle put-down generally satisfies the heckler and ends the problem.

Of course, there are the sincere questions also, an inevitable and important element of any seminar-type meeting. In fact, it is the opportunity to ask questions and discuss problems with the presenter that is one of the attractions that draws attendees to seminars.

QUESTIONS AND ANSWERS

As an expert consultant, you will be expected to furnish answers to most, if not all, questions on all subjects in areas in which you represent yourself to be expert enough to present and lead a seminar. Whether you invite them or not, there are going to be many questions directed at you during the presentation. You will have to handle them all in one way or another, and it is probably a good idea to have some kind of policy established for this.

64

From a marketing standpoint, the question-and-answer session is perhaps the most important element of your seminar. If you handle the spontaneous questions well—that is, satisfy the questioner and others that you have answered the questions wisely and knowledgeably—you will be asked for your card, and you will probably get calls later (or be invited to call someone) with a consulting assignment or two resulting. Even furnishing information by mail or telephone often constitutes an excellent sales lead and ought to be encouraged.

Some speakers request participants to hold questions until later, during a question-and-answer session. Others will accept questions spontaneously at any time. In my own case, I program at least one question-and-answer session as a planned feature of my own seminars. Still, I invite participants to interrupt my presentations with questions or comments as they feel the need to do so. My rationale is that it is best for everyone, presenter and audience, to clear up any misunderstanding or lack of understanding immediately and prevent the confusion that would otherwise occur. However, the fact is that I also enjoy answering ques-

tions and discussing specific points with participants more than any
other part of the seminar. That is where I am truly doing perhaps the
most good, answering individual questions about individual problems
and, in some cases where I think it advisable or necessary, inviting the
questioner to seek me out during a break or at the end of the session. If I
have the necessary information in my office but not in my briefcase, I
will promise to send it on when I get back to my desk.

To me, this type of interaction is truly group consulting, at least in
its counseling and problem-solving aspects. I am delighted to promise
individual attendees that I will call them later or send them some bit of
information they have asked for. In fact, on some occasions, when I have
found that a large number of attendees are interested in getting certain
items – perhaps the addresses and telephone numbers of some government agencies I have mentioned – I send a blank sheet around for individuals to enter their names and addresses, so I can mail the information
to everyone who wants it.

PUBLISHING A NEWSLETTER

The newsletter is a mass medium, although the mass is usually relatively
small and carefully selected. Nonetheless, through the newsletter, you
can reach a large number of people with your words and wisdom. The
situation is analogous to some degree to presenting a seminar, although
on a much smaller scale and sans the attendant spontaneity. Still, it does
furnish the opportunity for a kind of group consulting, including responding to readers' individual questions.

With modern equipment – highly capable computers, sophisticated
software, laser printers, and copiers – turning out a highly professional-
looking newsletter is quite easy. Figure 6-6 is an example of a first page
turned out with such equipment, using "only" the modern WordStar
word processor (not a desktop publishing program, that is) and a single
font family (Times Roman). In fact, many newsletter publishers believe
that it is a disadvantage to turn out a newsletter that is "too" professional – that is, too slick and polished looking. They think that a more
homespun look – a typewriter face, instead of the more formal type font
of the figure, and a ragged right margin, instead of a right-justified
margin – looks more spontaneous and friendlier. Whichever your choice,
they are equally easy to produce, and it is not much more difficult to use
desktop publishing software to produce a glossier newsletter, with illustrations and other refinements.

65

Even if only marginally profitable, newsletters can provide you with a number of advantages:

1. Newsletters allow you to keep your name on the desks of past clients.

2. They impress clients and prospects with your up-to-the-minute knowledge of your field.

3. They alert clients to new developments in their industry, the adjustments to which may require your guidance.

4. Newsletters serve as a means of advertising seminars, workshops, and other new services.

5. They offer you a vehicle to sell ancillary products, such as audio-cassettes, monographs, and books.

6. They provide excellent back-up for your brochures, proposals, and other marketing materials.

And if the newsletter should become profitable, all the better!

Newsletters vary widely in their size, format, frequency of publication, prices, and other characteristics.

Size

Size, as used here, refers to the number of pages of the newsletter, if we are talking strictly about the most popular 8½- × 11-inch format. Probably the most popular newsletter sizes are printed on one or two 11- × 17-inch sheets, which are folded to produce four or eight 8½- × 11-inch pages. There are others, larger and smaller, of course, but few run less than four pages, and most run to some multiple of four, so that they can be printed on an appropriate number of 11- × 17-inch sheets. Each such sheet, printed on both sides, is then a *signature* of four pages.

Format

Format refers to both the physical size of and the arrangement of type on the page. Figure 6–6 uses both single- and double-column text, right justified. It also uses a "name plate," that arrangement of lettering within the lines at the head of the page. Succeeding pages are also double-column, right-justified Times Roman text. Overall, the format is formal.

WRITING FOR MONEY

"No man but a blockhead ever wrote except for money."
--*Samuel Johnson, 1776*

No. 101   Editor/Publisher Herman Holtz
P.O. Box 1731   Wheaton, MD 20915   301 649-2499   Fax: 301 649-5745

EGO TRIP OR CAREER?

Getting published is always a most gratifying experience. Even the most seasoned and successful writer awaits publication of his or her latest work with great impatience and reads it with great satisfaction. Thus, in the beginning of a writing career, many writers willingly submit their work and permit it to be published without payment other than the ego gratification of getting published and a few copies to distribute to friends and relatives.

Eventually, for most who wish to make a career of writing, this proves inadequate compensation. For one thing, you find that you cannot make a career of writing without getting paid in more substantial form than ego boost and a few copies of the publication. For another and more significant consideration, the payment is, finally, the only real measure of the value of your writing. If the compensation reflects the worth, what does zero compensation say? Persuading someone to pay out cash for your writing gives you assurance that it has at least that much value!

A WRITING CAREER

There are four ways to earn money as a writer:
• Work on the staff of government agencies, companies, publishers, or other organizations.
• Write "on spec" and sell your work to commercial publishers.
• Work to order, under contract to produce custom work for clients.
• Be your own publisher.

MARKETS FOR WRITERS

You can easily combine these approaches, of course. Many staff writers and editors moonlight elsewhere, publish their own newsletter, freelance on-spec pieces, and do custom work for individual clients. Writing and editing are crafts that you can apply in many

ways. One reason that more writers and editors are not working regularly at their craft and earning money thereby is that most are almost completely unaware of the total market. Of course they know about publishers who buy short stories, articles, novels, and other full-length books, but they know next to nothing about the rest of a vast market for writing and editing, or even that it exists.

Consider the market in the business world alone, for example, with both individuals and organizations as prospective clients : Individuals want help in writing and editing resumes, reports, theses, dissertations, speeches, and other papers and presentations of various kinds. Companies, associations, and sundry other organizations want help in writing and editing some of these same things--e.g., speeches and presentations--as well as newsletters, reports releases, brochures, salesletters, proposals, catalogs, manuals, scripts, articles, and many other items organizations need every day to carry on their routine and non-routine business activities. But let's have a closer look at some of the possibilities.

Pieces for Business Periodicals

There are thousands upon thousands of "business publications"--trade journals (in both slick-paper and pulp magazine formats), tabloids in both slick paper and newsprint, newsletters, and some periodicals that appear to be hybrids of these styles. In fact, these represent a much larger market for writers than does the array of consumer-oriented (i.e., "general interest") periodicals that you find on newsstands in the supermarket and elsewhere. Trade journals alone, those slick-paper magazines that every industry spawns in abundance, represent a huge market with a voracious appetite for information. They want to know what is going on in their industry and in all other areas that relate to their industry--legislation, taxes, mergers, changes in personnel, labor movements, and whatever else is happening that affects the industry.

Figure 6–6.   Typical front page of newsletter.

Frequency of Publication

Newsletters are published daily, weekly, biweekly, semimonthly, monthly, bimonthly, quarterly, and semiannually. By far, the most popular publishing schedule is monthly, but there are many bimonthly and quarterly publications, too. For many newsletter publishers, especially those for whom the newsletter is only one of their activities and not the principal one, monthly publication is a heavy burden. The month flies by much more rapidly than it did before you started to publish a newsletter, and the deadline seems to be staring you in the face all the time, even immediately after you have gotten an edition mailed off to subscribers. That encourages many to opt for bimonthly or quarterly schedules.

There is ample reason to favor a monthly publishing schedule, however, if it is at all feasible for you to publish each month. But be realistic: If you are not absolutely sure that a monthly schedule will not become an intolerable burden, it may be wise to begin with a bimonthly or even quarterly publishing schedule and gradually organize things so that you meet those schedules easily and are prepared to face a more frequent schedule without trepidation. You can always increase the frequency of publication much more easily than you can decrease it, as far as subscribers' acceptance of change is concerned. Increasing the frequency suggests that you have had a high degree of success, while decreasing it suggests the opposite.

Pricing and Marketing Tactics

Magazine and newspaper publishers rely on advertising for their principal revenue and lose money on the cover prices of their publications. Unlike them, you have no advertising revenue. (Few newsletters do, simply because they cannot carry a significant amount of advertising.) Therefore, you must earn your revenue from profit on the subscription fees. That is a premise which you should accept up front. Decide first, however, whether you are most interested in selling a marketing or profit-oriented newsletter. If the former, you are probably more interested in recouping your costs; if the latter, you want to make money on the newsletter. The next few paragraphs contain suggestions for profit-oriented newsletters.

Newsletter subscriptions are not usually easy to sell, no matter what you may have heard to the contrary. You must work at it. Pricing has a great deal to do with it, of course. Obviously, you can charge more to subscribe to a daily or weekly newsletter than you can to a monthly or bimonthly one, so frequency of publication is certainly one criterion for pricing. Another is the quantity of information offered: An 8- or 12-page newsletter presumably merits a higher price than a 4-page newsletter. More important, however, is the intrinsic value of the content of your newsletter. Some newsletters merit extremely high subscription fees because their content is worth money to the subscriber (e.g., newsletters on investment), is hard-to-get information, is uttered by a recognized important authority, or has great value for some other reason.

There is also a special factor that not everyone recognizes: While the price of a newsletter is often set through some perceived value of its content, for many people the perceived value is at least partly the result of the price that is set! That is, in a great many cases, there is no reliable standard by which to judge the value of a newsletter other than the price asked for it, so we come to equate its price with its value or merit. Artificial though this may be in one sense, it is nonetheless a very real phenomenon and sometimes works to the newsletter publisher's benefit.

66

A great many people—probably most of us—are attracted to the idea of getting a bargain: We love discounts, and discount sales are among the most widely used and most successful marketing appeals. Thus, it is usually an effective marketing tool for newsletter publishers to establish a rather substantial list price and then offer a discount for subscribing to the newsletter. One way to decide on a price is to perform research and discover what the going subscription rates are for newsletters similar in nature to the one you plan and then use them as a guideline.

Besides pricing arrangements, many other inducements are used to sell newsletters. One solicitation that arrived in my morning mail recently offered me extra issues of a certain newsletter – 15 monthly issues for a year's subscription – as a bonus for subscribing promptly. Other offers have included free books and bonuses.

I have tried such gambits also. In one case, I offered three free consultations by mail or telephone with each subscription. I did so with my fingers crossed, aware that I could be swamped with requests, but the nature of newsletter sales being what it is, the number of requests I received proved to be perfectly manageable and not a burden at all.

Sources of Information and Features

Sources of information suggest features and vice versa. Once you understand this and establish your channels of information, you will probably find that it is no real burden to turn out an issue of a newsletter every month. In fact, in a very short while, your problem will not be finding information, but trimming an abundance of material to select what you can use and reducing it to fit the space you have. A newspaper or magazine publisher usually does not work with a fixed number of pages: The number varies widely from issue to issue. By contrast, although some newsletter publishers will publish an extralarge edition occasionally, most stick to a preestablished number of pages.

67

Bear in mind the main purpose of your newsletter: to advertise and offer your consulting expertise on a group basis. Of course, income and profit are a business objective of newsletter publishing, but you must not permit them to divert you from providing the maximum consulting service that the medium permits. Select your features on that basis—that is, with usefulness to the reader as the principal objective.

Thus, the essence of newsletter editorial management is as much editing as it is research and writing, and that means selecting the most useful and most important material for inclusion and then editing it to pare it to size. Put colloquially, a newsletter has to be "mean and lean": Text must be trimmed of all surplus verbiage, so that the style is almost staccato. Excising excess verbiage is the essence of editing, and it is in the editing of newsletters that it is practiced with great enthusiasm and to a greater degree than in most publications.

The following are a few suggestions for regular features you can use in most newsletters:

- *News items.* These are informational items that have a direct bearing on whatever the field is in which you provide consulting services—computers, marketing, office management, security, and so on. In writing new stories, you may wish to make use of the *sidebar.* (A sidebar is a relevant item that is printed in conjunction with, but is not part of, another story. For example, a newspaper story on a medical malpractice suit might be accompanied by a sidebar story on the history of malpractice lawsuits or on the most famous malpractice lawsuits of recent times.)

- *Letters to the editor.* There really is not enough room in a typical newsletter to reprint full letters from readers, but you might print abstracts of especially interesting or appropriate letters to the editor.

- *Question-and-answer columns.* Many questions will arise out of the letters to the editor, although you may also specifically solicit questions from readers. Answer them as informatively and completely as you can.

- *Current issues.* If there are controversial issues of the moment or new developments relevant to your field, these may be good fodder for discussions and opinions.

- *Editorials.* Editorials that bear directly on the subject of your consulting efforts are highly appropriate. You need not write all of them yourself, but can sometimes invite others to do guest columns and editorials.

- *Tips.* Relevant shortcuts, new ideas, new materials, new software, new hardware, and other items that are relevant and of interest always attract the reader's attention.

Sources of information for newsletters are plentiful, and in a short time you will be getting more than you can use. Here are just a few of the many sources there are:

- *Your own reading.* Little comment is required here. Read other newsletters as part of your everyday reading. (You can even exchange complimentary subscriptions with many other newsletter publishers!)

- *Letters from readers.* Encourage readers to write with comments, suggestions, questions, and ideas.

- *Press releases.* As you identify organizations that issue relevant press releases with any regularity or frequency, write and ask to be put on their distribution lists. You will get quite a lot of material to cull for your newsletter.

- *Electronic bulletin boards.* The conferences listed on some of the bulletin boards are rich sources of information and ideas. Don't quote anyone directly without permission, however, and verify any information, the accuracy of which you are not sure.

- *Contributions.* Call for these, and offer to pay modest sums for them — for example, $5 or $10 per item or a rate of 5 to 10 cents per word. You can post notices, with a description of the kinds of material you want, in writer's magazines — *Writer's Digest* and *The Writer*, to name two. Again, you will get quite a lot of material from which to choose, and you are not obligated to buy anything you don't want.

Production

With adequate computer hardware and software, you or any other experienced computer user can do the layout of your newsletter and run the spelling checkers, grammar checkers, on-line dictionaries, and any other software you use on it. Despite all this help, it will still probably be worthwhile to have someone do an editorial check of your copy before it becomes final.

What you thereby produce is camera-ready copy, copy that can be printed in quantity. But what is "quantity?" If you are sending out only 50 to 100 copies of your newsletter, you may wish to run them off on a high-speed copier and fold and mail them yourself. If you envision greater quantities being produced, then it is probably worthwhile to have the printing and folding done in a small print shop or letter shop.

Alternatively, you can make arrangements to print and mail your newsletter with any local letter shop or mailer. Many mailers have their own print shops and will handle it all for you — printing and mailing. Make a few telephone calls to printers, letter shops, and mailers listed in your local yellow pages, and inquire as to their services and rates. You will soon know enough to make a rational choice and arrange to have the portion of the job you want done for you.

OTHER PUBLICATIONS

It is as easy to publish other publications, such as monographs and even books of your own, as it is to publish a newsletter. These other products also are a means of presenting your services to others on a group basis. My own monographs, of which I have published many, are principally of the how-to-do-it variety, and tend to advise readers of opportunities for doing business with government agencies and winning contracts and even grants from the government. Later, I diversified into other areas, such as writing and publishing itself.

ANCILLARY CONSULTING PRODUCTS

The flip side of a consulting practice as a line of services is a consulting practice as a line of products. Products are part of consulting also, if you do not take a completely provincial view of consulting as a means of practicing your profession. Consulting products complement consulting services to make consulting a more complete and self-sufficient enterprise than it might otherwise be.

WHY CONSULTING PRODUCTS?

Group consulting involves the development and marketing of any or all of a diverse line of consulting products, principally seminar and workshop presentations, newsletters, and other publications. All of these products provide income, besides that afforded by consulting itself. That they are physical products is incidental to the philosophy and main objective of their presentation, however: You use those special media and products to broaden the base of your consulting services. They help make your knowledge, skills, and services available to many who would not be able to avail themselves of your assistance if they had to retain you individually.

In a larger sense, we all sell only services, whether we sell services per se or soap. Many marketing experts will argue convincingly that all that anyone has to sell *is* service; even when customers buy products, they do so because the products do or promise to do something for them, and not because they want to own or get any satisfaction out of owning the product. When they are involved, products are only the means of delivering the desired service. Thus, the rationale that seminars and newsletters represent services is by no means frivolous.

Accordingly, although in this chapter we shall address consulting products as such, it is well to keep in mind the services that they represent. Usually, these are products that are ancillary to your primary consulting services. They expand your practice in a dimension beyond that of pure consulting, at the same time furthering the consulting activity. Thus, they strengthen your practice, diversifying it and making you much more independent of the vagaries in demand that are an unfortunate, but common aspect of consulting.

68

Consulting is a profession that is typified by feast or famine. A line of products, such as group consulting, adds balance and stability, bridging the valleys between the peaks of activity. In a time of economic uncertainty, that is an especially important—perhaps even critical—consideration. Having this ancillary line and the income it produces can see you through economic downturns and enable you to survive until business conditions improve. Alternatively, it can see you through the difficult early months and years involved in founding your practice and getting yourself firmly established as an independent consultant.

KINDS OF PRODUCTS

The products discussed in the previous chapter—seminars, workshops, lectures, and newsletters—are of a somewhat transitory nature. One cannot recapture words uttered unless they are recorded, and while many people save and even bind together back issues of newsletters and other periodicals, they usually find it difficult or at least inconvenient to search out information that was published a long time ago. No doubt, those who attend seminars and other such presentations carry away with them only a fraction of the material presented by the speaker. That is one reason that those whose attendance is solicited are influenced to a large degree by the promise of a substantial package of printed handouts. However, at best, such handouts reflect only a little of the information a good presenter offers in a seminar or workshop: The presenter speaks and interacts with participants for about six hours in a typical day's seminar, providing spontaneously generated information and ideas. Only a fraction of what is said finds its way into print.

Audiotape Products

One way of surmounting the problem of transitoriness is to record the presentation on audiotape. Today, it is a rare office or household that does not boast a player for standard audiotape cassettes. In fact, more and more people have tape players in their automobiles and can listen to tapes while commuting and on trips. Over the years, I have accumulated at least four portable tape players, and I also have a radio/tape-player combination on my desk. I have a two-cassette tape lecture titled *How to Start a Business with Your Computer*, by Paul and Sarah Edwards. I have a three-cassette seminar on tape titled *Consulting*, by the late Howard Shenson, as well as three Shenson tape seminars of much greater duration on marketing consulting services, presenting seminars, and consulting on grantsmanship. I also have a set of Dottie Walters tapes on public speaking. In addition, I have some videotapes that other consultants – for example, Rene Gnam, the expert on direct mail – have sent me, although relatively few consultants create videotapes as products, due to the great expense and time required.

Some of these tapes are developed from scratch as new and independent products. Others are by-products of lectures of various kinds.

69

Audiotapes make a great consulting product. But if you make a recording of your seminar, it is most unlikely to be ready for duplication. We are not professionals at the audio and tape cassette game, so we must turn to the professionals for help. Our tapes must be edited professionally, probably with dubbing of music and suitable announcements. It is wise to retain an audio expert to do the initial recording of your live seminar: The result will be better when done with professional equipment by a professional sound engineer. In any case, such a tape set is a viable product. Even participants often buy them so that they can have a permanent record – a virtual transcript – for later reference.

Many are hybridized: Raw recordings of a seminar presentation are made, and they are then turned over to a good audio studio for editing and conversion to a set of cassette tapes.

Tape cassette sets, often accompanied by some written documentation, such as an instruction manual and an outline of what is on the tape, bring quite excellent prices. At one rather small seminar of about 15 people that I attended, the presenter offered his own tape cassette set at $250 and promptly sold about 10 sets. Even small sets of two or four tapes can bring about $65 to $150 when presented well in custom-made cases with accompanying documentation.

Printed Products

Despite the popularity of audiotape cassettes, printed materials provide a firmer base of ancillary products and are likely to constitute the bulk of such products that you create and sell. More buyers are attracted to printed than to audio materials because printed material is more familiar than tapes and because no special equipment is required to use it.

Books.   Books are probably the preeminent printed product. However, the term *book* has multiple and highly variable interpretations: It applies equally to the mighty tome of several thousand pages, the more modest one of many hundred of pages, the familiar model of 200 to 400 pages, and the many smaller models, some as slender as 100 or even fewer pages. Further, it applies to volumes that are 9 × 12 inches or larger, those that are 6 × 9 inches, and those that are the size of a paperback or even smaller. Again, it applies equally to expensive cloth-bound editions with sewn signatures, to volumes with "perfect" (glued) bindings, using three-ring binders, and to those bound with plastic or metal "combs" and staples, binding methods that enable anyone to bind his or her own books with inexpensive office equipment. Thus, the use of the term *book* is so comprehensive that it must be defined each time we use it so that we can communicate clearly with each other. When I use the term in any but a general sense, I look for a definition of just what kind of book it is to which I am referring.

Monographs.   A monograph, or report as it is referred to popularly, is usually a rather brief publication that is typically 5 to 20 8½- × 11-inch pages dealing with a single subject. It is an informal publication that is prized strictly and entirely for its content, rather than for the way it looks. Thus, a monograph lends itself well to self-publication.

70

For the well-equipped office, the production of monographs is no problem, especially compared with conditions of only a dozen years ago. Then it was necessary to carry an inventory, even for a modest array of 25 to 50 monographs, if orders were to be filled promptly. With a modern computer and laser printer system, that is no longer necessary. You can now "inventory" your reports as files in your computer and print out copies as you need them to fill orders. You no longer need to have stacks of paper or bound sets in pigeonholes.

Following are just a few illustrative titles of monographs from different fields of expertise that I have written and published myself. Each deals with a single subject, although even there, the coverage of the subject is relatively broad. (Many monographs are even more sharply focused on their subjects than these are.)

Grants and Other Federal Assistance
Business Plan Guide
Understandings, Contracts, and Agreements
Freelancer's Guide to Newsletter Markets
Basics of Proposal Writing
Small Business Opportunities in Government Contracting
Making Money in Direct Mail

Figures 7–1 and 7–2 illustrate the front pages of two reports that I market myself. The second of these reflects the greater capabilities of the later equipment – for example, the two-column, right-justified copy with proportionally spaced text. These added refinements are achieved at no added difficulty, because the equipment available has become more sophisticated.

CREATING BOOKS

I sometimes wonder if there is a single literate adult in the United States who does not have a book manuscript written and gathering dust or one that he or she is now writing or plans to write. Many people would like to write a book and have it published but hesitate because they are unsure of how to proceed or fearful of rejection.

HERMAN HOLTZ

P.O. Box 1731   Wheaton, MD 20915   (301) 649-2499

HOW TO WIN
U.S. GOVERNMENT CONTRACTS

by Herman Holtz

Ask any experienced proposal writer for the secrets of success in Government marketing and chances are that you will get something such as this:

Never bid a job you know nothing about before seeing it in the *Commerce Business Daily*. You can't win without advance marketing, etc.

Watch your proposal cosmetics--typing, reproduction, covers, margins, and other such details.

25 percent or more of the contracts are wired in advance. You haven't got a chance for these.

Don't bid if you haven't got an "understanding" with the customer.

That's the essence of conventional wisdom about proposal writing and Government contracting. It's right, for most cases, but not for all. It's right for the average situation, where the proposal writers are just that--proposal writers. What that means is that most proposal writers do a workmanlike job; they present a sound plan by a qualified bidder at a reasonable price. Just that and nothing more. But that's not enough:

Many of the other bidders do as much. Many submit proposals that are competent, acceptable, and essential equal to each other. A decision to select one is usually difficult, and other considerations than being competent--being good enough--usually drive the final decision.

In short, *none* of the proposals, in most competitions, are superior--not inspired by nor based on superior strategies, none truly clever in either concept or execution, none *demanding* attention and somehow dominating the field.

Once in a while, such a proposal appears, and the apple cart is upset. Wired procurements become unwired. The "rules" dictated by that conventional wisdom become irrelevant--bad advice. A dark-horse bidder wins unexpectedly, a competitor who ignored the rules advocated by the experts and ran off with the prize.

At the risk of bragging, I must defend my thesis by telling you this: In writing proposals that have won over $300 million in government contracts for my former employers, clients, and my own account, I have almost always learned of the solicitation through the *Commerce Business Daily*, with no advance work and so "special arrangements." I won each of these on the basis of a proposal that the customer believed merited the award.

Figure 7–1.   Example of a monograph or report.

HERMAN HOLTZ
P.O. Box 1731   Wheaton, MD 20915
301 649-2499   Fax 301 649-5745

A FEW TIPS ON HOW TO SUCCEED AS AN INDEPENDENT WRITER

by Herman Holtz

Writing is like prostitution. First you do it for the love of it. Then you do it for a few friends. And finally you do it for money.
                    -- F. Molnár

WHAT ABOUT THE RULES OF WRITING?

Freelance is the popular term for the independent writer, but I far prefer the term *independent*. It spells out more firmly that the freelance writer is independent, a free agent, controlling his or her own life, when, what, how to work, and for what rewards.

I have been writing for more years than many people have lived, and I have been doing it full time as an independent or freelance writer for a respectably large number of years, with many articles, columns, and books to my credit. One result of this is that I am constantly asked questions about writing professionally and independently. The questions come from hopeful beginners who are not necessarily beginners or tyros as writers--quite the contrary, many are highly proficient writers--but are usually quite naive about freelance or independent writing. Certain questions are of the *deja vu* variety: I hear them over and over. I am going to try to answer a few of those here, and I am going

to extrapolate from these a few questions I think the hopefuls *should* have asked. (Not too surprisingly, the hopefuls often do not know which are the most important questions they ought to have asked.) First will come those routine items; later, the more critical and important ones.

MANUSCRIPT FORMATS

I have been urged by countless alleged experts to prepare my manuscripts--margins, headers, footers, titles, and other trivial details--according to their standards. All nonsense, except the admonition to double- or triple-space copy so the editor can make his/her cabalistic marks. It is a must to double- or triple-space copy. (My own practice is to double space, trying to maintain some control over paper and postage costs.)

Many of the guidelines laid down were influenced by the Stone Age practices imposed on us by the Underwood and Remington typewriters. Most of us (I hope) now use word processors and printers. What

Figure 7–2.   Another example of a report in a different format.

Consultants are no exception to this categorization, and I am going to proceed on the assumption that you fit one of the categories mentioned – that you are working on a book of your own or need a bit of encouragement to begin doing so. If I am mistaken, and the idea has never even crossed your mind, perhaps what I have to say will persuade you to think along these lines. I hope so. As a consultant you have an advantage over many: You are an expert at something, expert enough to be paid for helping people solve problems and make things happen. You almost surely have knowledge that others would like to share. Those others may be your professional peers. They may be clients and prospective clients. They may be the lay public. You will have to decide for whom you will write your book. Or perhaps you will write three books, one for each of those classes of reader.

71

One way to create a book is to collect all the articles, papers, and reports you have written over the years and organize them into a series of chapters, adding introductory material and transitions, of course. If you have been publishing a newsletter, back issues of that publication alone may be a rich source of material. If you have been publishing monographs, they are another source. You may be surprised to find that you have a great deal of material to which you own rights. (If any of the articles you have written were published in the trade press, you can generally retrieve all but the first serial rights, which were exercised when the article was published and which leaves you free to publish the material again.)

A great many of the books created every year are of the "how to" genre and the closely related "how it works" genre. Their purpose is to teach the reader how to do something, for example, incorporate a company or design a computer program. Related genres of reference books are the "where to find it" and "how to find it" varieties. Just make sure that whatever book you write is on a subject in your field of expertise.

THE TOPIC THAT NEVER FAILS

If there is any such thing as a surefire formula for writing a successful article, report, or book, it is to write a how-to book on the right topic. If you can identify a problem that a great many people are aware of and would like to have a solution for, and if you can come up with a practicable solution for the problem, you have the elements for a successful monograph or book. Thus, when Jerry Buchanan of Vancouver, Washington, was plagued with gophers digging holes on his property, he investigated means for combating the pesky things. He discovered that the problem was a most common one and difficult to solve. Nonetheless, he conducted rather lengthy research and found practicable answers. He solved the problem and wrote a monograph explaining his solution. After selling 14,000 copies of that report at $2 each, he had the basis for a publishing enterprise that became his new career!

Presumably, the subject of gopher control does not merit coverage beyond that of a monograph or report. One might, however, write an entire book on controlling unwelcome intruders generally, with gopher control as one chapter. Naturally, the coverage of a subject will be broader in scope and greater in depth for a book than it would be in the typical monograph. However, the principle is the same: To write a book or a report, it is necessary to select a subject about which you can develop the necessary amount of the right information for the kind of reader you wish to reach and the objective you wish to accomplish. I would never write a book on copyright law, for example, because, as a layman writing to other lay persons, I don't have that much to say about the subject that would be of interest to writers and specialty publishers. Only a lawyer, writing for other lawyers, could find a bookful of material to present on that subject. But I can and have written a monograph on the subject, covering the essential points of the topic that are of interest to writers. On the other hand, I have written a number of books on subjects about which I had a great deal to say to readers who wanted a great deal of information. I always make sure, however, that the subject I pick is one on which I can reasonably present myself as an authority.

In sum, then, in preparing to write a book, you must consider questions such as the following: For whom will you write? What does he or she wish or need to know about the subject? Does the subject justify or require a full-length book, rather than an article or monograph? Are you enough of an authority on the subject to defend yourself against the inevitable attacks that will come (especially if you are writing on a controversial subject or you have a controversial position to assume)?

You must also think in terms of market: Is there a market for your subject? Would there be enough readers who want to buy a book about it? Don't permit yourself to be lured and misled by your own interests, which may be atypical. Producing a book, by whatever means, represents a substantial investment in time, effort, and money. The commitment should not be entered into lightly. Satisfy yourself first that there is an ample market for the book. Look into competitive books on the subject. If there are none, be forewarned: Perhaps there is not enough of a market to sustain even one book, let alone several. Be encouraged only if there are a few other books on the subject, but even then, consider the probabilities.

WHAT IS AN "AMPLE" MARKET?

Ample is a relative term, not an absolute one. In regard to publishing a book, the question of what is ample depends on the variables involved. One such variable is who is publishing similar books? If commercial book publishers are doing so, they will probably invest at least $15,000 to $20,000 in each book before getting back one cent. They will probably have to sell at least 3,000 to 4,000 copies to reach the break-even point and then begin to turn a profit. Thus, an ample market for them is going to mean enough prospective buyers of the book to make it likely that they will sell out the first printing (probably 4,000 to 5,000 copies), so that the book then becomes profitable. That in turn probably means that there ought to be at least 200,000 to 400,000 people who are reasonable prospects for buying the book.

If you publish a book yourself, the economics are a little different. You may decide to keep your first printing down to 2,000 copies, manufacturing a so-called trade paperback (a "quality paperback," as opposed to the mass market bodice ripper with the lurid cover). Having kept manufacturing costs down and having done much of the work yourself in getting the copy ready, you may have been able to keep your out-of-pocket investment down to $5,000 or even less. If you then sell the 2,000 copies at $14.95 each, you will get a gross profit (not counting your labor) of about $25,000. You may or may not consider that to be ample reward. Of course, if you sell out the entire printing, it is likely that you will order a second printing and continue to sell the book.

On the other hand, you can keep the out-of-pocket investment even smaller, if you wish to. You can print the book in 8½ × 11-inch format, by high speed copier, and bind it by some convenient and inexpensive means, making up a few dozen copies at a time to service current orders. In that case, the publishing is virtually self-supporting. I myself have published successfully in this manner. Moreover, doing it all yourself

·cuts the out-of-pocket costs so that you enjoy a substantial markup on each sale.

72

If you plan to self-publish and sell your book primarily through the mail, the ring binder format is your best bet. Although preferably laid out semiprofessionally with desktop software, your book pages need not be particularly fancy and need only be punched for the three-ring binder, with the reader supplying his or her own. Granted, your book won't jump off the shelves of Barnes and Noble, but it makes for a professional package. Many consulting "best-sellers" are still sold in this format through the mail.

PRESTIGE OR PROFIT?

If you are willing to make the necessary effort to self-publish a book and the additional effort to market it personally (see shortly), self-publishing can prove to be highly profitable. It may well prove to be more profitable than publishing via an established commercial book publisher, although that is not necessarily true: Publishing is risky, no matter who does it. It's more like show biz than like any other business: Your book is entirely at the mercy of how the public reacts to it, and that is almost always unpredictable. The publishing business has at least as many stories of brilliant successes and dismal disasters resulting from miscalculation of popular reaction as does show business. Still, the odds are in your favor if you self-publish and do it as conservatively as possible. But perhaps profit per se is not your only—even your main—objective in birthing a book of your own. You may have another goal.

For any professional in any field—but especially for the independent practitioner, who usually depends heavily on his or her personal reputation—the prestige of authoring a serious work on a serious subject is an important consideration. If that is your prime consideration in turning out a book, you are well advised to seek publication by one of the well-established commercial book publishers. Publishing by one of them means a professionally printed and bound book, with distribution to the book trade: Your book will appear on the shelves of bookstores and libraries throughout the world and will be read and reviewed both by your peers and by many scholars in your field. It will carry with it a mark of prestige that you can never achieve via self-publishing, where the reader knows that you have paid to be published, and so publication of the book is not a measure of its merit.

73

Being published by a publishing house does not preclude marketing your own book directly. As the author, you will (or should) be entitled by contract to buy as many copies of your own book as you wish to at a 40-percent discount from the cover price. One consultant I know, a rather prominent lecturer and author, always asks his publisher to give him his royalty advance in printed copies of his book at manufacturing cost. He thus gets several thousand copies of each of his books at the lowest cost possible, and he sells them at their cover price in back-of-the-room sales at his lectures and seminars. The whole venture is highly profitable for him.

MARKETING YOUR PRODUCTS

The old platitude about building a better mousetrap and having the world beat a path to your door is a myth: Nothing sells itself, no matter what overenthusiastic salespeople say. Build the best mousetrap ever, and charge the lowest price imaginable for it, and you still have to market it. Try standing on a street corner with a sign offering to sell dollar bills for 75 cents each, and see how few people will take advantage of your bargain. The dollar bills won't sell themselves.

Some things are easier to sell than others. Some people are easier to sell to than others. And some times and circumstances are easier to sell in than are others. These are all largely unpredictable factors, so you must always address marketing as though all the factors are working against you; that is, you must make your maximum effort.

The principles for marketing your products—newsletters, books, tapes, monographs, or other items—are the same as those for selling your services. The most effective motivators are emotional ones that appeal to the prospect's self-interests. The late Elmer Wheeler, acclaimed over and over as America's supersalesman and honored by innumerable dinners and awards, helped a general-store merchant in a rural area dispose of a huge surplus of longjohn underwear by putting a sign on them saying, "They don't itch!" He explained his marketing philosophy by an expression that has since become a virtual platitude of the sales and advertising professions: "Sell the sizzle, not the steak."

74

If you plan to speak anywhere, bring your line of products! Professional speakers usually hold back-of-the-room sales of their items at the end of their presentation or during breaks. It is best to have an assistant handle this, armed with a cash box, receipt forms, and, if you are in a position to handle credit card charges, the forms and machine necessary for that. Many professional speakers report that these sales produce profits equal to their speaking fees and often exceed them. In fact, many state that condition as the minimum necessary to make the presentation a satisfactory one.

If you are publishing a newsletter or presenting seminars, you are in an advantageous position to sell the sizzle. Subscribers to your newsletter and participants in your seminars are already customers, and established customers are by far the best prospects you are likely to have for any product you offer. In fact, there are newsletters that do not turn a penny's profit on the newsletter itself, but that pay for their existence by being a highly effective medium for selling other items, usually books, audiotapes, videotapes, and monographs.

Double-Duty (Piggyback) Mailing

Direct mail plays an important part in all of the preceding activities. It is how you solicit newsletter subscriptions. It is how you fulfill the subscriptions. It is how you fill orders for your products from readers of your newsletter. It is how you announce and solicit orders for your products to others, including the readers of your newsletter. And it is also how you announce your seminars and solicit registration and attendance at them. And speaking of seminars, I hit on an idea that paid off handsomely: I made my seminar mailings do double duty as solicitations for newsletter subscriptions and orders for my books and reports.

A good return on mailings for big-tag items such as registration for a seminar is one or two percent, even when mailing first class, the most expensive rate, as I always prefer to do. Bulk mail is cheaper on a per-piece basis — only a little more than one-half the first-class cost — but more costly in the end because you usually must mail several times as many pieces. I would therefore expect to get only a fraction of one percent response to a bulk mailing and would feel it necessary to mail 15,000 to 25,000 pieces to get an acceptable return. That is pretty costly, even at bulk rates.

A one-percent response to 5,000 pieces mailed out means 50 sales, a profitable margin, generally. Still, it is possible for some campaigns to bring in considerably less, perhaps only 25 or 30 registrations, against a mailing cost of about $1,500 for postage alone, without counting the labor and the printing costs, let alone the costs of running the seminar. The cost of postage continues to mount steadily, making it one of the major costs of doing business by direct mail.

Deeply conscious of that cost and the burden it represents, I conceived the idea of enclosing other sales literature with the mailing of registration forms for seminars, offering newsletter subscriptions and self-produced books for sale. It was my theory that some who could not register for the seminar, for whatever reason, might still be interested in these other items. The added cost of the enclosures was minimal, since I would incur the same postage cost as if they were not included in the mailing. The concept proved to be practical and successful: I was gratified to find that I always got enough response on these other items to underwrite the entire cost of the mailing at least. And that was the minimum benefit; the others were that I gained additional newsletter circulation and built a widening awareness of my entire program. The idea even proved to be a kind of insurance policy, removing much of the risk of seminar ventures because it covered one of the major expenses – printing and mailing the solicitation itself. Combine that with the seminar and the back-of-the-room sales, and you are virtually assured of the success of the seminar as a business venture. In fact, the back-of-the-room sales program is a cogent argument for making the seminar registration fee as modest as possible, to encourage maximum attendance – that is, a maximum number of prospects for those sales.

CHAPTER 8

THE EXPERT WITNESS

Among the kinds of clients any consultant may have are attorneys and their own clients: plaintiffs and defendants. In this role, the consultant usually provides his or her special expertise in support of legal efforts that are themselves in preparation for and direct support of litigation. Now the consultant becomes known as an expert witness. However, he or she will never actually take the stand in most cases. The term *expert witness* is often another name for a legal consultant—not a consultant who is also a lawyer or legal expert, but a consultant who provides expert support services to lawyers, both in and out of the courtroom.

THE EXPERT TAKES THE STAND

If you watch TV, you know what an expert witness is, at least in a TV drama: The expert witness sits on the stand and testifies that the gun exhibited is the murder weapon, that the fingerprints match those of the defendant, that too much of a given drug might kill a human, or that he or she considers the defendant to be sane. The evidence and opinions given by the expert witness are calculated to help sway the judge and jury to the prosecution's or the defense's case, depending on which side the expert witness represents with his or her testimony. Cross-examined and challenged by the attorney for the other side, in the TV drama the expert witness must often duel verbally with the opposing attorney, contributing valiantly to the suspense created by TV's typical courtroom combat.

It is all very gripping, but in real life the role of the typical expert witness is usually quite different: It is rarely that dramatic or that combative. In fact, if you are ever fated to be an expert witness, you are not likely to be working on or testifying in a murder trial or other criminal case, unless you happen to be a ballistics expert or are otherwise expert in some function or activity that is most useful to and common in criminal prosecution and defense. It is far more likely that you will be called on for considerably more mundane activities, helping attorneys in accident cases, lawsuits, and other everyday civil actions. You will be asked to testify to a lengthy catalog of monotonous, nit-picking details in some totally routine, low-key exchanges in a sparsely attended courtroom. In fact, you may not even be asked to take the stand at all, because so many cases are settled out of court, often minutes before the trial is scheduled to begin. (Legal strategies on both sides of civil actions mandate settling within minutes of the beginning of a trial, sometimes in the corridors outside the courtroom.) As a consultant serving as an expert witness, you are undoubtedly an expert, but the word "witness" need not be taken literally: Even in those cases where you do take the stand, you have usually spent a far greater amount of time helping the attorney in various tedious aspects of preparing the case than you will ever spend on the witness stand. Nonetheless, it is courtroom-related work done outside of the courtroom that represents the real business opportunity in the area of consulting as an expert witness. Indeed, this kind of consulting may be so profitable an element of your practice, that it may even become your consulting specialty.

75

It is estimated that 90 percent of all civil cases brought to trial or settled out of court involve some expert testimony. As both cases and our society become more technical and complex, the need for "litigation consultants" will grow. Many consultants now make a good living almost entirely in this area.

HOW CONSULTING MAY LEAD TO
THE COURTROOM

Hardly anyone ever starts out to become a consultant. It is not a normal career goal. Most of us are led to consulting careers as a result of serendipity, circumstances requiring a career change, or a decision arrived at after some years of experience in our specialized field. The same thing is usually true for those who become expert witnesses, whether they are expert witnesses only occasionally or make a regular career of such work. Thus, choice or chance may lead you to your first experience as an expert witness, as it did in my own case, which may or may not be typical.

Several years ago, I received a call from a Chicago attorney. He had read one of my books on the mail order business, he explained, and was defending a man charged by the federal government with mail order fraud. He had called to ask whether I would testify in court as an expert on mail order. I discussed the case with him, to get an idea of what it was all about, and agreed tentatively. We then exchanged correspondence, and I received documentation from him in which I became familiar with the more intimate details of the case. I found that I agreed with the defense's position and could testify for the defendant in good faith. I therefore agreed to be an expert witness in the case. (I would not have agreed to testify on behalf of the defendant had I thought the defendant guilty.)

In the case, the U. S. Postal Service charged that the defendant was making false and fraudulent promises to people he solicited by mail to enroll in a program to guide them in establishing mail order businesses of their own. In particular, the government believed that his promise that the people could earn as much as $300 a week was unrealistic and fraudulent.

Primarily, the attorney for the defendant wanted me to testify that I myself had earned that much in mail order, and I considered it an achievable goal for anyone who was truly willing to work at implementing the defendant's scheme. (I wondered why the government had singled out this one individual to prosecute for advertising that was quite similar to that of his many competitors. I learned later that the government's case was the result of and based on a single complaint by one of the defendant's customers.)

I fully agree that the promises made by many who offer such plans to their prospective customers are often inflated; success in mail order isn't as easy to achieve as advertisers would like their prospects to believe, and their advertising is often vague enough to be misleading. Still, that overly optimistic tone, the broad characterizations, and the somewhat extravagant promises are characteristic of most of our advertising and are rarely deemed to be illegal; if they would be more often, then two-thirds of all advertisers and their copywriters could be dragged into courts. Certainly I could testify in all honesty that $300 a week was a realizable goal for anyone venturing into a modest mail order venture if they worked energetically at it. I could certify that I had earned that and more in my own small mail order ventures. I therefore agreed so to testify, out of personal successful experience in conducting a number of different mail order campaigns and in what I had learned about mail order businesses.

The prosecution had brought in its own expert, of course. I was not permitted to hear his or her testimony; I was required to wait in the corridor until it was my turn to testify, a typical procedure to prevent witnesses' testimony from being tainted by hearing the testimony of other witnesses. However, the interrogation I underwent later at the hands of the prosecutor when I was finally summoned to the stand made it clear enough to me that the expressed opinions of the prosecutor's own expert were based on experience in large-scale, multimillion-dollar, direct mail campaigns and projects. This case, however, involved the campaign of a rather typical small direct-mail operator, quite a different thing, and one that needed to be pointed out if the judge was to get a clear and unbiased picture. (There was no jury.) I found it necessary to qualify my own observations and opinions again and again, by pointing out the vast and numerous differences between the major direct-mail campaign and the small, home-based mail order venture. Many of the standards for one are totally inappropriate and unrealistic for the other and cannot be used as a standard for judging the other, as the prosecution was trying to do.

The experience and testimony of the prosecution's expert witness was not really appropriate for this case, and although I could not make direct references to it, for I had not heard it, I could easily enough infer from the cross-examination and the leading questions of the prosecutor what that expert's testimony had involved, namely, many pompous and portentous references to regression analysis, demographic profiles, and other costly big-league backup work that was entirely impractical for the small, home-based mail order dealer. The prosecutor and his star expert witness were trying to hang the defendant out to dry because he had not backed his simple little mail-order system up with six-figure research and analysis measures such as Publisher's Warehouse or *Reader's Digest* might have used. I thought it a travesty, and I was quite glad to have the opportunity to spike their guns, since I personally believed the prosecution's case was completely unjust.

In my innocence (it was the fist time I had served as an expert witness), I charged only my normal daily consulting fee, which was at that time $500, not knowing that expert witnesses usually command much larger fees than that. I learned only much later how much injustice I had done myself in this respect! Too, I had been called in at a late date and went to sit on the witness stand with virtually no preparation or preliminary work. Later, with true 20/20 hindsight, I could even see where I might have helped my client develop a much stronger case had I been brought in earlier to help.

76

If you are hired as an expert witness, make sure that you charge an appropriate fee. As one consultant I know who frequently does legal work puts it, "Double your normal consulting fee for the time you spend on the stand. You'll earn it!" Another reported that the hours are long and the lawyers are mean, but, he observed, one can earn $200 an hour. For many, even that is a modest fee and a gross underestimate: In practice, there are many specialists who command as much as $5,000 a day for their services, and $10,000 for a day in court is not unheard of. Generally, the client is glad to pay the fee, for it is usually worth every penny to him or her.

This last point is something that needs to be emphasized, for it is a most important consideration. The attorney may make the mistake of bringing you in much too late in the case for you to make all the contributions you otherwise could have made. If you feel in a particular case that this is so, you should point it out to the attorney and suggest that he or she call you in much earlier in future cases. Try to point out where and how you could have helped the attorney prepare a much stronger case. Be as specific as you can in demonstrating what you could have done in terms of investigation, helping prepare other witnesses, and – most especially – developing strategies.

WHO CAN BE AN EXPERT WITNESS?

Just about anyone who is an expert in anything can be called on as an expert witness in almost any kind of legal proceeding. It may be an arbitration, rather than a full-blown courtroom trial, but it also involves a great deal of related work that takes place outside of the courtroom and usually prior to any courtroom appearance. I found again and again that those who have served as expert witnesses remark on the fact that they are paid for their work whether they do or do not ever take the witness stand.

Legal proceedings are concerned with such a broad area of human relations and activities that virtually no activity or function can be ruled out. In one case, a customer sued a computer dealer in small-claims court, charging misrepresentation and fraud. He claimed that the computer he bought was not what the dealer charged him for and represented it to be. The dealer disputed that, so the customer retained a computer consultant to examine the computer in question and write a report describing it in detail. The report was introduced as evidence, serving to provide the expert's testimony in support of the client's case, without the consultant expert ever being required to appear in court.

There are some expert-witness consultants who have developed unusually specialized expertise that is extraordinarily useful and thus very much in demand in litigation. For example, one scientist is an expert in interpreting blood spatters at murder scenes, as a result of research he has done. He has virtually created a science single-handed, and his testimony is often instrumental in findings at murder trials, so he is called upon regularly to serve as an expert witness in both criminal investigations and courtroom proceedings.

Other experts have specialties that are considerably less dramatic. One individual I spoke with estimates that he is one of perhaps five people who knows the subject of some specific kind of computer software well enough to discuss it without resorting to jargon – that is, to explain it in lay terms. He is therefore called upon frequently in cases where that special knowledge is useful to one of the litigants.

More often, the expertise called for is not at all uncommon. In movies and TV dramas, it is often a medical expert, such as a psychiatrist, who sits on the stand and defends his opinions against the onslaughts of an opposing legal gladiator. But a philatelist, mining engineer, metallurgist, lapidary, furrier, farrier, architect, seamstress, shoemaker, paperhanger, etymologist, geneticist, or almost any other specialist might be called upon to testify as an expert. In one case in which the plaintiff had been injured in a car wash and was suing the insurance company, the attorney sought out an experienced car wash owner as an expert witness to help prepare the defense. Almost anyone may prove to be a help to one side or the other in a legal proceeding, but the work generally is a form of consulting. Even if the individual does not ordinarily function as a consultant, for the time he or she is an expert witness, the person is a consultant. And so, just as consulting itself is not a profession as much as it is a way of practicing your profession, whatever that is, being an expert witness is a way of consulting. It is consulting with the legal community as you might consult with anyone, with the added condition that your consulting, in this case, might include a courtroom appearance now and then.

WHAT DOES IT TAKE?

Among the many things you may be called on to do as an expert witness, depending on just what it is at which you are expert, is carry out supporting research – investigations, studies, surveys, and tests to develop useful evidence for your client's case. You are likely to be called on to make formal written and verbal presentations, be deposed, aid your client in preparing questions for depositions by others, interview witnesses on matters of fact, help your client develop strategies, prepare other witnesses who are to testify for your client, and otherwise carry out a wide variety of duties in which your special skills and knowledge are essential. Much of the stress must be placed on the word *expert,* rather than on *witness,* in understanding what you must do when retained by an attorney to help a client.

77

One experienced consultant who has served as an expert witness advises, as his first injunction to anyone who aspires to serve as an expert, to be sure that you are truly an expert. The opposing side will do their best to discredit your expertise if they cannot discredit your testimony. In fact, the stronger your testimony is, the more likely it is that you will find yourself attacked – that is, your credentials as an expert and perhaps your honesty and objectivity as well. You will need to have great confidence in yourself and be able to remain calm under pressure.

A large part of your effectiveness lies in your ability to be credible and persuasive, and an exterior of calm confidence helps greatly in this regard. You must smile indulgently at the attorney who seems intent upon destroying you, and you must appear undisturbed by the attack, regardless of how you feel internally. The jury probably has no more than a partial understanding of the technical issues and therefore is basing its judgment only partially on the logic of your testimony. The jury will also form opinions based on external appearances, comparing the calm and unruffled expert witness against the impassioned opposing attorney, who has, presumably, boned up on the subject so as to appear equally expert. If you are lucky, he or she may appear to be just a bit too frantic and passionate.

In addition to the aforementioned desirable personal traits, it helps greatly if you have a naturally inquisitive and analytical nature. The abilities to write and speak fluently in general and also in your area of expertise are assets in more than one way: They are skills you can use to good effect in carrying out several of your many functions as an expert witness, but they are also great assets in marketing your services as an expert witness. Prospective clients – trial attorneys – will inevitably try to judge your credentials as a witness per se – how you will come across to a jury from the witness stand – when they are considering retaining you to help them. They will naturally tend to the consultant who presents the calm, rational exterior and delivers his or her presentation with quiet confidence.

Tutorial skills are also a great help, because a large part of your job will be to educate your clients and the jury, explaining the basis for your expert opinions on various aspects of the case. You will be called on to enlighten, as well as opine, by your client and by opposing attorneys taking your deposition, as well as later by the jury, if you do, in fact, finally testify in court.

Credibility is vitally important in testifying in court, of course. It inevitably lies in your formal credentials, to a large degree, as well as in your demeanor and your presentation. Those credentials include formal education and related academic degrees, special training, honors and awards, licenses, professional affiliations, patents, publications, and any other achievements you can cite and point to, as well as the personal trait of having a calm and confident demeanor during depositions and court-room appearances.

GETTING STARTED

To get started in becoming an expert witness, consider the work as a specialized form of consulting, for it is just that. You will use your expert knowledge and skills in probably a wider variety of ways than ever before. The likelihood and frequency of your being called upon to be retained as an expert witness will vary according to at least three key factors:

1. Relevant demand—how often your kind of expertise is normally needed and called for in legal situations.
2. How common or how rare your expertise is—in other words, how many competitors you have in your specialized field.
3. How effectively you market yourself as an expert witness.

There is a fourth consideration that is rather specialized, and that is your personal image, visibility, and reputation. This consideration is related to items 2 and 3. You may, for example, be only one of many thousands of capable brain surgeons, but if you have persuaded others to perceive you as the absolute best in the field (e.g., if you have gotten a lot of favorable press coverage), you have become a rare specialist, perhaps the one and only brain surgeon with as much of a reputation. You are then unique, and your word carries far more weight than that of any of your peers. This may appear to be a cynical observation, but it is a practical truth, and we must recognize it for what it is.

That fellow who analyzes blood spatters, for example, can be kept quite busy as an expert witness because murders and murder trials in which there are blood spatters are common enough, and he has made himself one of a kind: No one else can speak on the subject with as much authority as he can. On the other hand, customers do not sue computer dealers and need consultants to evaluate their purchases every day, and computer consultants are also in plentiful supply. Hence, if you are a computer consultant who wants to be an expert witness, you will have to market yourself energetically or perhaps find some special niche connected with your special field. On the other hand, there are plenty of computer-related disputes of other kinds, usually related to software and custom contracts—for example, lawsuits charging breach of contract. Some attorneys specialize in computer software-related litigation, involving thorny questions of copyright and contractual obligations. That alone is a full-time legal field.

If you are a one-of-a-kind expert or even one of a few-of-a-kind experts whose help would be useful in many cases, clients may come seeking you out, with little marketing effort required on your part: Word of mouth may do the bulk of the marketing job for you. Other than that, if you want to make expert witnessing an important part of your practice, you will have to develop and pursue an organized marketing program, as you (presumably) do in selling your services generally. Once again, that story about the better mousetrap and the world beating a path to your door is myth and fantasy: In real life, the world almost never comes beating on your door to buy what you have to sell, nor do they even respond to mere invitation. You must *woo* them, and you must do so energetically if you want their dollars.

Of course, it may take a little time for you to become the world's most outstanding authority in your field and the most sought-after expert to testify at dramatic trials. Still, it is possible that your first experience as an expert witness will come to you serendipitously, unbidden and unsought after, as in my own case and that of many other consultants. Circumstance selected me when that Chicago lawyer needed a mail order expert, and I happened to have adequate credentials to undertake the job. However, if you wish to make expert-witness consulting a major part of your practice, you will do well to depend on your own efforts, and not on the fortuitous accident we call serendipity. To get started successfully vending your expert consulting services as an expert witness, you will almost surely have to organize a specific effort to do so.

One computer consultant told me that his father had retired from the insurance industry after a 45-year career there and has now become an expert witness in insurance-related cases, handling a variety of duties for insurance companies and attorneys. He flies all over the country on these assignments and stays busy doing what he enjoys, being a consultant expert in his own field and earning a substantial income in doing so.

Logically enough, the first step in getting started is to decide what your expert-witness specialty is going to be. Although fate cast me unbidden and without premeditation as a mail order expert in a federal courtroom in Chicago, probably my greatest expertise is in marketing to the federal government and proposal writing. Marketing to government agencies happens to be the field in which I have most frequently consulted and lectured because my success in writing winning proposals was great enough to attract attention to me and lead to demand for my services. It is the area in which my credentials are most impressive, and were I to seek assignments as an expert witness, I would cast about for assignments that made use of my knowledge and experience in the field.

To get started as an expert witness, I would first conduct some research to arrive at an estimate of how many lawsuits involve proposal writing and government contracting – for example, when a company that loses in a contract competition sues the government or otherwise has a contract-related dispute that winds up or threatens to wind up in litigation. I would want to know how often one side or the other retains consultants to serve as expert witnesses in these cases. I would study the records and statistics to see whether patterns emerge, perhaps identifying a desirable niche in expert witnessing. I would also want to know where, geographically, most such lawsuits are entered into, if there is any kind of pattern with respect to locality.

All of that information, plus my own policies and preferences in connection with traveling and the kinds of cases I would prefer to work with, would give me some idea of how wide a net to cast in marketing my services—that is, how to define my geographical area of service and the range of subjects in which I could claim adequate expertise to stand up to the demands of being an expert witness. Or my research might help me identify a more specialized niche than that in which I have heretofore consulted and lectured: We are often unaware of great marketing opportunities waiting to be discovered. (Before I became a proposal consultant, I was totally unaware of how many people in large and small companies would gladly pay me substantial fees to help them write proposals. My discovery of the market was quite accidental—all but forced on me by friends and circumstances. Later, I learned a corollary—that there were many organizations, large and small, for profit and not for profit, that would enthusiastically hire me to present seminars and instruct attendees in the art of proposal writing.)

It might take substantial research to gather all the information I would need to launch a campaign to become a full-time expert-witness consultant, but the information to plan this campaign ought to be readily available. Court records, open to the public normally, would be one source of such information. Probably, public data bases, both those serving the legal profession (LEXIS and WestLaw are two leading names in the field), and other public data bases, would furnish useful data. Further important sources would be the various registries and directories of consultants offering their services as specialists in government contracting and proposal writing. There are a number of such registries, as well as a number of related organizations, that could furnish such data. It is also possible that any inquiries I made in any association to which I belong and of the subscribers to several of the electronic bulletin board conferences in which I participate would produce useful data.

Of course, having yourself listed in these registries and directories, joining relevant associations, and making your interest known widely to others are themselves approaches to marketing your services. Another

78

In marketing yourself as an expert witness, you should cover at least these activities:

1. Add your name to appropriate registries of consultants who are interested in legal work. The largest of these is the Technical Advisory Service for Attorneys (TASA), at 428 Pennsylvania Ave., Fort Washington, PA, 19034, telephone (215) 275-8272.
2. Use direct mail techniques to notify law firms that have handled cases in your area of expertise. A minimal amount of research can help you identify these.
3. Place a dignified ad in attorneys' periodicals.

approach is to make mailings to law firms, especially those which appear to specialize in the areas most likely to require your services. Any such mailings should be dignified and include a tasteful brochure and letter.

The methods you use to attract clients should be the same as those you use to market your services generally. Use the same PR activities as a part of your marketing effort: Public speaking and writing articles for respected journals, for example, lend you prestige and bring you to the attention of many people, including attorneys and people they talk to. You may have to seek out occasions to speak publicly. One excellent way is to volunteer to speak (without a fee) at law seminars and other occasions when it serves your purpose. Writing a "serious" book is even more productive in elevating your visibility and bestowing on you an impressive image of professionalism and great authority in your field. It is not as difficult a feat to accomplish as you probably think it is.

In doing these things, always remember that your clients—those who seek you out and hire you—are usually lawyers, even if your fees are paid directly or indirectly by their clients. You therefore must write articles and books that are likely to be read by lawyers. You do that either by writing for journals that are read principally by legal professionals or by titling and slanting the articles and books you write to appeal to and attract the attention of legal professionals. (Even lawyers read other kinds of books and periodicals than trade and professional journals.)

You can also place discreet advertisements in periodicals read by attorneys. It would probably be helpful to advertise your services under more than one category; for example, besides offering your services as an expert witness, offer your services as an expert consultant, investigator, researcher, and analyst in your special field. In the early stages of a case, an attorney may not yet be thinking in courtroom terms and may be looking for an expert only in terms of such preparatory work as those categories suggest. Lawyers have quite a lot of need for investigative work.

Networking methods work well here in marketing your services. Make it your business to become acquainted with as many lawyers in your area as possible, and try to network with them. Make sure they know what you do in support of the legal profession. In general, you can pursue the networking methods discussed in Chapter 3 to make direct contacts and win referrals. In this connection, you might consider organizing a special interest group (SIG) of expert-witness specialists within an association of consultants or, for that matter, within any other association where it is likely that a significant number of members are already offering services as expert witnesses or are interested in doing so.

Most of these techniques are direct marketing methods, methods that result in prospective clients calling you directly for direct negotiations. Some of the registry and directory listings are free or may cost you something, but they also result in your getting calls directly from the attorneys who will be your prospective clients. Other registries, such as TASA, are brokers for your services. The client must reach you through these organizations, which will mark up your fee and bill the client directly, so you will get paid by the broker. Of course, you can choose to confine yourself to such brokers, avoid registering with a broker and pursue all assignments directly, or use some combination of the two, taking advantage of every opportunity to win assignments. On the other hand, you may develop some regular clients, in time, who have frequent need of your help, and you may then choose to confine your practice to these clients alone, as some consultants do.

NEGOTIATIONS AND CONTRACTING
TO START WORK

Whatever your marketing methods, the first contact for your services as an expert witness will normally be from an attorney, by mail or telephone, usually the latter. After the customary introductory chat, you will be asked about your interest in serving in some advisory capacity. The term *expert witness* may or may not be used at this time; it may be much too early to think about that aspect of the case.

The Initial Considerations

In pondering whether you ought to accept the offer, you must consider whether you have any conflicts – for example, will you be asked to adopt a position contrary to your true beliefs? Will you have a schedule conflict? Do you have conflicting interests of any kind?

Another thing to consider is whether there will be time for you to do a proper job. It may be, and often is, the case that you are being called on at five minutes to 12. Can you then handle this as a last-minute, dire emergency? Will you be forced to take shortcuts that will hurt your own reputation and image?

Follow-Up Activity and Considerations

You probably cannot make all the necessary decisions on the basis of the first contact. You will have to know more by reviewing the documents of the case or having a face-to-face interview with the attorney. Possibly, you will even have to do some outside investigation. This can take a great deal of time, and you are entitled to be paid for your time. You may find it necessary to express an interest in the assignment, but withhold acceptance until you have investigated further.

79

You are entitled to be paid for the time you spend reviewing the case and reaching a decision regarding whether you will accept the assignment. Make sure that this is clearly understood when you discuss your fee. At the same time, the client is entitled to get something for his or her money, even if you decline the case: You will be expected to submit a formal report and opinion. But unless you can agree immediately and make a firm commitment in advance, you should state a figure for your time and effort in reviewing the case and offering an opinion on it.

The Question of a Retainer

When you accept a case, regardless of other considerations, you will have presumably reached agreement on a fee, and you will have estimated the total cost and expenses, as nearly as you can anticipate them at this time. You are now entitled to a retainer, which is really an advance payment against the anticipated total billing, before you do anything. It is wise to ask for this and, in my opinion, unwise to proceed without it. That could easily lead to collection problems later.

My own practice in this regard is to require approximately one-third of the anticipated total billing in advance, one-third at some agreed-upon midpoint, and the final one-third on completion of the assignment. Other consultants have different, less liberal conditions: They track payments made against hours or days expended and require additional payments when the payments already made are essentially expended for the hours or days already provided. In any case, you should keep an accurate log of your time spent on the assignment, to avoid confusion. Whether or not your retainer is "used up," you should submit a clear time record.

80

There are many contingencies that are difficult and even impossible to anticipate in setting a retainer. One of them is waiting time: You have no reliable way of anticipating how long you may be required to wait, chafing, in an anteroom, to be called to testify, or how long a trial will be continued, postponed, or otherwise delayed. Thus, you must usually keep your charges open ended, never committing yourself to more than your best estimate when the matter of fees and charges arises. Flat "for-the-job" rates or other fixed-price arrangements are impracticable for the most part; only rarely will you be able to do more than estimate the hours you will need to get the job done. In fact, you should be charging portal to portal, including travel time.

FEES AND EXPENSES

As already noted, fees vary widely, according to several factors. As a class, physicians appear to charge the most for their expert testimony and related services, especially in malpractice cases, where many and probably most physicians are reluctant to testify at all. (One, in my own experience, charged $400 for a 10-minute physical examination and a two-page report.) You can charge by the hour or by the day, as you do in your consulting work. (Very likely, those who are "star" expert witnesses charge by the day, while most of us tend to set our rates on an hourly basis.) That retired insurance executive I mentioned earlier charges a relatively modest $150 an hour and manages to average about $50,000 a year in his retirement.

A Few Ethical Considerations

It occurs to some consultants who serve as expert witnesses that they ought to charge a greater fee when the side for which they testify wins. That's a bad idea for more than one reason, but the first reason is enough: That kind of fee setting makes it appear that the expert has sold his testimony and thus is not testifying objectively or honestly. A judge would be quite unhappy to hear this, and a jury would be inclined to have a sharply reduced faith in the expert's testimony. *Any* form of contingency fee is objectionable for that reason, and is, in fact, barred by law in some jurisdictions.

On the other hand, some expert witnesses do charge more for the time they spend in court than for the time they spend in other activities related to the work. Some consultants have maintained that there is some justification for this, such as having to wait endless hours on a hard bench in a corridor while waiting to be called, enduring verbal batterings from opposing attorneys, and undergoing great stress in general.

You may be working for either side. You should charge the same rate when working for the plaintiff as you do when working for the defendant, or you will appear to be less than objective. It is, of course, important not only that you be objective in this work, but that your objectivity be readily apparent.

81

Make up a formal schedule of litigation support fees and terms, and hand it to clients or enclose it with your initial response. This sets forth your base fee, on an hourly or daily basis, your requirements for retainers or advances and travel expenses, your policy regarding payment for depositions, and any other condition relevant to your fees and expenses. Try not to make any special concessions. When I have been asked to do so—for example, to work without an advance retainer or deposit—I decline quietly, stating clearly that it is a matter of fixed policy and I cannot make changes or exceptions to the policy. So far, this has proved to be an effective argument.

When you are deposed by the opposition, the opposing attorney must pay your fees, including travel time and expenses. Time spent in preparation for giving your deposition, however, is billed to the attorney who has retained you.

CHAPTER 9

SALES PROMOTIONS

Every business venture needs sales promotions of one sort or another. Many of the classic methods of sales promotions—advertising in the media, for example—are rather costly, and often prohibitively so, for the independent consultant. There must be more suitable—that is, effective but less costly—ways to promote one's practice.

USING DIRECT MAIL

There are many kinds of marketing and sales promotions for consultants. As described earlier, the various consulting products and services may be used as profit centers in themselves, or they may be used as marketing tools. Direct mail, for example, is one means of marketing products and services. Philosophically, this multibillion-dollar industry represents proactive, rather than reactive, marketing. That is, instead of waiting for a prospective client to respond to your advertising by calling or visiting your office, you "go out" to call on the prospect. Direct mail is a way of, in effect, knocking on doors, using literature as surrogate salespeople making the calls.

    For the most part, consulting contracts do not result directly from advertising solicitations of any sort, not even those made by direct mail. That is, consulting is not a "one-call" business. You might advertise a TV repair service in the newspaper or by direct mail and have customers, sold by your advertising copy, call and say, "When can you be here to service my TV?" It rarely happens that way in selling consulting or other professional services of any kind: A prospect interested in a new office management system, counseling on corporate communications, or investment advice is normally going to proceed with some caution and want to know more about your services, your promises, your guarantees, your credentials, and your rates. That usually means several contacts or exchanges in meetings before coming to a decision on whether to contract with you. Thus, selling your services as a consultant usually requires that you help the prospect build a sense of confidence and trust in you. That is something that you cannot ordinarily do in a single presentation.

In short, direct mail will not often produce sales – consulting contracts – for you any more than newspaper advertising or TV commercials will. If the promotion works well, it produces sales *leads,* leads that have to be followed up. That is all you can ask for and expect, and that is what you must aim to achieve.

82

Direct mail is an excellent marketing tool for consultants and professionals because you can target potential clients with absolute precision, have complete control over your message, and monitor the cost of sending each message to each prospect. Far from being "junk mail," the consultant's mailings can build in all the professionalism desired – even watermarked pages and an engraved letterhead.

TARGETING YOUR PROSPECTS

Besides direct mail, the mass media offer another avenue for sales promotion. However, when you advertise in any medium, print or broadcast, you may be limited in how or how much you can target your services to specific prospects. The publisher or broadcaster will furnish some guidelines offering demographics and other information to help you place your advertisement, but the targeting is still relatively inexact. All such advertising is broadcast advertising, even in print, in the sense that you are appealing to a diverse and general audience. Things are a bit better when you advertise in trade journals or other special-interest periodicals. You can then begin to think in terms of "narrowcasting," to at least some extent. You will reach only dentists and those involved in one way or another with dentistry when you advertise in a dental trade journal. You may even narrow the targeting a bit more if you find a journal that is aimed at oral surgeons only or at those concerned with dental prostheses only. Even so, you can target prospects far more selectively and precisely with direct mail. You can, for example, confine a mailing to a single area code or even a single neighborhood, something you can't do in most other media. (You could even limit your mailing to those named Jones or Greenstein if you had any reason to do so.)

KNOWING YOUR COSTS

Marketers who sell advertising space or time in the mass media – in printed periodicals and on radio or TV – are fond of telling prospective advertisers how inexpensively they can reach prospects. The marketers like to point to astronomical numbers of readers, viewers, and listeners and break costs down into terms of a penny or two per individual reached. But are these individuals really prospects, or are they only readers and viewers or listeners? That is, how many of those readers, viewers, and listeners are truly prospects for what you wish to sell? Obviously, in a broadcast commercial or print advertisement in some periodical, you reach many people who are not prospects and who don't and won't even listen to or read your copy. However, when you make a mailing to 5,000 prospects whom you have selected as all being true prospects, you are making calls at 40 cents each. When you spend $2,000 for a print advertisement or TV commercial, you may be reaching readers and viewers at two cents each, but how much does it cost you to reach the true prospects among those readers and viewers? It's hard to say, though it may be costing you a dollar or two for each true prospect. So another advantage to direct mail is knowing your true cost per prospect, given well-documented mailing lists and careful selection of lists to use. But how does one come to know these costs? The answer is, with testing, and even then, the results are not always exact or completely reliable, but they do give you some idea of your costs per prospect.

TESTING

Testing is a sine qua non in all advertising and promotion, but it is never easy to do. It is probably easiest to do and produces the most reliable results in direct mail campaigns. In a closely targeted mailing campaign, without testing you never know how well you are doing, except in a general sense. And even then, you don't know until you can't do much about it. For example, it can take many months to try out a campaign, run test advertisements, review results, possibly run follow-up test advertising, and settle on the final copy and program before rolling out (mounting the full-scale advertising campaign). But in print advertising, so many periodicals have deadlines for receiving advertising copy of two months or more before the date of publication. Thus, by the time the advertisement is printed, the results of the tests may be completely unreliable. In direct mail, however, you can generally judge results within about three weeks after running the test mailings. Then you can run the follow-up test mailings, if any, immediately, and do the rollout about three or four weeks later.

83

Never underestimate the importance of testing in direct mail, and don't make the common mistake of using testing to prove your own pet theories. You must keep your mind open: You are not trying to find out how good or bad your initial estimates are; you are trying to find out what works best in producing the response you want. But you must also know precisely what it is that you are testing: It is one thing to test your copy—the sales presentation itself—and quite another thing to test your offer or what you are selling. To do the latter, you must:

1. Know precisely what you are testing.
2. Test only significant or important items.
3. Test each significant item individually.

The Basic Rationale of Testing

The premise upon which testing is based is that your sales appeal must have a principal motivator—that the success of the appeal depends on the degree of success you achieve in identifying and presenting that item which will most effectively induce the prospect to buy. The most effective motivator in any given case may be any one of many things: price, convenience, effectiveness, or anything else.

To some degree, what is the most effective motivator depends on what you sell. Probably, the majority of automobile sales are based on price—on the customer's perception that he or she is getting the "best deal," which usually means the biggest bargain (the best final price, the biggest trade-in offer, or other blandishments). Selling something that is easily identifiable as a unique model invites cost comparisons, so it may be assumed that prospects will do price shopping. That doesn't mean that they may not be motivated by other factors as well, but these factors will probably be secondary considerations. Thus, the automobile dealer might do well to test "lowest price" versus "biggest trade-ins," to see which produces the better result, and then do follow-up testing with other motivators, such as better service or more encompassing guarantees.

84

Price appeals are risky in the direct marketing of consulting services: They clash with the professional image you want to project and may do you a great deal more harm than good. On the other hand, you can advertise maximum competence and capability or the most modern equipment (if equipment is a factor in your work), or you can offer a free initial consultation or assessment of need, invite readers to register for a free introductory seminar, or offer other inducements that are in keeping with your professional image.

Know Precisely What You Are Testing

Whatever you decide, you must decide in advance what items you must test for, and you must design the tests to test for those items specifically. The key items in your presentation that you ought to consider are the following:

- *Your promise.* Just what do you offer? *Specifically,* what do you promise (e.g., guaranteed results, the most efficient program, or the swiftest results)?

- *Your proof or backup.* What evidence do you provide that you can and will deliver exactly as promised? Logical argument? General credentials? Past accomplishments? Testimonials? References?

- *Your copy.* Besides what your copy *says,* you may find it useful to test how persuasive your copy *is* — your headlines, your blurbs, your text, and in fact, your brochure as a whole.

- *Special inducements.* If you offer something special as an inducement – say, a free seminar, a free initial consultation, or a free
  needs assessment – it would be useful to test the effectiveness
  of these as motivators.

There are many other things you can test, but probably, all of the
important items fall into one of the preceding categories. What is important is to select whichever you believe to be the most likely motivators
and test them with as many test mailings as you believe necessary and
can afford to run. You try to make all the mailings as nearly identical as
possible. That is done by dividing your mailing up into several groups,
using mailing lists as much like each other as possible. (One way is to
break up a single mailing list into several pieces selected at random.)
Then you mail the same package to each test group selected, except for
the one item you wish to test – the headline, the price, the promise, the
proof, the guarantee, the offer, the proposition, or any other variable you
think important enough to test for.

Test Only Significant or Important Items

You must be careful to test only significant items, based on the nature of
your market and list size. Some campaigners are delighted with a 0.23
percent improvement in response that resulted from using two-color
printing, or a 0.019 percent difference resulting from using teaser copy
on the exterior of the envelope. Perhaps that amounts to a significant
number of dollars in a multimillion-dollar campaign, but it isn't likely to
make much of a difference to you in your program, mailing only a few
thousand pieces of literature and seeking a few dozen responses, rather
than several thousand orders. Accordingly, you need to test only items
that are likely to make a major difference in response in your program.
You can fine tune your program later to get even better results, if you
wish, but you should start out trying only to find what works reasonably
well for you.

Test Each Significant Item Individually

You can't test your entire sales package and evaluate the results on a
wholesale basis. That is, you can't break your package down into several
subpackages and measure the differences in response to each, for you
will have no idea why one package pulled a better response than an-

other. Instead, what you must do is change only one item at a time to see what difference the change makes. What makes one subpackage give so much better a result than the others? Is it the wording of the promise that makes the difference? The price? The guarantee? The packaging? The testimonials? The special inducement? The presentation? Some other variable? Getting the answer is what testing is all about.

FINDING THE WORDS

Successful sales and advertising appeals are based on making powerful promises and convincing the prospect that you will make good on your promises. Thus, one important aspect of testing a direct mail campaign (or any promotional campaign, for that matter) is finding the words that have the greatest impact in making the promise and are the most persuasive in backing up the promise with evidence of your ability and intention to deliver what you promise. Without those, all promotion is less than maximally effective and more often than not totally ineffective.

Examine the advertising copy you come across. What does it promise to do for you? How does it try to convince you that it will deliver on its promise? What is the evidence offered?

In effect, through promotions, you "ask" your prospects what they want by trying out different ideas and monitoring the results to see what your prospects respond to in the greatest numbers. They know it when they see it, and only when they see it, as a rule, so you must parade the ideas before them.

FINDING THE SERVICES

The preceding section assumes that the service you offer has a market and that you are simply in search of the right words – the right presentation – to help your prospects recognize their need for what you offer. But if you are launching a new consulting practice and basing everything on your assumption of what the market is like in terms of needs for services, you may have to first test that assumption. Let me cite my own case as a rather typical example.

I got into consulting when appeals from friends for help in writing proposals became too numerous for me to accommodate in my spare time. I was compelled to begin saying no, whereupon I began to get offers to pay for my time and help. Still, I found later that the demand for proposal-writing help was spasmodic, with too many peaks and valleys to be satisfactory as a full-time consulting practice. Only over a period of time, as I tested and discovered the marketability of proposal-writing seminars and publications, did I succeed in fashioning a full-time consulting practice based on my knowledge of marketing to government via proposal writing and related activities.

Usually, you can offer a variety of services, based on whatever your professional or technical specialty is. You may have begun a practice based on some perceived service or set of services that really are a mirror image of whatever kind of duties you performed in a career position before launching a consulting service. But that does not guarantee that there are enough prospective clients waiting to order those services. That is, it is quite possible that your prospects truly do not perceive a need for or want what you offer, no matter what terms you find in which to make the presentation. You must always consider such a possibility – the possibility that there is simply not a large enough market for the kind of service you offer.

85

If responses to a promotion indicate that there is not enough of a market for your services, you must determine the services your prospects do want. To do so, compile a broad list of prospects, mail your promotions to each person on the list, and analyze what kinds of services have the greatest appeal and what kinds of prospects are most interested in them.

In that case, your quest in analyzing response becomes one of seeking to identify the services your prospects do want. That is kind of a chicken-and-egg problem, since the answer to the question of what your prospects want is tied to what kind of prospects you are addressing. Accordingly, if yours is a new, as yet untried practice, make sure to mail your promotions to a fairly broad list of prospects, and analyze both what kinds of services have the greatest appeal and the profiles of those who respond.

RESPONSE ANALYSIS

Most people selling merchandise by direct mail enclose order forms and gauge response by simple measures: the number of sales that are made and, where the size of orders vary, the average order size. They usually also measure how well each mailing list produces orders and try to perceive any patterns in the responses that will be helpful – for example, whether there are customers that have any characteristics in common. And if they sell a variety of items they also want to determine which items sell best.

Measuring the number of orders placed and the average order size does not work out well with direct mail (or other advertising and promotion) to sell your consulting services. As mentioned earlier, your initial contact with a prospect will not often produce an immediate sale. The response you want and should strive to get is an expression of interest that represents a sales lead. The whole purpose of the mailing is to find prospects who want to know more about what you can do for them and what it will cost. The mailing should be designed to elicit responses from such prospects; therefore, the item to be measured is not sales, but inquiries. Moreover, these must be *interested* inquiries, rather than casual ones inspired merely by curiosity.

86

Direct marketing efforts for consultants often require some rethinking of what a sale is, compared with similar promotions for other products. If you are offering some special inducement, such as an invitation to attend a free seminar you are offering, each response represents a "sale" in that it represents a registration for your seminar. That is a good short-term or immediate measure of response. The long-term and more significant measure, however, is how many of those respondents become clients. That is the final measure of the effectiveness of that special inducement and your direct mail effort.

PROFILING YOUR CLIENT

Measuring the number or percentage of responses to a mailing is only one aspect of the response analysis. You also want to get a good look at the best prospect for your services: You want to get a profile or definition of your quintessential client. Doing so is an important key to improving your marketing.

It is usually difficult, in the beginning, to define your typical client. You start with an estimate of the kind of prospect that is most likely to become your client. Perhaps you started your consulting practice with the expectation of doing business with the same kinds of customers your former employer did business with. This is a common enough assumption by those launching independent consulting practices. Quite often, we find that it is an unwarranted assumption, a premise that must be proved. When I started to pursue clients for my government-marketing/ proposal-writing service, I assumed that my best prospects would be the kinds of companies that I had worked for or that my former employers had done business with. Those were companies that wrote many proposals in their pursuit of business. They were mostly electronics companies pursuing high-tech research and development contracts for radar, missiles, aircraft, computers, and sundry other military hardware in the aerospace/electronics milieu of the vast defense establishment. (I had been employed by such companies as GE, RCA, Philco, and other companies that provided support services to these aerospace/electronics giants.) In time, as I monitored responses to my direct-mail campaigns, I came to learn that the prospects I had the greatest success with were not these firms, but were companies developing custom software for mainframe computers. (The personal computer was not in existence yet.) For some reason, such companies appeared to feel the greatest need for my help in developing proposals.

87

Your direct marketing can do double duty if you use it to help you profile your market. Offer extras to respondents who give you information on, say, the size of their business or the percentage of their total contracts with government agencies. Or devise a sample "poll" of client's key concerns and needs. A number of free newsletter issues, a free 15-minute phone consultation, or some other offer will increase your responses.

My error was in overlooking the undisputed fact that change is continuous and inevitable, and nowhere is that a more significant truth than in the world of high technology: No field in modern times has expanded and diversified as explosively as has the computer field and all the satellite industries and activities it spawned. Even in the relatively few years I had been immersed in electronics and aerospace programs, computer technology had been outgrowing all other electronics-based industries phenomenally, but a great deal of that growth was due to massive government financing.

I can't say yet why that now so obvious truth escaped me. I could guess at it, although without any certainty, and that is itself a significant factor that points up the need to do response analysis. I did learn quickly enough, however, that software developers were better prospects for my services than hardware developers were. Why that was so isn't important. What is important is keeping your mind open so that you can find the answers that will enable you to improve your marketing steadily. The more you know about who and what your clients are, the better you can attract and serve more of them. Perhaps even more significantly, until and unless you do know precisely who and what your clients are, you are not in total control of your practice, especially the marketing aspect of it.

WHAT DO YOUR CLIENTS WANT TO BUY?

The W. H. Hoover Company was in the leather goods business and had no thought of inventing or manufacturing vacuum cleaners when it was launched in 1907. The Radio Corporation of America, RCA, was founded by David Sarnoff to market Thomas Edison's invention, the phonograph. The Philadelphia company that started out making storage batteries to be used in automobiles became Philco, a major electronics company that ultimately was acquired by the Ford Motor Company. And Elisha T. Otis had no more intention of perfecting and manufacturing elevators than IBM's Tom Watson had of manufacturing computers when he started in business. A very large percentage of businesses—perhaps even most of them—develop into something far different than their founders envisioned and set out to do originally. There is thus an excellent chance that, if you have been consulting for some time, what you are doing now is not what you started out to do or did at first! In fact, if you are starting now or recently started your practice, there is a large possibility that you will be offering quite a different service a year or two from now than you originally planned. Indeed, your survival as an independent consultant may depend on your adaptability and willingness to change as is necessary. The stubborn resistance to change is the Achilles heel of many ventures.

THE NEED TO GROW (AND WHAT THAT MEANS)

It has become an article of faith in these fast-moving and rapidly changing times that the company still selling what it sold 10 years ago—or even 5 years ago, in many cases—is verging rapidly on obsolescence or has already achieved it. Change and the need to adapt steadily to it are now accepted as inevitable, a fact of business and professional life. (Would you buy the personal computer of 1982 today? Or patronize a dentist using 1960 tools and methods?)

Another way that aphorism is expressed is by saying that a business must grow – that a business that does not grow will perish. Many people take that to mean that a business must expand in size, but that is not what is meant by growing. Expanding in size, in many cases, is simply swelling. Growing means changing appropriately – adapting to whatever conditions dictate a need for change and changing accordingly. It may mean adopting new marketing methods, improved packaging, better employee plans, modernized products and services, or many other things, but in all of them it means positive change.

The reason for changes are many – serendipity, technological development, and other unforeseen events – but none is so significant as the perception that the client wants something you had not originally envisioned or foreseen. I did not plan to be a marketing consultant and certainly not to help people write proposals; the demand for help, despite my protestations that I did not have the time to help others in this manner, forced the decision to be a consultant on me. Nor did I plan to become a lecturer and lead seminars on the subject; that also evolved as result of my response to demand and my perception of needs. Most significantly, I did not contemplate a full-time career writing books. That evolved from a first book on marketing and proposal writing, which was itself the result of a bit of serendipity. The important thing is not that these changes evolved, but that I adapted my activities to them as I perceived the need or market for them. Of course, what I refer to here as demand might be also called opportunity, for it certainly was that, even if I did not at first perceive it as such.

The changes that represent growth sometimes appear to come about in spurts, as occasional events without timetables or even predictability. In fact, however, change is continuous; it is our *recognition of* and *reaction to* change that is intermittent. Personal computers, for example, improved almost daily for a dozen years after the earliest models appeared. However, practically speaking, one could not buy a new model every few months – that is, whenever an important new improvement appeared – so most of us bought a new model only every few years, usually lamenting after a short time that we had not waited just a bit longer to make the change! It took me about 10 years to move up through three improved models, and the same pattern obtained in my acquisition of ancillary equipment: I am now using my fourth printer, third modem, third copier, and first fax machine. (My fourth printer, however, is also my first laser printer.) I lamented each time that I did not wait just a little longer to buy each of these, but each represented an improvement in my efficiency and my capability to serve my clients. The point is that change and the need for change are continuous, but the points at which you adopt changes in terms of your own practice are a matter of your judgment.

I KNOW IT WHEN I SEE IT

Unfortunately, history records plainly enough that there are many practitioners who cling stubbornly to their original and often outdated notions, even when it ought to be plain to them that the time for change has long since arrived. It is that resistance to change, that refusal to adapt to even the present, much less the future, that has destroyed and will continue to destroy many flourishing businesses, even businesses as large as major airlines and chains of retail stores. The more fortunate ones are acquired (e.g., RCA, acquired by GE), while the less fortunate ones (e.g., Robert Hall) simply cease to exist and are soon forgotten.

Such disasters are due to a failure to perceive what is happening, sometimes simply to a stubborn refusal to listen to the customers and learn what they want. A major objective of your response analysis should be to find out what clients want to buy – what kinds of services or products you should be offering. You find this out by offering them many choices and observing which they prefer. No one knows better than the client what he or she wants, although the client may not be able to tell you in precise terms what it is. Those clients of mine who wanted help with proposals were often not aware that that was what they wanted. They responded infrequently and unenthusiastically to my offers to help them write proposals. They did want to win contracts, however: They were well aware of that, and when I offered to help them do that, they became interested. Now they truly "understood" (i.e., *appreciated*) the need for help in writing effective proposals. The lesson here is simple enough: You must find language that the customer understands.

Many clients know what they want only when they see it. In fact, that's the way it is for many of us. Sometimes we don't know enough to know what we want – we don't know what we can have because we don't know all the alternatives. (When an Army surgeon asked me if I wanted a piece of shrapnel removed, I was stunned: How could I know? I had to ask what the alternatives were before I could respond. P.S.: I still have the shrapnel in my leg.) That puts it up to you to help your prospective clients "see it." The process is often known as educating the client, and it is very much a part of marketing.

RELATIONSHIP MARKETING

The notion of asking your clients what they really wish to buy is not a new one; there simply has never been a really good mechanism for doing so until now. Among the newest marketing developments, however, is *relationship marketing.* The central idea behind this term is to develop a closer relationship with your clients than you may have maintained in the past. The objective is primarily to know your clients better and to be able to understand their wants and needs better. The principal mechanism for doing this is establishing a dialogue with your clients and prospective clients, gathering a great deal of data about them (much of it provided by the clients themselves), and entering the data into a data base established for the purpose. This becomes the *marketing data base,* and the system is thus often referred to as *data-based marketing.*

The problem of building marketing data bases is not difficult, as far as equipment is concerned: Today's desktop computers can accommodate large data bases—marketing data bases of a size quite adequate for the typical independent consultant. The chief problem is getting information—finding and implementing something to provoke a dialogue and get clients to provide the feedback you need.

Large corporations initiate various programs that invoke such feedback. They launch contests in which contestants provide information about themselves. They offer rebates, which also require requesters to furnish certain information. They create clubs, groups, and other such organizations that will cause individuals to register and provide information. Once, years ago, long before I knew what a data base was, let alone what would one day become known as data-based marketing, I created something along those lines: I invited the subscribers to a newsletter to become my "associates," an invitation to which a great many responded. Perhaps I unwittingly invented data-based marketing! In any event, it is an idea you might wish to consider for your own practice, as it offers a means for establishing an unusually close relationship with your clients and may prove to be an effective mechanism for marketing your services.

88

If you do a good job of assembling a customer profile from your responses, you're on the way toward establishing a relationship marketing program. The goal is to amass a data base of information using today's desktop technology to help point you in the direction of your customers' distinguishing characteristics and needs.

In some ways, the large corporations enjoy some advantages of size: They can launch those national contests, clubs, rebates, and other such programs. On the other hand, there are measures you can use that are impracticable on the macrocosmic scale of the supercorporations. For example, you can sponsor many minievents, such as breakfasts and lunches with officials of associations and with civic leaders, a telephone campaign whereby you place a follow-up call to your clients to verify that your earlier meeting did everything that it was supposed to do, free evening seminars with prospective clients, and any other such events that you can conceive and stage. (On one occasion, I appeared as a guest on a local TV show, and it brought so many inquiries, that I staged a series of miniseminars to which I invited all who had questions they wished to ask or inquiries they wished to pursue.)

The point of all this relationship marketing is that the more you know about your clients and prospective clients – their problems, needs, aspirations, goals, and wants – the more effectively you can respond and market to them and that there are many ways to gain this knowledge. Far too often, we market to what we think the client ought to want – what we want the client to want – rather than to what the client does want. That is the most common failure of marketing. The alternative is clear enough, and today it is not difficult to implement that alternative: We perform testing, offering alternatives and measuring how the prospects respond to each alternative, as an indirect means of asking the client what he or she really wants.

NICHE MARKETS

It is quite possible to infer something here that I do not wish to imply. You may think that, once you complete your testing and find the combination of elements – what you offer, what you promise, and what you ask for it – that respondents like best, you drop all the alternatives and roll out with that package. In fact, that is often precisely what many campaigners do, and it is just as often all wrong to do so. If the package in question is an overwhelming favorite, and all the others produce quite poorly, that may be the sensible thing to do. But suppose that one package produces quite well, but two of the others also produce reasonably well. It is then possible that you have discovered two additional markets. At least, this possibility is well worth investigating. You should analyze the results to see whether there are any distinguishing characteristics of those who responded to each package that was mailed – especially any characteristics that might distinguish one group of respondents from another. If you find any, you have probably uncovered a niche market, a segment of your market that responds to some specific element of your presentation. But whether you do or do not uncover a niche market in the normal course of your testing and response analysis, you should be aware of and on the alert for the discovery of niche markets.

89

Relationship marketing, if properly done, creates not just one customer profile, but several. Using this technique, you can begin segmenting your customers into separate niches, each with its own strategy. However, don't fall into the trap of simply chasing the biggest segment alone; the knowledge you obtain about smaller subgroups is also valuable.

I discovered that small software-development companies were a niche market for my services in developing proposals for government contracts. This is not to say that they were my sole market – I helped many other kinds of companies win contracts – but they responded especially well to my offers to help them develop proposals.

On the other hand, for training people in writing proposals, my best clients were the large software-development firms. I also delivered my lectures and seminars at conventions, in community colleges, and elsewhere, but it was the large software-development firm that was my best prospect. Either it had a large in-house staff for me to train in successive sessions, or it had multiple offices and wished me to make my training presentations to the staffs of each office.

Both of these were rather broad-based niche markets. Most markets meriting the name are considerably narrower in scope, smaller in size, and—probably most characteristically—narrower and more specialized in their needs.

A true niche market is one that has special needs to which you can appeal and which you can satisfy. Let us suppose, for example, that you are a personnel specialist. You know how and where to recruit personnel of all kinds for short- and long-term needs. You are familiar with all the appropriate federal and state laws that must be complied with in staffing. But you have a very special competence in finding some particular category of hard-to-find personnel, perhaps rocket scientists, calligraphers, or migrant fruit pickers. Then you might do very well to seek out and specialize in those niche markets, the employers of and seekers after such specialists.

A niche market is not always dictated or defined by some specialty you possess and can offer. It can be the other way around: You may discover a small segment of the market that has a special need that is not very well satisfied by the current and typical suppliers of that market. Perhaps you do not originally have that special ability to find and recruit rocket scientists or calligraphers, but you discover that there is a substantial niche market for them. You then woo that market, while you develop a special ability to satisfy its needs. The result is the same as the other way around: You have virtually captured a market you can call your own. This is a valid approach to marketing; even the larger companies are beginning to recognize the importance of pursuing niche markets.

CHAPTER 10

CONTRACTING VIA JOB SHOPS AND BROKERS

The ideal business situation for the typical independent consultant is to work on projects contracted directly and independently with clients. But many consultants, especially those starting new practices, are not nearly as effective at marketing their services directly as they are at performing them. Or they deem their time to be too valuable to spend in marketing if they can avoid so spending it. Hence, many consultants turn to a variety of alternative marketing methods whereby others, who are marketing specialists, find assignments for them and take fees or commissions for their services.

BROKERAGE IS A TIME-HONORED BUSINESS

There are few businesses or industries that do not have brokers of some sort, although they are not always known by that term. They are also called *finders, dealers, agents, representatives,* and *commission merchants* and are known as well by many other terms (including *job shops* and, sometimes, even "body shops," or sellers of "warm bodies"), but their basic function is invariably the same: They sell something to be provided by someone else. They are middlemen and middlewomen, in the vernacular, functioning between the provider of the goods or service and the buyer. In some situations they work as agents for or representatives of one party or the other, but they also often work as total independents, representing themselves only. The literary agent who sells a writer's books or plays is thus a broker. The agent who finds work for an actor or entertainer is a broker. The agency that furnishes models for advertising purposes is a broker. The local copy shop that arranges to have your business cards or wedding invitations printed by a larger or more specialized printer is a broker. The local business service that accepts your parcel for shipment by some common carrier is a broker, as is the travel agency that books you on a flight or a vacation tour. The tailor shop that sends your clothes off somewhere for dry cleaning and your shoes somewhere else for lifts or heels is a broker. Sometimes they are paid commissions, while sometimes they pay wholesale prices and charge retail, earning a profit or markup as their fees. Whatever it is called, they earn the difference between what the customer or client pays and what the provider is paid. Thus, they may or may not do billing and handle the money in the transactions.

In light of all this, it should come as no great surprise that there are brokers who sell your own specialized services to clients and earn fees or commissions for themselves by doing so.

90

Unfortunately, many consultants feel compelled to condemn brokers; ironically, they are usually the ones who take the greatest advantage from the brokers' services. Yes, there are unscrupulous brokers, but the vast majority are honest, and the broker is entitled to be compensated for his or her service. Only you can be the judge of what value the business the broker provides you with.

None of this is to say that brokering is not an honorable enterprise, that brokers do not serve a legitimate function and provide a useful purpose, or that they do not merit their earnings. Unfortunately, a great many of those who turn to brokers regularly or even only occasionally for help in getting work to sustain their enterprises are inclined to criticize and even denounce brokers as exploiters and parasites. They begrudge the broker his or her fees, while obviously acknowledging the need for and utility of the broker's service by taking advantage of it to find assignments. But while there are some unscrupulous brokers who will take advantage of both clients and consultants when they get the opportunity to do so, that should not constitute a reason to condemn all brokers, as some consultants seem inclined to do. Marketing – getting business – is an honorable and useful function – a valuable function, in fact – and the marketer is entitled to be compensated for his or her service. Still, there are various opinions. One consultant raises the point by asking what it is about working through a broker that one might find advantageous, as compared with selling services directly to the client.

The answer to that question depends entirely on your personal view. Some of us so dislike marketing that any alternative is preferable. Others perceive that marketing for yourself has its drawbacks: What you pay a broker, whether directly as a commission or indirectly as a markup of your own charges, is in lieu of what it would cost you to go out and do that marketing for yourself. It costs money to market, no matter who does it, you or someone else. Also, there is a risk in marketing for yourself: There is that clear and distinct possibility that your entire marketing effort and expense – advertising, time, travel, and the rest of it – will not win any business. Then you have a double loss: money and time. On the other hand, when the broker earns a commission or markup on an assignment he or she has provided for you, it is for guaranteed work that is at no risk to yourself. Try to take a balanced view, therefore, and perceive both the pros and the cons of using the services of brokers in winning work assignments.

JOB SHOPS AND BROKERS

In 1991, the 25th Silver Anniversary Convention of the National Association of Temporary Services celebrated 25 years of existence as the pre-eminent association of companies in the temporary industry. The convention saluted an industry that boasts an annual payroll in excess of $10 billion and employs more than a million people working as temporaries on any average business day of the year.

Supplying temporaries of any class or category is not a business or industry in which only a few large companies are dominant. On the contrary, because it does not take a great deal of capital investment or highly specialized requirements to enter this business and provide temporaries, the industry is characterized by only a few truly large suppliers and many small ones. There are, in fact, more than 1,000 companies supplying temporaries operating out of 7,700 offices across the United States. Basically, it is a small business by its nature, but it is large in the aggregate as a national industry.

Some substantial portion of the one-million-plus work force this industry represents consists of office temporaries, working on short-term assignments as secretarial and clerical help. Just about everyone knows of these people, mostly women, as the familiar "office temps" or "Kelly Girls." For those who are not really familiar with this industry, the very word "temp" is a code that refers to an office worker. That's because a great many people do not know that there are many other kinds of temps, especially technical and professional specialists. Nurses are one very visible example: There are many short-term needs for nursing services, and many nurses prefer to work on individual assignments, rather than in permanent staff positions. But there are many other examples as well. The shortages of skilled people, the sharp advances in technology, and the demands of many huge government defense contracts in the 1950s spawned the sudden growth of needs for scientists, engineers, architects, computer programmers, technical writers, editors, illustrators, draftsmen and draftswomen, administrators, and sundry others, to meet contract obligations. Although most of these had always been career positions, many specialists accepted short-term assignments, running from a few weeks to several years. Predictably, brokers sprang up to help satisfy the demand for these individuals' services.

The providers of engineering and other technical specialists of various kinds initially, and computer programming and other specialists later, soon became known as *job shops.* Originally, the term was applied to machine-tool shops that specialized in subcontracting portions of contracts from large firms (e.g., machining the tail-fin assembly of a small tactical missile) and otherwise handling a variety of individual jobs, usually as subcontractors. Consequently, providers of engineering, computer, and other technical specialists as temporary workers became, colloquially, *job shops,* and those who were employed by and worked on assignments from these shops became known as *job shoppers,* a term that has stuck stubbornly to the industry and is well understood today by those working within it. (The term is often used somewhat derisively, even by those who apply it to themselves.)

AS THE CLIENT SEES THE SERVICE

Typically, the contractor who needs a number of specialists, but only for a relatively short term—for example, for the life of the current contract or for some single phase of a contract—doesn't want to hire such people as permanent employees. Recruitment of permanent employees is expensive: It costs money to run advertising and to pay recruiters and employment agencies, and it takes time, which is also costly. Further, it costs money to terminate employees, to furnish notice of their termination, and to give them severance pay. It is often much more in an employer's interest to hire a consultant or contractor than a permanent employee. Then, you and your services are simply a purchase, handled not much differently than the purchase of a machine or a shipment of supplies: There is no withholding tax, FICA, sick leave, insurance, and all the rest of that kind of administrative overburden. Too, if you are unsatisfactory as a subcontractor or temporary employee, it takes only a telephone call to the job shop to terminate you immediately. There is no notice or severance pay required and no unpleasant confrontation: One need not continue to suffer a less than satisfactory employee because of the well-known reluctance to confront the employee and tell him or her of the termination. (And even that is not the whole reason for the reluctance to fire unsatisfactory employees: Today, fired employees have a tendency to sue employers, another costly result, even when the employer successfully defends the lawsuit. This also discourages terminating marginal or unsatisfactory employees.)

91

There are benefits for both the client and the consultant in working through a job shop. The client avoids many financial, legal, and personal burdens involved in hiring a permanent employee, and the consultant usually gets a higher fee and a frequent change of challenges, scenery, and pace.

To gain all these benefits, which translate into a substantial cash value, the client is willing to pay a higher rate for a consultant than he or she would be willing to pay a permanent employee doing the same job. Even at a higher direct rate of pay, the client can save money and minimize problems.

Sometimes the client hires a few consultants or subcontractors directly, under individual contracts, but generally, the client is not suitably equipped to do this, particularly when he or she needs a number of specialists. So the client turns to a professional supplier of such help, a job shop, and the job shop recruits the people needed, sometimes by a concerted recruiting campaign and sometimes by the simple expedient of calling individuals whose resumes they have on file. The job shop is equipped to do this, with thick files of resumes and people trained in the field of recruiting and placing a variety of technical and professional specialists. These personnel recruiters run help-wanted advertisements, and make many telephone calls to the people whose resumes they have on file. Many even help their recruits write a resume and prepare them for interviews with the client. (Yes, interviewing high-priced specialists for important assignments before accepting them either as contract labor or as independent contractors and subcontractors is a normal practice and should not surprise anyone. Even with the option of readily terminating contractors who are not satisfactory, clients prefer to interview aspirants and satisfy themselves that they are competent and compatible with the client's general environment.)

Normally, the technical and professional temporaries go out on assignment as employees of the job shop – true W2 employees, with taxes withheld and salaries paid every week, even though they enjoy only minimal, if any, fringe benefits. (Usually there is health or hospitalization insurance, and sometimes there are even a few sick leave and vacation days.) Their status as employees of the job shop normally is coincident with their employment by the client: It begins on the day they report to the client and ends on the last day of their assignment, unless the job shop has another assignment to send them on immediately. In return for giving up the advantages of being a regular employee, job-shopping specialists usually earn a rate of pay that is from one and one-half to two or more times the rate they might reasonably expect to be paid as a regular employee. (Job shoppers are often offered permanent staff jobs by clients, but usually decline the offers because the salaries are usually substantially less than they are earning as temporary employees.)

AS MANY CONSULTANTS VIEW
THE ARRANGEMENT

Many consultants and other specialists prefer to work as job shoppers for one reason or another. Some prefer the higher direct income to the indirect income of typical fringe benefits and the greater job security of regular career employment. Others choose subcontracting and job shopping because they dislike the marketing aspect of consulting – the search for and selling of their services to prospective clients. Still others work as truly independent consultants, but turn to this indirect means of finding assignments occasionally, when they cannot find direct contracts or are just starting out as consultants. Yet others become a kind of independent, one-person job shop, selling themselves directly as temporaries working on the client's premises at an hourly or daily rate.

The job shop operates between Heaven and Earth: It is not a brokerage in the classic sense, for it actually *employs* the consultant and carries out the minimal functions of an employer. Yet, in a broader sense, it is truly a brokerage in that it provides the consultant and his or her services, but nothing else: It does not take on project responsibility, work on a fixed-price contract, or commit itself to some end product or result. In fact, the job shop is responsible only for seeing that the "warm body" shows up on schedule and for nothing else.

Interestingly, marketing your services as a consultant-temporary, either via a job shop or directly, is not the only way in which you can market yourself on the basis of an hourly or daily rate or through another organization. There is another middle-person arrangement in vogue today, the true labor broker, someone who makes no pretense to being an employer of the consultants he or she provides to clients, but merely provides the labor. Labor brokers have come on the scene to provide help to clients on a somewhat different basis than that of employers of consultants whom they assign to the client, although the difference is transparent to the client: The labor broker contracts with the client to provide consultant specialists or temporaries to serve on the client's site, rather than contracting for a fixed-price job of some sort. That is, like the job shop, the labor broker does not normally undertake to deliver an end product, but only to provide qualified specialists—consultants, working as temporaries. In this arrangement, the temporaries are not employees of the provider, as they are in the case of job shops: They are independent subcontractors, what are known as "1099" contractors. That is an allusion to the government form 1099 which the client must supply to the IRS and to the contractor. And since, in this case, the temporary is a subcontractor to the broker, he or she must be furnished form 1099, which the broker also provides the IRS, showing information on money paid the consultant-temporary, who is an independent contractor paying his or her own taxes.

The client does not normally care whether the temporary is an employee of or a subcontractor to the provider: The consultant represents temporary labor services, a quasi-employee on a temporary basis. The services tend to be based on an hourly rate, although each individual negotiates for his or her services individually with the job shop or broker and may prefer to negotiate a daily or even weekly rate. Trying to strike average or typical rates is difficult, since the rates vary with location or geographic area, with the type of work, with what is normally paid to direct employees for similar work and responsibility, and with the individual situation and person. In a brokerage arrangement in its purest form, the broker ought to be marking up what he or she pays the individual consultant 10 to 15 percent, according to the opinions of many in the industry, although there are undoubtedly some who mark up their subcontracts considerably more than this. In a job shop arrangement, the conditions are quite different, since the job shop is liable for the employer's share of taxes and other obligations, as well as typical overhead. The job shop probably experiences an overhead rate of 30 to 35 percent, so the markup of the hourly rate paid the individual is likely to be 10 to 15 percent above that.

92

Newcomers to brokerages should beware of being exploited. Because it is so difficult for shops to increase their markups otherwise, both brokers and job shops can and do increase their markups when they recruit newcomers. Almost invariably, the newcomer is totally unschooled in the way brokers and job shops do business and asks for or is persuaded to accept a rate well below the maximum he or she could have gotten based on the broker's or job shop's charges to clients. (Where a number of job shoppers are employed on an assignment, those new to the business are often dismayed to learn that others are getting considerably more than they are.) If you contemplate winning some of your business by this route, be sure to make inquiries to find out what you ought to ask for and demand as your minimum. You may find out that the rate is considerably higher than you suspected.

THE ECONOMIC PRESSURES

It's a competitive business: brokers and job shops vie fiercely for clients. This competition puts downward pressure on the rates job shops and brokers can charge clients, of course, and thus constrains markups. But it also puts downward pressure on the rates offered the consultants. The result is that these rates are not linked to rates paid permanent employees, so the rate you might get in that capacity is not a guideline to what you can ask for and get in the temporary situation. For some years, there was an acute shortage of engineers and many other kinds of specialists. That put the specialist in the driver's seat in negotiating rates for assignments, and experienced job shoppers knew how to turn that to advantage and exact top rates for their services. Today, the situation is stable, and the individual must be competitive in his or her demands once again. It can be important to know how to negotiate, but you must also know the condition of the immediate market and how that affects your bargaining power at the moment.

93

Argument rages today among many consultants as to whether they are entitled to know the rates at which their services are sold to clients. Some maintain that intermediaries such as brokers and job shops are understandably entitled to keep that information confidential, while others insist that they have the right to know the rates at which their services are being sold. Some report that intermediaries resist pressures to reveal their rates and markups, while others say their own intermediaries are free with information about their selling prices. There seems to be no uniformity in how various intermediaries regard the confidentiality of their rates, so as a rule, ask what the selling price is anyway.

THE IRS TAKES A POSITION

So far so good: Brokerages and job shops sound like a good way for everyone to get what he or she wants. The client gets help at an acceptable cost, the broker or job shop earns an acceptable fee or markup, and the consultant does not need to go knocking on doors to get work and income to meet his or her needs. But apparently, the IRS does not believe that it gets what it wants or should have in many of these arrangements. The IRS does not always agree, for example, to recognize the temporary employee as an independent contractor simply because the employee says that he or she is an independent contractor. The IRS may say that the temporary is actually an employee disguised as an independent contractor and thus not entitled to the normal business deductions. Moreover, the IRS may say that the temporary is an employee of the client or of the broker, depending on whether the consultant has contracted directly with the client or with a broker, and may go after the client or the broker for withholding tax, FICA, and anything else an employer is normally liable for.

This is not to say that the IRS's judgment and decisions in the matter are entirely arbitrary: The agency does furnish some rules and guidelines – the well-known 20 questions of the IRS regulations for determining whether you are an independent contractor or an employee. Some of the key considerations are where you work (on your own premises or on the client's premises), what responsibility you have (to furnish only undefined services or some specific product or outcome), from whom you take directions or orders, and how many other clients you have. Working on the client's premises entirely or primarily, being committed only for general services rather than to a specific project or product, taking directions and orders directly from the client, and having only one client for the year or for most of the year are all suggestive of being an employee and not an independent contractor. The last is almost a catch 22: If you work on long-term assignments – that is, have only one client on a long-term basis – that is prima facie evidence to the IRS that you are an employee and not an independent contractor at all. So to overcome the problem, you may feel compelled to accept short-term assignments only, and those from a variety of clients. Doing so, however, raises your marketing costs and increases your idle time, thereby raising your overhead costs.

94

One factor the consultant must keep in mind in going out as a "temp" is the increasing tendency of the IRS to see temporary consultants as employees of their clients, rather than as independent contractors. If you fall into this category, you can lose deductions and get hit with withholding and other taxes. Your exposure to such a decision is less with shorter term assignments. Study section 1706 of the IRS regulations concerning consultants to help clarify your position.

The net effect on clients is an increasing reluctance to hire independent consultants by contracting with them. The effect on brokers is to drive many into becoming job shops and acting as employers of record, rather than contracting with consultants as independent 1099 contractors or subcontractors. In many cases, clients concerned over the position the IRS takes, as well as over general business and legal considerations, began to require independent consultants to be incorporated before the clients would agree to contract independently with them. (The presumption was that incorporation was evidence that the consultant was an independent contractor, but it seems to have had rather little effect on IRS thinking in determining who is truly an independent consultant and who is an employee thinly disguised as an independent consultant.) The result seems to be that, increasingly today, at least in some areas, both clients and brokers prefer to hire consultants as W2 temporaries. Word comes from independent consultants in the Phoenix, Arizona, area, for example, that most brokers in the area have switched all their contracts over to the W2 arrangement and that many consultants living in that area commute from as far away as San Diego to accept assignments as true independent contractors. And so the distinction between brokers and job shops grows more and more indistinct, as the pressure on brokers to become job shops grows and clients become more and more bearish about contracting long term with independent consultants who will work on the client's premises without clear and specific project responsibilities.

PRIME CONTRACTORS VERSUS BROKERS

As with brokers and job shops, the distinction between labor brokers and prime contractors is often not clear. A prime contractor often hires subcontractors. For example, RCA, prime contractor to the U.S. Air Force for the huge BMEWS (Ballistic Missile Early Warning System), awarded some 360 subcontracts. The practice is not unusual: Most large prime contracts are satisfied by a large number of subcontracts, and your "independent" contracts are often just that—subcontracts to help your client fulfill his or her prime contract. But a prime contractor undertakes a specific project, entailing total responsibility to produce some end product or end result. Subcontractors are also committed to specific products or goals, and not just services in general.

Now, there are many contractors of specialized services who hire subcontractors and who work wholly or partially on the client's premises. That does not of itself make them labor brokers. Probably, the sensible distinction is that the true contractor has a permanent staff of individuals skilled in whatever are the kinds of services the contractor offers or the projects the contractor is willing to undertake, and the contractor's own permanent staff manages the work and directs the efforts of the subcontractors hired, whereas the labor broker has only marketing and administrative permanent staff, who undertake none of the work but subcontract every task of the project.

95

It may seem that it should make little difference to you whether you hire out as a 1099 (independent contractor) consultant or as a W2 (payroll employee) consultant. In fact, however, if you have significant expenses that you must pay out of your own pocket—expenses for travel, licenses, seminars, hardware, and software, for example—it does make a difference: You can't write off those expenses as a W2 employee. Either you must get your employer of record to pay the expenses by compensating you for them, or you must "eat" them yourself. In the latter case, you had better take those costs into consideration in negotiating a rate for your services. Furthermore, you might wish to bear in mind that if you are a W2 employee, your employer must pay the employer's share of FICA, whereas if you are an independent contractor, you must pay it all. At today's rates, this is not a small sum of money.

A key question revolves around what the contract with the client calls for. Does it specify a result or product, or does it call simply for services? A true project contract will specify the product or other result required, and the contractor will decide when, where, and how his or her services will be performed to produce the specified result. And that test has to be as valid for the contract between the independent consultant (or independent contractor) and the labor broker as it is for the contract between the labor broker and the ultimate client.

RATES OF PAY

As noted earlier, as a job shopper you are likely to earn from about one and one-half to two or even three times the hourly rate you would earn as a "captive" or "direct" (terms used by job shoppers to describe permanent, staff employees) employee. (I went from $4.00 per hour—it was 1960—to $6.50 per hour in one jump in this manner.)

If the job is too far from your home for you to commute daily, requiring you to undertake extra living expenses (50 miles was the determining distance when I was so employed), you should be paid per diem allowances. In 1960, was $56 per week, or $1.40 per hour, and it was not entirely adequate even then, although it was a boon for some who traveled to the jobs with their own house trailers or similar vehicles.

Rates can vary rather widely, depending on how good a negotiator you are. I negotiated the then top rate of $6.50 per hour, not because I was a good negotiator, but because I really didn't want to work out of town, and the job shop wanted me more than I wanted the job! (I discovered later that I happened to have some credentials the client thought especially useful for him, and he pressed the job shop to persuade me to accept the assignment.)

It is important that you learn to be a good negotiator. Unless conditions change considerably, you will not be able to rely on economic pressure to help you get the top rate.

96

Everything is subject to negotiation. Although a broker or job shop may intimate that rates are fixed, they are not. Always assume that you can negotiate just a bit better rate for yourself.

CONTRACTS: ASPECTS AND PROBLEMS

Consultants hiring out as temporaries via job shops, being W2 employees of the job shop, do not usually sign contracts. Those accepting assignments from brokers as 1099 independent contractors normally are required by the broker to sign a contract. The contract must stipulate the financial considerations, of course, as well as the term of work, the place and working hours, and other items normally found in any contract. But there are also some special elements, at least two of which need careful consideration.

First, there is the exclusivity clause, in which you agree that you will not accept contracts directly from any other client during the life of the contract. Brokers may also ask that you agree to refuse to accept other work independently from the client for some period following the expiration of the contract. Such clauses seem to be in direct conflict with your status as an independent contractor, of course.

Then there are termination clauses, which also can be treacherous. Of course, the other party will try to keep all the initiatives for termination of the contract and leave you few, if any. Such clauses require careful scrutiny and careful thought.

In sum, it may be well worth the cost to have an attorney examine the contract and advise you before you sign on the dotted line.

Job shop operators are also concerned that you do not take advantage of a short-term assignment to go to work subsequently as an employee of one of their clients. And they are concerned that the client does not take advantage of the job shop's recruitment of temporaries to find new permanent employees at no cost to itself. Therefore, job shops may ask clients to sign agreements limiting their freedom to hire temporaries as direct employees or requiring them to pay the job shop a placement fee, and they may also ask you to sign an agreement limiting your freedom to accept a permanent job with any client on whose premises you are working as a temporary.

MARKETING YOURSELF AS A JOB SHOPPER

As noted before, a great many consultant specialists have been attracted to job shopping as a way of professional life. They like being able to move about the country. (Some even own house trailers or vans, so that they take their living quarters with them.) They like being able to take frequent vacations between assignments. They like the sense of freedom and independence they have. And they like being able to concentrate their energies entirely on their work and never having to worry about marketing their services. (Actually, the latter isn't entirely true: They do have to take certain steps to ensure that they work an adequate number of days to produce income.) Accordingly, they follow certain practices that have become a kind of sine qua non for those who pursue job shopping seriously:

- Keep a current resume on file with a number of job shops.
- The day you report to an assignment, the first thing to do is to call all job shops you know of and advise them where you are and how you can be reached.
- Immediately update your resume to reflect your newest assignment, and mail copies of the resume to all job shops you know of and keep on your mailing or resource list.
- "Touch base" with every other job shopper on the assignment, and get briefed on all news of interest, including (as far as you can manage it) learning what others are getting in the way of hourly rates and per diem allowances.

Having your resume on file at many shops can lead to unusual situations. On one occasion, a certain job shop sent me to General Electric Company's Missiles and Space Division to be interviewed as a technical writer. I reported to the GE offices in Radnor, Pennsylvania,

══ **97** ══

If you are a career job shopper, keep a list of job shops, and leave up-to-date resumes on file with them. Especially do this with job shops where you are frequently employed and sent on assignments. That is one means of maximizing your opportunities for assignments.

and was duly interviewed. At the conclusion of the interview, I was asked to report for work the following Monday. But as I was about to leave, the interviewer said, "Whom do you work for? We have copies of your resume from a half-dozen job shops, and I don't care whom you work for, but I have to know whom to pay for your services."

Slightly stunned, I named the shop that had sent me in for the interview, although I could have named any shop, I suppose. But I thought my decision was the ethical one to make. (I must confess that at least some job shoppers are not as ethical as they might be, operating always on the premise that job shopping is a dog-eat-dog proposition, which, they believe, entitles them to indulge in rather sharp business practices.)

I worked always as a technical writer, generally regarded as one of the many engineering specialties and one in which there seemed, at the time, to be plenty of work available at all times. In any case, I never had any difficulty finding assignments.

Many others whom I knew preferred to work as engineers, but couldn't always find suitable assignments when they were at liberty. On the other hand, many veteran job shoppers I knew were competent and could function well in a number of specialties. Therefore, for many, the solution was to have a number of resumes, each of which offered their services in a different capacity. They had resumes extolling their virtues as engineers, designers, draftsmen, technical writers, technical editors, and sundry other technical and professional specialists. One man I knew had, in fact, 12 different resumes and could function acceptably well in all of them. He was thus able to work on one assignment or another with few idle periods of any length.

THE ONE-MAN OR ONE-WOMAN JOB SHOP

Many experienced career job shoppers have abandoned sending their resumes to established job shops and have begun to circulate their resumes only to companies at which they think they can win assignments as individuals contracting directly with the clients. They make up lists of those companies on whose premises they formerly worked and lists of other potential clients they know or have learned of through the grapevine. Thus, they cut the broker or job shop out of the picture altogether, both saving the client some money and earning more for themselves.

98

If you are in a situation in which a client wishes to hire you to function in general terms, handling a variety of duties without a clear-cut objective, it may be helpful for tax purposes to specify in your contract the development of a report as the product of the assignment, even if the assignment is long term and is to be conducted entirely on the client's premises. It is also helpful, however, to contract for at least some of the work to be done on your premises, using your own equipment.

However, there is a problem virtually built into this arrangement vis-a-vis the position of the IRS: One test of the individual consultant as a true consultant or contractor, rather than a temporary employee disguised as an independent consultant, is the assumption of responsibility for a project with a specific product that emerges at the end. Admittedly, many projects involve no truly tangible product, but it is always possible (and in government contracting generally required) to specify some kind of a product, be it a length of magnetic tape, a few floppy disks, or a written report of some kind. So you must make sure to produce something tangible on every assignment, to satisfy the IRS. (This is rarely a problem in technical writing assignments, for a specific product is always at stake: a manual, a proposal, a report, an illustrated parts breakdown, or some other kind of documentation.)

CHAPTER 11

INFORMATION AND GOING ONLINE

The quality of the business decisions, plans, projections, reports, and whatever else you produce for yourself and for your clients is not an independent variable. It depends heavily—indeed, almost entirely, in many cases—on the quality of the information you have and can use in whatever processes you employ to produce end results.

THE SEAS OF INFORMATION

I once worked for a company that was a division of a major corporation, a conglomerate. The division that employed me specialized in designing and manufacturing custom machines to automate various industrial manufacturing operations. One of their projects called for designing and manufacturing a machine to pack chocolates, delicate and expensive confections that must, understandably, be handled with great care. The machine that evolved from the effort worked well, fortunately. The company executives were so delighted with the results that they ordered the marketing staff out to seek more orders for this wonderful new boon to the bonbon industry. Before long, the sales force had brought in orders for two more machines.

At this point, everyone in the company saw a winner, and management, encouraged by an enthusiastic marketing director, went on to order the manufacture of three more machines for inventory, so that future orders could be filled promptly as they came in.

Months later, the three machines built for inventory were reposing quietly, gathering dust in a cavernous warehouse: No more orders had been forthcoming, despite energetic marketing. Concern then grew and a formal market study was ordered. The market research report was devastating: There were only six bonbon candy manufacturers in the entire world large enough to afford and justify the purchase of a half-million-dollar (1964 dollars) machine such as this, and the company had already saturated the market by capturing a full one-half of it. Obviously, the company was stuck with three white elephants.

The failure was really one of information – the lack of it, that is: No one in our marketing department had contemplated doing the proper market research in advance, to find out what the true market potential of the machine was. It was a typical seat-of-the-pants marketing decision, a high-risk decision and a resulting disaster. What was particularly inexcusable was that the pertinent market information that would have prevented the disaster was easily available, even in those days before today's great information era. A visit to a local library or even a call to Dun & Bradstreet would have elicited the right information.

In a much happier experience a few years ago, a client of my own, who was in the steel-fabricating business, had developed some interest in doing business with the government. The client asked me to investigate the federal government market for steel shelters – for example, sheet steel enclosures of various sorts purchased by government agencies for any purpose whatever.

In response to the client's request, I used a local information service to which I was a subscriber that could provide access to a public online data base called "CBD ONLINE." The service is a computerized version of the federal government's publication *Commerce Business Daily*, in which agencies advertise their procurement needs and opportunities to compete for contracts. I asked the service to search the data base for the previous few months' notices of solicitations and awards of steel shelters. The search took about an hour of computer time and cost approximately $90. It took only another hour or two to sort, edit, organize, and compile the results into a report to my client, who now had the information he needed to proceed in developing the company's marketing plans as reality, and not fancy or wishful thinking, dictated.

Of course, it isn't always marketing information that you and your clients want to research and gather. You may be scheduled to have a meeting with a client who expects you to produce, on demand, information on other subjects in which you are reputed to be knowledgeable. Here are just a few of the many other kinds of data you may seek or lists you may need to gather quickly to satisfy your or your clients' wants:

- Labor rates in some other city or some specific profession.
- Associations within some industry.
- Profiles of major cities.
- Speakers' bureaus.
- News of the hour.
- Information on meeting facilities.
- Standard Industrial Code numbers.
- State or local government procurement offices.
- Patent and trademark searches.
- Legal precedents.
- Statistics on almost any subject.
- Weather reports.
- Sources of certain rare materials.
- Books in print.
- Articles and monographs.
- Lists of who's who in one field or another.
- Today's opening quotations on commodities.

The list could easily go on for many pages and could become a great deal more detailed and demanding. Moreover, you may be seeking full text, abstracts, or only bibliographic listings, and you may even need it "yesterday," which brings up an interesting question: How important is it that you get the information you need *now*, and not tomorrow or sometime later? Often, that is the real problem: not the availability, but the immediacy, of information. You don't have time to go to the library and spend even an hour or two browsing there, hoping you will get the information and that it will be up to date. You need the information right now, at your fingertips, so to speak. For those who have gotten aboard the online express, spending a lot of time getting information is a thing of the past. More and more, it takes less and less time to gather the information we need. (We probably spend much more time today deter-

99

> In our technological society, the speed with which consultants can obtain data will be a key to their success. We are in an era of information — surrounded by it, immersed in it, perhaps even drowning in it because so few of us have yet learned how to swim in it, and it gets deeper almost daily. But we must learn to do so. We must learn how to go online if we are even to survive, much less prosper, as professionals — as experts and consultants to others.

mining what kind of information we need than we do gathering the information.

ONLINE LITERACY

For a time, as the personal computer caught on and was being installed in millions of offices and private homes, we were being urged and even harangued by many writers to become "computer literate." No one managed to explain that idea with any great success. Just what did "computer literate" mean? Did it mean becoming something called a "power user," a truly proficient computerphile, a maven of the monitor and keyboard? Or was it sufficient to learn how to use a word processor and do a few simple sums via the keyboard and monitor? To be computer literate, must you be able to call up your local bulletin board and join in the gossip and political arguments there? We never knew at just what point one becomes computer literate and at what point he or she can brag of being a power user or a maven of some degree. Perhaps it is something like language literacy: Those who can read comic books may be deemed literate, but only as long as they confine themselves to comic books and do not attempt to read papers by theoretical physicists or novels by Russian writers.

Never mind; it's unimportant now. It is no longer enough to be merely computer literate, in whatever sense of computer expertise the term is used. The technology is moving much faster than anyone anticipated. Consequently, most of us, especially we who are consultants and must always be at the leading edge of our own professional specialties, must master the most essential tools available today. We must learn to exploit the incredibly rich resources awaiting us as online capabilities. We must become "online literate," part of the online society.

AN APOLOGIA

Many of you reading this are presumably already expert in computers and thoroughly familiar with online operation. To all of you, I beg your indulgence as I plod through some most basic fundamentals for those who have not arrived at this happy state and who need the information that many of us accept as primary education, and I ask you to be patient. I believe that before we reach the end of the chapter, I will have offered something of utility to everyone here, even those who use a keyboard daily, and made it worth your while to be patient.

THE ONLINE SOCIETY

That we have become a computerized society is no secret to any literate adult today: Even those who have never had direct, personal contact with a computer and keyboard must be aware of the presence of the personal computer everywhere today – in offices, in stores, in institutions of all kinds, and in private homes. The high-tech era of the past few decades has spawned a few catchwords and catchphrases that have persisted and been used often enough to become clichés. Some of the shibboleths that come to mind immediately are *technology transfer, information explosion,* and *knowledge industry.* We find that we are also being assured that this is the *Information Age,* another term pronounced with all the solemnity of one announcing a new Ice Age or a new Industrial Revolution, with the latter comparison not entirely inappropriate. Perhaps this is, indeed, a new Industrial Revolution or, perhaps, even that same Industrial Revolution merely at the doorstep of a new, advanced phase.

The modern personal computer has given most cogent emphasis to the idea of technology transfer. Nowhere has the concept become more of a reality: Modern chip-based computer technology has been married to many older technologies as a result of the microminiaturization and minuscule power requirements of computer circuits today. The new products, miniaturized to a degree not even dreamed of a few decades ago, have replaced or modernized our radios, typewriters, telephones, calculators, cash registers, and a great many other things to an extent that makes many of these familiar devices virtually new inventions with only ancient roots in the technologies from which they sprang. And not the least of the revolutionary developments has been the impact of the present-day computer on the information explosion and concomitant knowledge industry. Where once only a handful of large organizations could afford to own computers or knew even what to do with them, today those large organizations have computers by the dozens, and millions of individuals have their own computers in their homes and offices. The effect on world society has been profound, meriting the overworked word *revolutionary.*

As a matter of fact, we had been advised of the arrival of the information explosion and knowledge industry for several decades. The announcement was based on the growing knowledge of what the computer could do and be. It had become a growing conviction ever since it became apparent that the computer – the behemoth mainframe computer of a few decades ago – was here to stay and was a far more significant development than anyone had suspected in the beginning. It was reported that IBM founder Thomas J. Watson, far less prescient than his later success suggested he had been, had remarked in 1943 that he saw a world market for about five computers. Data processing was pronounced a fad by a Prentice-Hall business book editor in 1957, who predicted that it wouldn't last out that year. As late as 1977, Ken Olson, president of Digital Equipment Corporation (which was to become, eventually, a major player in the computer industry), said he saw no reason for anyone to ever want to have a computer in his or her home. And in March 1949, with the pioneer ENIAC computer with its 18,000 vacuum tubes and 30 tons of weight clearly in mind, a writer in *Popular Mechanics* magazine made the understatement of the year (or maybe the century): An article he wrote for the magazine predicted that in years to come, the most modern computers would weigh as little as 1.5 tons.

Obviously, no one understood where we and our computers were heading, or what our future would be, even when it became clear that computers were here to stay and would be a continuing influence. But we had at least reached the point where we had begun to understand that the computer was something more than a giant adding machine or supercalculator. (The ENIAC [Electronic Numerical Integrator and Calculator] had been funded by the Department of Defense during World War II, to calculate artillery trajectories, a complicated mathematical problem.) We had just begun to grasp the simple fact that the digital computer had an unparalleled capability for helping humans gather, sort, analyze, compile, organize, store, and retrieve information of all kinds – that it could do in minutes what human beings could not do in hours and in hours what human beings could not do in months. (In fact, we would eventually learn that the computer could do many things that people could not do at all without the computer.) But the best was yet to come: We had hardly gotten under the outer skin of this new technology.

With the advent and early maturation of what has long outlived the name but is still erroneously called the *personal computer* (it is, in fact, much more than that: It is also the main computer today for millions of small businesses and other organizations), the knowledge industry reached a dimension never envisioned in the day of the behemoth we now refer to as the mainframe. Today, millions of individuals – virtually anyone and everyone – can gain *direct* access to the mountains of data that are available through a computer. Even a so-called laptop or note-book model can plug into an incredible array of information and communications resources by "going online." Alfred Glossbrenner, in the first edition (1981) of *The Complete Handbook of Personal Computer Communications,* was reporting on 600 data bases offered by 93 online services, he tells us eight years later in his third edition of that book. In the later edition, he reports information on 4,024 data bases offered by 586 online systems, with the numbers still expanding rapidly. (You can see by these numbers alone that many online systems provide access to many data bases.) With your personal computer, a modem, and a dial-up telephone connection, you can reach any of these services and the data bases to which they provide access from your own desk and retrieve any information available there. You can view the information on your own monitor's screen, store it on a disk, print it out on paper, or all of these.

Does this seem rather mysterious? Probably to the uninitiated it does. But even if you have yet to press a key on a computer keyboard for the first time in your life, you have probably gone online in one way or another, although you may not have realized that that was what you were doing. Consider the following actions, which have become quite everyday for most of us.

When you go to an ATM to withdraw cash from your account or to borrow cash against a credit card, your transaction is verified and approved – or disapproved – via online communication between the ATM computer and whatever other computer is capable of examining your account and authorized to issue an approval or disapproval. You are online when you press the keys to identify yourself by your PIN (personal identification number) and order the transaction. It doesn't matter where you are: You can be at the other end of the continent, in Canada, or anywhere else in the world; if there is an ATM available, it will go online for you to deliver what you ask for.

Online communications are used to verify your credit card purchases and other transactions while you wait at the register counter in a store, no matter how far you are from home or from the bank that issues the credit card. They are also the means by which an automobile dealer calls a credit-reporting bureau and gets while-you-wait approval for financing your new automobile. When I couldn't find my special discount card while purchasing a book at Waldenbooks recently, the clerk found my name and membership in minutes, using his personal computer to query the company's central computer. When I wanted to find out what was available on the subject of data-base marketing, I enlisted the aid of a national library research program while seated at my desk in my own home. Within minutes, I had a lengthy listing of book titles on my computer screen. In those few minutes, I had queried computers and searched indexes and catalogs in libraries from California to Massachusetts. I have used the online capabilities of my computer to make airline and hotel reservations, to look up a name and address or telephone number in another city, and to communicate directly with friends and acquaintances all over the world.

I subscribe to several electronic bulletin boards, on which I exchange ideas and information with others. (I check several of these for messages the first thing every morning.) You need no longer be a specially trained expert to do these things. You do, however, need to understand the shape and structure of the online universe we have fashioned and the several major elements that define it. On the other hand, you do not need to understand, even in a general way, the elemental technology transfer that has taken place between the computer and the telephone, which is at the basis of all data communications. However, you will probably be more comfortable having some knowledge of what the elements are and how they interact with each other.

THE TELEPHONE-COMPUTER MARRIAGE

Telephone lines are the essential common ingredient in all online activities, and both conventional dial-up lines and dedicated lines are used. Computers "talk" to each other — transfer data — via telephone lines; however, the computer and the telephone speak different languages. Computers speak *bits* and *bytes*, which are electrical pulses. In a sense, they speak a very simple language, with only two basic elements: a pulse and the absence of a pulse. (In computer engineering, the two elements or signals are often referred to as "marks" and "spaces," although they are also referred to as "1's" and "0's" or "high" and "low" and by other mutually exclusive pairs of terms.)

The two signals are combined to make up bytes, combinations of eight bits. The bytes are in turn combined in an almost infinite number of combinations corresponding to words, numbers, and symbols of various kinds. All of these are silent, appearing only as pulses and spaces — voltage rises and spaces between rises — and telephones speak only in sound languages. Since the telephone can't hear the bits and bytes, or pulses and spaces, a device called a *modem* (a contraction of the technical terms *mo*dulator and *dem*odulator) is brought in as a translator. The modem changes the bits and bytes into an audible sound — a *carrier* that varies its tone according to the bits and bytes — for transmission from the sending computer and then reconverts the variations in sound to bits and bytes for the computer at the receiving end of the transmission. The process is much like the interpreters at the UN translating the languages spoken there from one to another. (Your fax machine also uses a modem designed especially for fax transmissions. Special modems that handle both fax transmissions and other computer-based transmissions have been growing in popularity lately, even further developing the computer-telephone marriage.)

THE THREE CLASSES
OF ONLINE COMMUNICATION

There are at least three different meanings to "going online" for computer users. For many, it refers only to local electronic bulletin boards, colloquially called BBSs, for "bulletin board systems." For others, it is an online utility service that functions as both a BBS and an information service. CompuServe is undoubtedly the largest and best known of these, but there are others, notably GEnie, Prodigy, America Online, and Minitel. And finally, there are the online public data bases and services offering access to them, services devoted primarily to providing archived information. It is this latter class of online communication, electronic libraries, with which we are most concerned here, but the others are not insignificant, and we shall explore them too. But we ought also to recognize a relatively little used class that we will probably use more and more sometime in the future, as the technology continues to grow and makes it less formidable a task for most: communicating with another individual directly via a hookup between personal computers. This is done to some limited extent even today. For example, some writers already transmit copy to their publishers in this manner. Most organizations, however, are not yet prepared to handle this kind of communication on a regular basis.

The BBS

There are thousands upon thousands of electronic bulletin boards in operation in the United States. Every metropolitan area has hundreds, and they are generally listed in computer magazines. The majority are in individual homes, operated as a kind of hobby, free of charge to users. (A few charge a small fee.) Typically, they are message-exchange centers with forums or conferences. For example, a typical BBS might have conferences devoted to general purposes, writers, small business, real estate, investments, history, a foreign language or two, economics, news, advertising, and any of many other special interests. In some cases, the entire BBS is dedicated to a special interest.

In addition to active daily conferences – echanges of messages among participants – most BBSs carry files that the user may "download," or copy to his or her own computer. These can be text files or programs, also called software. The files are accumulated as a result of users "uploading" them – that is, sending copies of them to the BBSs to be posted there for others to download and try out if they wish to.

═ **100** ═

Bulletin board systems, or BBSs, can be an economical source of software for your specialty. Such programs, often known as shareware, can be downloaded to your personal computer. You can try the files out and pay for them on the honor system if you decide to adopt them.

A few bulletin boards are operated by organizations, such as dealers who advertise their existence in this way and even accept orders submitted via the BBS. Some BBSs are operated by computer clubs, as a service to members. There are also BBSs operated quasi officially out of government offices. The operators ("sysops," for "system operators") are usually government employees operating the systems in their spare time.

For most users, participation in BBS exchanges is both recreational and useful. It is also an excellent, low-stress learning process in communicating online. For that alone, BBSs are worth getting involved with.

The Online Utility Service

Online utilities such as CompuServe and GEnie charge fees to users, from flat fees for certain prescribed usages and services to "connect" fees for each minute of time online with the service and extra fees for connection to special data bases that are not part of the utility, but must be accessed via the utility. I generally exchange messages with others on CompuServe's Working from Home, Computer Consultants, and Journalism forums, but there are dozens of others, some of which I log onto occasionally.

Many services and data bases are available to users without paying extra charges. The following illustrate items available on CompuServe. Basic services are identified and are included in the basic online connect charge ($12.50 per hour in most cases); extended services, for which extra charges are assessed, are identified with a (+).

COMMUNICATIONS/BULLETIN BOARDS contains the CompuServe Mail service (basic), a "real-time" CB (Citizens Band) Simulator (+), CLASSIFIEDS (basic), many discussion forums (+), clubs and special-interest groups, and a FEEDBACK feature that lets you leave messages for the Customer Service Department.

NEWS/WEATHER/SPORTS offers reports from wire services, major newspapers, and newsletters from various sources. Included are the Associated Press Online (basic) and Hollywood Hotline (+). The Executive News Service (+) is a special feature providing an electronic "clipping" service for stories of interest from the AP, UPI, and other news wires. Local weather reports (basic) are available for most National Weather Service stations, with weather maps.

TRAVEL AND LEISURE caters to people on the move. It contains special features such as Travelshopper (basic), EAASY SABRE (basic), and the Official Airline Guides Electronic Edition (+), all of which provide airline schedules, seat availability and reservations, car and hotel information and reservations and an assortment of other services. You can also choose your hotel in ABC Worldwide Hotel Guide (+) or search through information on local attractions for many destinations, plus other business and leisure travel services. You may visit the Travel or Florida forums (+) and "Make a Friend" at your destination.

The ELECTRONIC MALL® (basic) is CompuServe's shopping service. CompuServe offers free shopping in the MALL: Connect time charges are waived for all members. It gives 24–hour-a-day, 7-day-a-week shopping within the comfort of your home or office via the MALL, where dozens of nationally recognized merchants provide information and products to meet your needs. Also available is the Softex Software Catalog (+), where software can be purchased and delivered electronically to your personal computer, as well as SHOPPERS ADVANTAGE CLUB (basic), a discount home shopping service offering name-brand consumer items. CONSUMER REPORTS (basic) is a valuable resource when you want to research an item before you make a purchase.

MONEY MATTERS & MARKETS (GO MONEY) is the financial area of the service. It includes stock market quotes and information, as well as banking and brokerage services, tax and insurance information, corporate reports, earnings and economic discussion forums. Use the Quick Reference Words provided in parentheses to access these financial services. Use the ticker symbol HRB to receive surcharge-free reports. REFERENCE leads you to electronic reference materials such as encyclopedias and government publications. It also takes you to educational services for teachers, parents, and students, as well as to special features relating to issues concerning special education and the handicapped. Grolier's Academic American (basic), U.S. government publications (+), and demographic information (+) are just a few of the services available. The Phone*File (+) service is much like an online telephone book that has information on over 80 million households in the United States.

COMPUTERS/TECHNOLOGY is home for a number of discussion forums (+) about specific kinds of computers and software. It also contains a research and reference section and directions for using your own Personal File Area (+) on CompuServe.

BUSINESS/OTHER INTERESTS (+) is for corporate executives and other professionals, such as those in law, health, aviation, engineering, and data processing. Newsletters, periodicals, discussion forums, and a variety of informational features are available for professionals in these fields.

Libraries, Files, and Downloading

The listing of services given in the previous section is a rather typical potpourri of information available on online utilities, although CompuServe is probably the most comprehensive of that genre, and one of the most useful features of any such utility is the library section of each forum (or conference).

There are usually a number of libraries, up to a dozen, each addressing a different interest within the spectrum of interests of the forum overall. Subscribers are free to upload files to these libraries and download files from them. Many of the library files are immediately readable and usable when they are downloaded, but others are compressed and can't be used until they are decompressed. Those unfamiliar with the systems are often frustrated by this. (I can easily recall my own frustrating first experiences with it!) A brief explanation is thus in order.

Most files, especially those that are all or nearly all text, have a lot of "air" in them (as they say in publishing): blank spaces, partial lines, etc. They can be compressed, often to not much more than one-half their normal size, to take up less room in storage and to speed up uploading and downloading them. (That reduces costs, since you are paying "connect time" costs for every minute or fraction of a minute you are on-line.)

Almost without exception today, these compressed files are "zipped." That is, their names end in the file extension ZIP. (A few of the older files used an earlier system, but these are not often found today.) Any file with the extension ZIP must be "unzipped" before use, and you can do this with the shareware file PKUNZIP.EXE, which is usually available on any BBS or online utility that carries ZIP files. Fortunately, many of the files that do the "unzipping" end in the extension EXE and are identified as "self-extracting." That means that you need merely type the main title, omitting the EXE, as though it were any command program, and the file will decompress itself.

ONLINE PUBLIC DATA BASES AND DATA-BASE SERVICES

The terms commonly used to describe and define public online information facilities are far from standardized. Accordingly, we shall have to define them for ourselves here and explain what the systems are and how they relate to each other. First of all, a *data base* is any collection of information that one chooses to assemble as a unit or designate as a data base. I can designate my entire filing cabinet (I have only one in my small office) as a data base if I choose to, but it is far more convenient and sensible to divide it into numerous data bases—for example, one of all my book proposals, another of all my royalty statements, another of all my correspondence, and so forth. But that is all paper, and when we use the term *data base* here, we are generally referring to information we have compiled into a computer file.

Be that as it may, you decide arbitrarily what you wish to designate as a data base. Each data base can be of whatever size and organizational structure you wish it to be, as simple as a mailing list or as complex as a personnel file.

What we refer to as an "online public data base" is a file of information that is stored in a computer somewhere and is accessible to the public, for a fee, from any other computer. That is, you or anyone else may use a telephone line to call the computer in which the data base is stored, examine that information, and copy whatever is of interest to you.

You do this by naming one or more keywords. If I wish to determine how many books have been written about the War of 1812, I can call up one or more library data bases and ask for a list of books that are about that war. Or I may search the data base for a book by a specific author or by a specific title, if I know either of those. Recently, I uploaded a file to an online library that contains a proposal-writing manual. I issued four keywords: PROPOSALS, MARKETING, GOVERNMENT, and HOLTZ. Naming any of those keywords in a search of that library will retrieve the title of the file in question, identifying it so that the searcher may then download it. That is what keywords are for.

CBD ONLINE is a data base of all the issues of the federal government's publication, *Commerce Business Daily.* LEXIS is a legal-information data base. An electronic version of the Official Airlines Guide exists as a data base. LEXPAT offers patent information. NEXIS offers complete texts from the *New York Times.* NewsNet is a data base of newsletters.

In some cases–for example, NewsNet–you can access an electronic data base only directly; in other cases, you can access a data base through a number of online utilities or electronic libraries. CBD ONLINE, for example, is available through at least six different *gateways,* as such utilities are often called. For example, when I wish to go through a local library cataloging system to a library data base in California or Massachusetts, there is a pause while a message appears on my screen: "Trying a connection." Then, either I am connected to the other data base, or I get a message asking me to try later, which means all lines to the other data base are in use at the moment.

SUBSCRIBER SERVICES AND PUBLIC DATA BASES

Following are a few of the many online subscription services available. In all cases, it is best to inquire about the rates, services, and types of data bases that the organization has. The information listed is that reported at the time of writing and is subject to change. In any case, a written or telephone inquiry is necessary to gain full information.

BRS/Bibliographic Retrieval
Services, BRS/After Dark
1200 Route 7
Latham, NY 12110
(518) 783-1161 and (800) 833-4707

Two services, offering over 80 data
bases on science, medicine,
education, business, and other
subjects.

BRS Executive Information Service
John Wiley and Sons, Inc.
One Wiley Drive
Somerset, NJ 08873
(201) 469-4400

Data bases summarizing recent
major business articles from 600
periodicals, abstracts of other
business articles, and related
information.

Data Resources, Inc.
2400 Hartwell Avenue
Lexington, MA 02173
(617) 863-5100

Commerce Business Daily online and
other business data bases, including
Value Line.

Dialog Information Services, Inc.
Dialog Information Retrieval
Service and Knowledge Index
3460 Hillview Avenue
Palo Alto, CA 94304
(800) 227-1927 and (800) 982-5838

Hundreds of business data bases,
including *Commerce Business Daily*
online, agricultural data, data on
computer and electronics
industries, and general news. Can
be accessed via Tymnet, Uninet, or
Telenet.

Dow Jones News/Retrieval Service
P.O. Box 300
Princeton, NJ 08540
(800) 257-5114

Twenty-seven data bases on
business/economic and financial/
investment services.

Dun & Bradstreet Corporation
299 Park Avenue
New York, NY 10171
(212) 593-6800

Timesharing and such business
services and information as D&B is
already well known for.

GTE Information Systems, Inc.
12490 Sunrise Valley Drive
Reston, VA 22046
(804) 478-7000

Electronic mail, intercomputer
communications/network service,
medical, pharmaceutical, and
clinical practice information, and
stock quotes.

ITT Dialcom
1109 Spring Street
Silver Spring, MD 20910

An electronic mail system with
access to airlines flight information,
news, and other data bases.

Mead Data Central
9393 Springboro Pike
Miamisburg, OH 45342
(513) 865-6800

LEXIS, LEXPAT, and NEXIS.
LEXIS is a legal research service,
LEXPAT a patent search service,
and NEXIS a news service offering
several business magazines and the
AP and UPI National and Business
wires online.

National Library of Medicine
8600 Rockville Pike
Bethesda, MD 20209
(301) 496-4000

MEDLINE and MEDLARS data
bases, medical information
provided to physicians and
hospitals (but available to and
subscribed to by others), including
diagnostic assistance.

NewsNet
945 Haverford Road
Bryn Mawr, PA 19010
(215) 527-8030 and
(800) 345-1301

Business information utility
distributing a variety of online
business newsletters and wire
services. Provides search services
also.

Nielsen Business Services
A. C. Nielsen Co.
Nielsen Plaza
Northbrook, IL 60062
(312) 498-6300

Offers its Nielsen Retail Index, a
data base pertaining to inventories
and other information about retail
trade in food, drug, health, alcohol,
cosmetics, and related lines.

TRW Information Services Division
Business Credit Services and Credit
Data Service
500 City Parkway West
Orange, CA 92668
(714) 937-2000

Reputed to be the largest consumer
credit-reporting service. Operated
in association with Standard and
Poor and the National Association
of Credit Management (NACM).

United Information Services, Inc.
20 North Clark Street
Chicago, IL 60602
(312) 782-2000

A service to programmers to sell
their software online through an
authors' program. Includes related
information shared among
subscribers.

Westlaw
West Publishing Company
50 West Kellog Boulevard
P.O. Box 43526
St. Paul, MN 55164
(800) 328-9352

An information service for law
offices. Searches citations, other
legal information, and news
services.

ON THE PRACTICAL SIDE

In principle, an online data base sounds simple enough. In practice, it is
not so simple. It is a complex process that can be quite expensive, with
connect time running as high as hundreds of dollars per hour for some
data bases and $20 or more per hour for even the less costly ones. In
practice, the time to download the information you want is usually
relatively small, compared with the time you spend searching for the
information. The charges begin when you go online with the host computer, and they continue whether or not you are getting any good use out
of being online. The experienced specialist will therefore spend as much

time as necessary devising a *search strategy* before going online, so as to minimize online time.

101

Prices for online services can be steep. The charges begin when you go online with the host computer, and they continue whether or not you are getting any use out of being online. The experienced specialist will therefore spend as much time as necessary devising a *search strategy* before going online, so as to minimize the time logged on. There are also a few books available that are directed specifically to helping you develop your skills in doing this, and these are listed in the appendix. I recommend that you turn to them for serious study of the field of research via online public data bases.

Because of the costs, if you are going to make serious use of online information facilities, it is worth your while to learn how to use them efficiently. One way to sharpen your skills is, as suggested earlier, to sign on to a few of your local BBSs and log on to them as often as you can. You will thereby develop a facility in intercomputer communication, searching, and downloading.

══ APPENDIX ═══════════════════════

REFERENCES AND MISCELLANEOUS DATA

This miscellany of assorted guides and references will help you put some of the ideas and suggestions of previous chapters to work for you.

WHY A REFERENCE FILE?

When challenged in a court of law about his knowledge of some matter under discussion there, Henry Ford retorted that he saw no need to clutter up his mind with details when he could press a button on his desk and summon someone to get the information for him. Others have at times observed that one of the most important outcomes of a formal education is the knowledge of where and how to seek out needed information. This appendix includes a number of items to which you may need to turn for guidance or for searching out the details of some important subject. In some respects it may be the most important part of this book.

Among the items offered here is a list of reference materials the modern consultant ought to have in a personal library. If you do not already have a substantial library of books and other materials to help you along the road to success, you may turn to these as the seeds of your own reference library and add to them steadily.

BIBLIOGRAPHY

Bjelland, Harely. *Using Online Scientific and Engineering Databases.* Blue Ridge Summit, PA: Windcrest/McGraw-Hill, 1992.

Cousins, Jill, and Robinson, Lesley. *The Online Manual.* Cambridge, MA: Basil Blackwell, 1992.

Crowe, Elizabeth, and Waldinger, Paul. *The Electronic Traveller.* Blue Ridge Summit, PA: TAB Books, 1992.

Everett, John H., and Crowe, Elizabeth Powell. *Information for Sale: How to Start and Operate Your Own Data Research Service.* Blue Ridge Summit, PA: TAB Books, 1988.

Glossbrenner, Alfred. *The Complete Handbook of Personal Computer Communications,* 3rd ed. New York: St. Martin's Press, 1990.

———. *How to Look it Up Online.* New York: St. Martin's Press, 1987.

———. *Alfred Glossbrenner's Master Guide to Free Software for IBMs and Compatible Computers.* New York: St. Martin's Press, 1985.

———. *Glossbrenner's Guide to Shareware for Small Businesses.* Blue Ridge Summit, PA: Windcrest/McGraw-Hill, 1992.

———, and Rugge, Sue. *Information Broker's Handbook,* Blue Ridge Summit, PA: Windcrest/McGraw-Hill, 1992.

Goldman, Nahum. *Online Information Hunting.* Blue Ridge Summit, PA: Windcrest/McGraw-Hill, 1992.

Harper, Rose. *Mailing List Strategies, a Guide to Direct Mail Success.* New York: McGraw-Hill, 1986.

Holtz, Herman. *Great Promo Pieces.* New York: John Wiley & Sons, 1988.

———. *The Direct Marketer's Workbook.* New York: John Wiley & Sons, 1986.

———. *The Consultant's Guide to Winning Clients.* New York: John Wiley & Sons, 1988.

———. *The Consultant's Guide to Proposal Writing,* 2nd ed. New York: John Wiley & Sons, 1990.

———. *Speaking for Profit.* New York: John Wiley & Sons, 1987.

Hughes, Arthur M. *The Complete Database Marketer, Tapping Your Customer Base to Maximize Sales and Increase Profits.* Chicago: Probus, 1991.

Johnson, Eric and Reichard, Kevin. *Using Computer Bulletin Boards.* New York: MIS Press/Henry Holt, 1992.

Lewis, Herschell Gordon. *Direct Mail Copy That Sells.* Englewood Cliffs, NJ: Prentice-Hall, 1984.

Newman, Edwin. *On Language.* New York: Warner Books, 1980.

Nimersheim, Jack. *pc Anywhere, the Complete Communications Guide.* Blue Ridge Summit, PA: Windcrest/McGraw-Hill, 1992.

Rapp, Stan, and Collins, Thomas. L. *The Great Marketing Turnaround: The Age of the Individual.* Englewood Cliffs, NJ: Prentice-Hall, 1990.

Rash, Wayne, and Kenner, Hugh. *Writing Well in the Real World: The Official Guide to Grammatik.* New York: Random House, 1992.

Rose, Lance, and Wallace, Jonathan. *SYSLAW: Your BBS and the Law: A Sysop's Legal Companion.* New York: M&T Books, 1992.

Scott, Tom. *The Bulletin Board Book.* New York: M&T Books, 1992.

Strunk, William, Jr., and White, E. B. *The Elements of Style.* New York: Macmillan, 1972.

Taylor, Steven. *Telecommunications on the Mac.* New York: MIS Press/Henry Holt, 1992.

Walters, Dottie and Lillet. *Speak and Grow Rich,* Englewood Cliffs, NJ: Prentice-Hall, 1989.

PERIODICALS

Meeting News
Gralla Publications
1515 Broadway
New York, NY 10036

Meetings & Conventions
Ziff-Davis
One Park Avenue
New York, NY 10016

Sharing Ideas
Dottie Walters
P.O. Box 1120
Glendora, CA 91740

DM News
19 West 21st Street
New York, NY 10010

Target Marketing
401 North Broad Street
Philadelphia, PA 19108

A RECOMMENDED PROPOSAL FORMAT AND GUIDELINES

Proposal writing appears to be both mysterious and formidable to many who have never participated in the art. That is one reason so many consultants shrink from using this essential marketing tool.

Some RFPs mandate a proposal format, and some companies have a standard format specified for their proposals, either of which you follow, as the case may be. In the absence of these, the following format is recommended as being straightforward, logical, and suitable for most applications:

1. FRONT MATTER
    Copy of Letter of Transmittal
    Executive Summary

Response Matrix
Table of Contents

2.   SECTION/CHAPTER I: INTRODUCTION

About the Offeror: A brief introduction to your firm, a thumbnail sketch of your company and qualifications, a reference to details to be found later, an opening statement.

Understanding of the Requirement: A brief statement of your understanding of the requirement, in your own language (don't echo the RFP), leaving out the trivial and focusing on the essence of the requirement. This provides a bridge (transition) to the next chapter.

3.   SECTION/CHAPTER II: DISCUSSION

Extended discussions of the requirement, identifying and analyzing problems, and exploring and reviewing approaches (with the pros and cons of each). Include similar discussions of all relevant matters – technical, management, schedule, and other important points, with worry items. This is a key section in which to sell the proposed program, make the emotional appeals (promises), explain the superiority of the proposed program, and demonstrate the validity of the proposer's grasp of the problem, of how to solve it, and of how to organize the resources. The section should culminate in a clear explanation of the approach selected, flowing directly into the next chapter. Include graphics, as necessary – especially a functional flowchart – explaining the approach and technical or program design strategy employed.

4.   SECTION/CHAPTER III: PROPOSED PROJECT

This is where the specifics appear – staffing and organization (with an organization chart) and resumes of key people. Also included should be the following:

Project management: Procedures, philosophy, methods, controls; relationship to parent organization, reporting order; other information on both technical and general/administrative management of project.

Labor-loading: Explain the major tasks and estimated hours for each principal in each task (use a tabular presentation), with totals of hours for each task and totals of hours for each principal staff member.

Deliverable items: Specify, describe, and quantify.

Schedules: Specify. (Use a milestone chart if possible.)

Resumes: Resumes of key staff, prepared for the project.

5. SECTION/CHAPTER IV: COMPANY QUALIFICATIONS

A description of company, past projects (especially those similar to the one under discussion), resources, history, organization, key staff, other resumes, testimonial letters, special awards, and other pertinent facts.

6. APPENDICES

A TIP OR TWO ON GRAPHICS

A good illustration requires little explanation, and that is the way to test the quality of any illustration. We ask, Does it require explanation, and if so, how much?

Another question to ask is, Is the illustration clear, or is it "clever"? Forget about clever devices and artistic considerations; the purpose of an illustration is to communicate information accurately and efficiently. If the reader has to puzzle over the meaning or study the illustration to understand it, the reader will probably set your proposal aside with a sigh and go on to the next one. A basic rule is: Make it as easy as possible on the reader. Cleverness is all too often the death of meaning and understanding and, therefore, the death of the sale.

For function charts, use the WHY? HOW? technique to generate the chart and to test it. Going from left to right (or from top to bottom if you prefer that), ask WHY? of each box, and the answer should be in the next box. Going in reverse, ask HOW, and the answer should be in the next box. If the answers are not very clear, consider adding boxes (for more detail) or changing the wording in the boxes. (Like text, charts should go through drafts, editing, reviews, and revisions.)

USE OF HEADLINES, GLOSSES, AND BLURBS

Proposals are not exciting literature and, at best, are fatiguing to read in quantity, as customers are compelled to do. Anything you can do to make things easier for the reader will help you, in the end, in at least two ways: (1) it will help you get your own messages across and pierce the consciousness of readers who may be reading mechanically and without full appreciation by the time they get to your opus and (2) it will enable you to earn the reader's gratitude, which can do nothing but help your case. There are at least three devices that will help.

Headlines

Use side heads and centered heads as freely as you can and as often as you can. Use them to summarize messages and to telegraph what a paragraph or page is about – what the main message is. But use them also to *sell*. That is, use the headline to summarize promises, benefits, and proofs.

Glosses

A gloss is a little abstract in the margin of a page that summarizes the text next to it. Usually, there is at least one gloss on a page, and often there are several. Like headlines, glosses can and should be used to help sell the proposal by focusing on benefits and proofs.

Blurbs

A blurb is very much like a gloss, except that it is not used as frequently and is thus somewhat broader in scope and, usually, of greater length. A blurb generally appears after a major headline (e.g., a centered head) or chapter title. Like headlines and glosses, blurbs should be used to sell, as well as to sum up information and communicate generally.

INFORMAL PROPOSALS

There are occasions that call for informal or letter proposals, so called because they are usually embodied in a letter of perhaps one to three or four pages. However, the informal proposal still ought to contain the major elements of the proposal in summary form: the introduction, the statement of the client's need or problem, comments, the proposed solution, and information on costs.

CAPABILITY BROCHURES

The capability brochure is somewhat of a generalized proposal and may follow the proposal guidelines, albeit in a general fashion that is less formal and less detailed. Its purpose is to demonstrate, in general terms, your capabilities to serve the client's needs, and it thus provides a profile of the kinds of services you offer and the resources you can bring to bear, including identifying associates you can call on for help and providing resumes for yourself and any associates you wish to identify.

MAILING LIST BROKERS

American List Counsel, Inc.
88 Orchard Road
Princeton, NJ 08543

AZ Marketing Services, Inc.
31 River Road
Cos Cob, CT 06807

Chilcutt Direct Marketing, Inc.
1701 East Second Street
Edmond, OK 73083

Direct Media
200 Pemberwick Road
Greenwich, CT 06830

Doubleday List Marketing
501 Franklin Avenue
Garden City, NY 11530

Kleid Company, Inc.
530 Fifth Avenue
New York, NY 10036

List Services Corporation
6 Trowbridge Drive
Bethel, CT 06801

Listworks Corporation
One Campus Drive
Pleasantville, NY 10570

Media Masters
51 Madison Avenue
New York, NY 10010

ONLINE Information Network
5711 South 86th Circle
Omaha, NE 68127

Penton Lists
1100 Superior Avenue
Cleveland, OH 44114

Qualified Lists Corporation
135 Bedford Road
Armonk, NY 10504

TransMark Lists
555 West Adams Street
Chicago, IL 60661

21st Century Marketing
2 Dubon Court
Farmingdale, NY 11735

Worldata
5200 Town Center Circle
Boca Raton, FL 33486

BUSINESS NAMES

The subject of business names seems to be a matter of great concern to many independent consultants. As mentioned in the text, there is a school of thought which holds that, the smaller the company, the bigger is the name. Many of the giants in business and industry – IBM, RCA, GE, ALCOA, General Motors, Dun & Bradstreet, Sears & Roebuck, Montgomery Ward, Hughes Aircraft, and Boeing, to name a few – managed well with simple names. There is probably extremely little to be gained from the invention and use of an extravagant name.

Much the same may be said for logos, especially those which are so clever and artistic that their meaning is completely lost on those who are supposed to be impressed and perhaps even awed by their very ultra-sophistication. I personally am bewildered at many of the devices used as logos today.

Generally speaking, your are entitled to do business under your own name – for example, *Jack Smith, Consultant,* or some such representation as *Smith Consulting Associates* – without anyone's permission. It is when you wish to disguise who it is that the client does business with by using a fictitious name for your business – for instance, Confounding and Confrontational Consultants, Ltd. – that you must reveal just who is behind the organization. You must *register* the business name with the state and sometimes also with the county and the city.

If you incorporate, the name under which you incorporate is already a matter of public record, so you don't have to worry about registering the name. In most states today, incorporation is a simple affair that you can handle yourself if you want only a simple close corporation. (Consult a lawyer and possibly your accountant for more details as to your various options and the pros and cons of each.)

My personal recommendation is that you not try to deliver a lengthy sales message in your business name, nor try to impress prospective clients with it. You will probably do better with a simple name: It suggests quiet confidence, rather than frantic effort. In most cases, your own name will serve quite well and will keep you free of annoying and unnecessary complications.

CONTRACTS AND AGREEMENTS

If you are not schooled in the business world, you may need a brief education in contracts, and the first thing to learn is that a contract is not a piece of paper. A contract is an *agreement.* It is wise and customary to define the agreement in detail in some permanent form, such as ink on paper, because human memory is somewhat fragile and some humans work at developing faulty memories. It is thus often necessary to use that piece of paper to remind the other party of what he or she agreed to. And in extreme cases, it is sometimes necessary to have a third party – a judge – look at the paper and try to determine exactly what the agreement was.

There are several types of contracts you may encounter, including the following:

- *Fixed-price, for-the-job contract.* In this form, the contract specifies what is to be done, by whom it is to be done, what the outcome is to be, what the term of the contract is, and how much money is to change hands between the party of the first part (you) and the party of the second part (the client).

- *Time-and-materials contract.* In this form, the contract specifies a *rate* – and provides for reimbursement of the cost of all materials required to do the job. Also, it usually gives an estimate of the number of hours or days that will be required to complete the task or at least puts a ceiling on the length of time needed.

- *Task order contract.* In this form, rates are specified, but instead of being hired to work at those rates, you agree to estimate specific tasks the client needs to have done, as they come up, using the rates specified in the contract for your estimates. When you reach agreement with the client on an estimate for a given task, you perform the task as per your estimate as a fixed-price job.

There are many variants of the preceding forms, but these are the basic types of contract that will usually be offered you.

TIPS ON WRITING DIRECT MAIL COPY

The following reminders function as a checklist of "dos and don'ts" to refer to when preparing direct mail copy:

- Always make things as easy as possible for the customer. For example:

  1. Make it easy to understand what you are saying. Use short words, short sentences, and short paragraphs. Put one thought in a sentence and one subject and one main point in a paragraph. Use examples and illustrations freely, especially on the more obscure points.

  2. Make it easy for the customer to order, ask for more information about, or otherwise reveal interest in your product or service. Provide a return postcard, telephone number, or other convenient means for responding.

  3. Make it easy for the customer to understand what you want him or her to do by *telling* the customer exactly what to do. A great many sales are lost by advertisers who fail to tell the customers what they want them to do – for

example, "Mail this card today." (Yes, it does make a difference in the response rate.)

- A cliche in direct mail (which is nonetheless a truism) is "The more you tell, the more you sell." Hence, don't stint on copy. Be sure to include a letter, a brochure or flyer of some sort, and a response device (an envelope and/or order form) as an absolute minimum, and there is no harm in enclosing even more. The experts claim that three-quarters of the response results from the letter and that a good circular or brochure can increase the response rate by as much as one-third. My own experience bears this out quite emphatically.

- Repetition — repeat mailings — pays off. Many who do not respond to a first, second, or even third appeal respond to a fourth or fifth one, and, up to a point, the rate of response often actually increases with the number of mailings. (Some experts report that results don't begin to fall off until as many as 10 mailings have been made to the same list.)

- Don't tell it all in the letter. Split the copy up among the various enclosures, or at least provide additional details in those enclosures. Make it clear that additional information and details are to be found elsewhere in the enclosures. Give the reader good reason to read everything if you want maximum impact.

- Geography makes a difference. Prospects who are nearby tend to respond better than those at a distance. Know nearby zip codes, and use them. But do conduct tests, for there are always exceptions. For example, when it comes to consulting and speaking services, there is some appeal — even a kind of mystique — to the expert from a distant place, especially if you are mailing from a major industrial or business center, such as New York, Chicago, Washington, or another major metropolitan area. If you are, take advantage of the fact by giving it prominence in your copy.

- If you use envelope copy — advertising and sales messages on the outside of the envelope — do two things:

  1. Use both sides of the envelope. If you are going to make a bulletin board of the envelope, you might as well get full use of it; copy on both sides pulls better than copy on one side only — if the copy is powerful.

2.   Now that you've served notice that the envelope contains
      advertising matter, why pay first-class postage? You
      might as well save money by using bulk mail or, at least,
      something less expensive than first class.

CONSULTANTS' ASSOCIATIONS

Many of those who belong to speakers' associations and to many other
kinds of associations and professional societies are consultants. But there
are also a number of consultants' associations, including the following:

American Association of
Professional Consultants
9140 Ward Parkway
Kansas City, MO 64114

American Association of Hospital
Consultants
1235 Jefferson Davis Highway
Arlington, VA 22202

American Association of Medico-
Legal Consultants
2200 Benjamin Franklin Parkway
Philadelphia, PA 19130

American Association of Political
Consultants
444 North Capitol Street, NW
Washington, DC 20001

American Consultants League
1290 Palm Avenue
Sarasota, FL 34236

American Society of Agricultural
Consultants
8301 Greensboro Drive
McLean, VA 22101

Association of Bridal Consultants
29 Ferriss Estate
New Milford, CT 06776

Association of Executive Search
Consultants
151 Railroad Avenue
Greenwich, CT 06830

Association of Management
Consultants
500 North Michigan Avenue
Chicago, IL 60611

Independent Computer Consultants
Association
P.O. Box 27412
St. Louis, MO 63141

Society of Professional Business
Consultants
221 North LaSalle Street
Chicago, IL 60601

Society of Professional Management
Consultants
16 West 56th Street
New York, NY 10019

SEMINAR TIPS

As one of the most important tools available to you to build your income
base and market your services, seminar production deserves some
thought. For that reason, a few tips and reminders are offered here for
ready reference:

- A typical day's session runs approximately six hours: three in the morning and three in the afternoon, with midmorning and midafternoon breaks of about ten minutes. The lunch break is usually from ninety minutes to two hours, depending on conditions.

- Back-of-the-room sales are an important seminar benefit to both you and your participants. They may be conducted prior to the start of the morning session, during the lunch break, and after the close of the afternoon session.

- Whether you sell books, tapes, or other materials, you should include handout materials as part of the seminar. Often, these are themselves a major inducement to registration and attendance. Because of that, it helps if they are available exclusively to attendees. However, in many cases you can get excellent materials free of charge from government agencies, associations, community groups, large corporations, schools, and other sources. Take advantage of the opportunity to include ample promotional material of your own, which leads to specific consulting assignments as a follow-up to the seminars.

- Often visual aids are also available from the sources just named—movies, slides, filmstrips, transparencies, and posters of various kinds. Be sure to inquire of all such organizations.

- One profitable idea is the miniseminar, which is focused sharply on a few well-defined topics or objectives. Several years ago, I held these two- to three-hour sessions for 10 to 15 people in my offices on Saturday mornings, charging what was even then a rather modest fee—$25. If your offices are at home and unsuitable for this purpose, you can usually arrange to rent an inexpensive room somewhere.

- A variation of that idea is to conduct two such sessions—one in the morning, another in the afternoon—so that you can register twice the number of attendees for a single day. (Your total cost is only slightly greater for two sessions, and your income is, of course, doubled.)

- You can sell your books, tapes, and/or other materials at the miniseminar as well as at the full seminar, making them especially profitable.

INDEX

227